LIVELIHOODS AT THE MARGINS

SURVIVING THE CITY

James Staples, Editor

Left Coast
Press Inc.
Walnut Creek, CA

Left Coast
Press Inc.

Left Coast Press, Inc.
1630 North Main Street, #400
Walnut Creek, California 94596
http://www.lcoastpress.com

Library of Congress Cataloging-In-Publication Data

Livelihoods at the margins : surviving the city/James Staples, editor.
    p. cm.
  ISBN-13: 978-1-59874-272-5 (cloth)
  ISBN-13: 978-1-59874-273-2 (pbk.)
  1. Urban poor--Developing countries. 2. Sociology, Urban--Developing countries.
I. Staples, James, 1966-HV4173.L58 2007
305.5'69091724--dc22   2007013873

05 06 07 08 5 4 3 2 1

Printed in the United States of America

The paper used in this publication meets the minimum requirements of American National Standard for Information Sciences—Permanence of Paper for Printed Library Materials, ANSI/NISO Z39.48—1992.

Cover design by Piper Wallis

Contents

Preface

This volume grew out of the Livelihoods at the Margins conference at the School of Oriental and African Studies (SOAS), University of London, in July 2004, a forum for drawing out ethnographic research with people who derive incomes in ways usually excluded from mainstream economic analyses. I had envisaged the event as a small one-day workshop to round off an ESRC-funded post-doctoral fellowship. I hoped the discussions it generated would help me to find wider frames of reference for my own work on begging in South India. However, I was overwhelmed by the level of interest in response to my initial call for papers. The stack was finally whittled down to 24 abstracts which, between them, spanned all the continents of the globe and represented a full range of disciplines across the social sciences. The terms 'livelihoods' and 'margins' clearly resonated. Interest from potential delegates was even higher. Nearly half of those who expressed an interest in attending had to be turned away from what became a lively two-day conference, held from 8–9 July. This volume at least brings to a wider audience a sample of the material presented during those two days.

I am grateful to all those who came along and contributed, in particular the speakers and the seven discussants: Christina Toren, Kit Davis, Johnny Parry, Barbara Harriss-White, Joanna Busza, Helen Lambert and John Gledhill. Their collective comments have helped reshape the representative selection of papers that make up this collection. Choosing just a few of them for inclusion has been a difficult task, thankfully made easier with the advice of Briar Towers, our initial commissioning editor at UCL Press, who helped steer me towards the specifically urban focus I have pursued in this book. Also worthy of special mention are David Martin and Duncan Franklin at SOAS for their help, respectively, with administering the conference and with getting the programme and papers online. Abstracts and background information on the conference can still be found in the anthropology pages of SOAS's website (www.soas.ac.uk/anthropology). I am also indebted to Rebecca Marsland and Atreyee Sen who, in addition to giving papers, very generously stepped in to help things run smoothly.

Finally, I am grateful to the ESRC (Award Number PTA-026-27-0342), the British Academy (ref BCG-38368) and SOAS (thanks especially to Richard Fardon and John Peel) for helping to fund the conference. This resulting book was edited during a post-doctoral fellowship from the British Academy (ref PDF/2004/51).

1 Introduction: Livelihoods at the Margins

James Staples

Livelihoods – what people do to get by – both in terms of fulfilling biological needs and giving meaning to their existence – is an area of enquiry salient to disciplines across the social sciences. For anthropologists the activities people carry out in a bid to survive and fulfil their desires are significant in constituting people as social beings. Observation and analysis of those activities, including the relationships they involve us in, how we relate to them, and how they interconnect at local and transnational levels, help to inform us about multiple socio-cultural issues. For economists, these same activities have first and foremost been viewed as rational and materialist: people's strategies for making a living offer real-life examples of the ways in which scarce resources are distributed. For those in the related fields of development studies (as well as for those working hands-on in development), analysis of livelihoods and the assets used by people to get by are increasingly being seen as pivotal in creating countrywide solutions to poverty and social exclusion.

Others, too, have become increasingly interested in livelihoods as an entry point from which to start making sense of the world at the onset of the 21st century. Geographers and scholars of migration from across the disciplinary spectrum plot how the pursuit of employment and other forms of livelihood activity relate to the ways in which people criss-cross the boundaries of nation-states (eg, Duany 2002; Thomas-Hope 2002). Sociologists, meanwhile, use data on work patterns to document and predict wide-ranging social trends. How people make a living – or how they *make a life*, in the widest sense – provides a point at which a large variety of different interests converge.

This book, which focuses on livelihoods in urban settings, is made up primarily of contributions from social anthropologists and scholars working under the umbrella of development studies. Some of the authors might place themselves within both those categories. It was a deliberate intention in selecting and ordering the chapters, however, to blur disciplinary borders, to encourage readers to explore in particular the correlations and disjunctures between anthropology and development studies and to see if, in juxtaposing different kinds of material, the result might be more than the sum of its parts. As some of the chapters show, development studies' expansion of the livelihoods concept offers anthropologists something useful to think with. Conversely, anthropology's multi-perspectival focus provides those seeking solutions with alternative ways of interpreting their data. But this is not just about a creative dialogue between disciplines. I also want to rupture the dichotomy routinely drawn between those in development and applied anthropologists on the one hand, and scholarly anthropologists on the other. As Mosse puts it:

> While some of the latter accuse the former of contributing to the reinforcement of ethnocentric and dominating models in development, some of the former accuse the latter of elitist irrelevance driven by the intellectual trends of Northern academia. Caricatures of mercenary consultants or 'feeble forms of politically correct anthropology' (Grillo 1997) abound, seriously misrepresenting the varied spectrum of positions from which anthropologists work and their individual capacity to combine engagement with policy and critical work. (Mosse 2005: 241)

The contributors to this volume reflect some of that variety, their work evidence of the scholarly *and* practical value of blurring disciplinary boundaries.

What their work shares – and what, to some extent, unifies the chapters – is an approach that is primarily ethnographic. That term may be used as a gloss for a variety of research methods. What for the anthropologist is the long-haul participant-observation of 'being there' is, for some of the harder-edged social scientists, research that draws on open-ended questionnaires as well as statistical analysis. Despite differences at the boundaries, however, for most of us ethnographic method falls somewhere between those two extremes, incorporating elements of both. I use the term here to describe qualitative analysis that draws on detailed first-hand research, conducted *with* people, on the ground, in cities across the world. The ideas, themes and theoretical positions discussed in the book emerge out of those ethnographic encounters, rather than predetermine how they will be read.

Before launching into a selection of fine-grained ethnography of livelihoods at the margins across a range of urban landscapes, I want to explore a bit further some of the key concepts that have framed the book, namely, what we mean by the terms 'livelihoods' and 'marginality'. In exploring and problematising these notions in a diverse range of contexts – all the way from Ugandan tour guides and drug dealers to Bolivian fish sellers – we find that there are a number of other themes that keep recurring. Two of these are encounters with the tensions that exist between explanatory models that favour structure and those that favour human agency, and the attempt to avoid either falling captive to a victims' discourse or allowing oppressors to hide behind the shield of cultural relativism. Each chapter also serves to chip away at a series of taken-for-granted dichotomies that often frame thinking about livelihoods. The conceptual distinctions between the rural and the urban, the formal and informal sectors of the economy, tradition and modernity, and the margins and the centre are rightly shown to be flaky. The final sections look more closely at some of these emerging themes, provide outlines of the chapters and draw out the threads that join them together.

LIVELIHOODS

The term 'livelihoods', as it is employed in everyday discourse to refer to the *means* by which people make a living, has an obvious relevance to economists. The search for income, whether in cash or kind, through which they can access resources to sustain themselves and their families, is a significant factor in understanding how people structure their everyday lives and in plotting their movements – sometimes across national boundaries – through space. And because of the centrality of economic activity to these pursuits, 'livelihoods' are also of clear practical interest to those whose work is concerned with tackling material poverty – namely, those working in development.

A dominant argument that has shaped this connection between a focus on economic factors and poverty alleviation is that 'economic growth is not only the most important anti-poverty strategy but is also the only strategy that can generate meaningful poverty reduction in very poor countries' (Mills and Pernia 1994: 11). This neo-liberal position, which holds that the metaphorical cake should rise to meet the demands of the poor rather than be cut up into different sized slices, takes centre stage in much of the literature produced throughout the 1990s (eg, Behrman 1993; Fields 1994; Mazumdar 1994; OSCAL 1996; Quibria 1993). Economies were conceptualised as needing to grow in order to meet the livelihood needs of the populations they served. To achieve such growth a broad understanding of macroeconomic conditions was seen as imperative.

Reduced to the mechanics of what people and institutions need to do in the capitalist marketplace in order to survive, 'livelihoods' appear to have only limited interest to anthropologists. The domain of economic activity, one might argue, is but one of a whole series of interconnected arenas through which social life is constituted and reconstituted. The old anthropological categories of religion, ritual, marriage and kinship jostle alongside economics in a combined and discursive effort to construct 'society'. Economics can be dealt with by the harder social sciences; anthropologists can be left to pick over the remains.

If, however, we resist the reduction of 'livelihoods' merely to the *means* of making a living and let it also refer, as it does in the older sense of the term in English, to *ways* of living, then the notion begins to have much wider relevance. There has been a clear move towards this over the last 10 years. Sorensøn and Olwig (2000: 2–4), for example, usefully call for 'livelihoods' to be reinvested with the socio-cultural since the means by which people make a living *only* make sense within their wider social contexts. Conversely, wider economic organisation – such as the trading associations we encounter in the final chapter of this book – only makes sense through understanding the social relationships in which it is simultaneously embedded.

Those working in development have also made strides over the same timeframe in reconceptualising livelihoods, as the burgeoning literature, such as the UK's Department for International Development's (DFID) expanding livelihoods website (www.livelihoods.org), and the International Institute for Environment and Development's journal *Environment and Urbanization* bear witness to. In his work on rural livelihoods development, for example, Ellis (1998) went beyond conventional economic models to define livelihoods as including social institutions (such as family or community), gender relations and property rights, as well as income (in cash and in kind), recognising that '[a]ny study of livelihoods ... requires an awareness of the wider spatial context of the unit of analysis' (Sorensøn and Olwig 2002: 4). Long, in bringing together these newer arguments, suggests that the livelihoods concept 'best expresses the idea of individuals and groups striving to make a living, attempting to meet their various consumption and economic necessities, coping with uncertainties, responding to new opportunities, and choosing between different value positions' (2000: 196). Livelihoods, in short, are about more than just achieving an income.

Researchers in development studies have been especially active in thinking out ways of using this broader definition of 'livelihoods' to address issues of deprivation – a category that has also been broken down into the dimensions of physical weakness, isolation, poverty, powerlessness and vulnerability (Chambers 1989). Others, in refining our definitions of poverty, have attempted to address how chronic poverty might be measured over time, highlighting the relevance of age, gender, ethnicity and education to the experience of material deprivation (eg, Mitlin 2005). A 'livelihoods framework' recognises that households construct their livelihoods within broader socio-economic and physical contexts, using social as well as material assets (Carney 1998: 4).

Assets, within this framework, include human capital, social and political capital, physical capital, financial capital and natural capital (Rakodi 2002: 14). Their inclusion as central to the analysis of liveli-hoods is intended to focus on what people have – and to build on that capital – rather than to identify them as passive victims (*ibid*). While we need to be aware that such an approach runs a real risk of obscur-ing the wider political causes of people's marginalisation, it does at least enable us to consider their agency in responding to that margin-alisation. These policy models also set out to nuance the rather static notion of deprivation – previously reduced to economic poverty – by placing much greater emphasis on 'vulnerability', a concept seen bet-ter able to capture processes of change (Moser 1996: 2, cited in Rakodi 2002: 14). The notion of 'social exclusion' – which can be traced back to Lenoir's (1974) study of those who fell through the French insurance-based social safety net and led to the excluded (*les exclus*) rather than the poor or unemployed becoming the object of social policy (Cannon 1997: 78) – has developed out of a comparable analysis. Vulnerability, like the plight of the socially excluded, is defined as a high degree of exposure and susceptibility to risk of stress and shocks, and little capacity to recover.

These aspects of a 'livelihoods framework' have been elaborated elsewhere in the literature (eg, Carney et al 1999; Radoki 2002). To summarise the guiding principles, such a policy framework is intended to put the priorities of the vulnerable at the centre: 'The first priority is not the environment or production but livelihoods, stress-ing both short-term satisfaction of basic needs and long-term security'

(Chambers 1989: 1). In shifting the focus of policy from outputs to people and what they defined as their priorities, sustainable livelihoods frameworks (SLF) challenge assumptions about what those priorities might be, and place them within a wider context. In particular, SLF analysis:

> ... highlights the importance of macro-micro links: how policies, institutions and various levels of government and non-government organisations affect people's lives in multiple ways, and the extent to which people themselves can influence these structures and processes (DFID 2000).

There is much to commend such an approach, and a number of authors in this volume use it as a starting point for thinking about issues that concern their informants' livelihood strategies. As a model-based approach, however, it has important limitations. First, as DFID's own guidance concedes, the SLF approach fails explicitly to address issues of politics, power and authority (DFID, 2001). If we confine ourselves to a consideration of people's own 'assets' and 'capital', we miss out on the wider conditions of their existence and, moreover, we let the institutional structures that force some people to the margins off the hook. We need, as Collinson (2003) argues from a political economy perspective, to understand vulnerability in terms of powerlessness as well as in terms of material need. A livelihoods approach sidesteps the wider historical and geographical perspectives required to answer the question of *why* particular groups of people are marginalised in the first place (*ibid*: 4–6). Arce draws broadly similar conclusions when he suggests that Chamber's sustainable livelihoods approach 'suffers from a peculiar narrowness' (2003: 203). It does so, he argues, in part because 'it focuses on the internal dynamics of net assets at the expense of contests over social value and actors' understandings of their own reality' (*ibid*).

One of the reasons for this narrowness, as DFID's guidance also accepts, is that the SLF approach is an oversimplification. Rather, 'the full diversity and richness of livelihoods can be understood only by qualitative and participatory analysis at a local level' (DFID 1999). Furthermore, because measurability is an important part of such analyses, 'assets' that in reality can only be fully understood in qualitative terms, by necessity become quantified. In short, people's assets are ultimately reduced to attributes that can be measured and then weighed against other factors. This might be necessary for designing widely useable policy that successfully addresses issues of vulnerability, but it does run the risk of treating other social factors as if they were qualitatively similar to purely economic factors. This is problematic because it is difficult to compare the advantage one might gain from, say, one's particular standing in relation to a network of people, with the amount of money one might earn from a particular activity. It is right that neither should be treated in isolation, but homogenising complex sociopolitical realities as 'assets' or 'capital' risks obscuring the very nuances of people's situations that we need to explore if we are to gain an understanding of their livelihoods. We need to find contextually specific ways of learning what particular 'assets' mean to particular people in particular situations. A relationship defined as 'social capital' or as an 'asset' in one context, for example, might become a burden in others. Deployment of other 'assets' might be reliant on external factors over which individuals have little or no control.

Several of the authors in this book have attempted to address these issues, whether they specifically refer to the SLF approach or not. Butler's exploration of young people's livelihoods on the streets of Rio de Janeiro, for example, considers how *revolta* – a Brazilian term which loosely translates as 'inner rage' – simultaneously aids and abets his informants' capacity to live as they wish (Chapter 3). Conticini's consideration of Bangladeshi street-living children's livelihood strategies (Chapter 4) likewise goes beyond conventional socioeconomic assets to include such ephemeral qualities as love and trust within his analysis, while Frankland (Chapter 2) reconceptualises the expatriate clients of the Ugandan guide and drugseller as a particular kind of asset or commodity. Kaiser's description of Sudanese refugees (Chapter 10), meanwhile, suggests uses *and* limitations of a livelihoods approach by setting refugees' capacities to exploit their resources against the limiting policies of their hosts. My point, then, is not that a livelihoods framework should necessarily be discarded; rather, that we should see it as a possible way in to thinking about different ways of living: as a methodological tool rather than as a rigid theoretical model. Some of the contributors to this book illustrate how that might be done in practice. Others, in adopting different approaches, show very clearly that there is more than one way of addressing questions of livelihoods.

MARGINALITY

The other main theme of this book is, of course, marginality. As a category of analysis, the term is going to prove a slippery one, but suffice it for a general definition to state that the livelihoods of all those discussed here are in some sense excluded, either from the wider social groups with which they identify or from the geographical locations in which they make a living. Most of them are also thought of – when they are considered at all – as victims: as groups of people who, as a consequence, ideally need rehabilitation that will draw them from the peripheries and back towards the centre.

A related danger in drawing an analytical distinction between the margins and the centre – or between the periphery and the core, as Wallenstein (1974) conceptualised it – is that we end up with 'Orientalism all over again' (Washbrook 1990: 492). Talk of the margins, and the orientation of policy towards bringing people closer to the centre through economic growth, creates a new kind of 'other': those implicitly deemed as lacking the dynamics needed to transform their lives. As several chapters illustrate, however, people are seldom marginal because of their failings or by simple accident of geography or time. They become and remain marginal because it suits those at the centre that this should be the case. As Kaiser (Chapter 10) shows, certain categories of people – in the case she describes, refugees – have literally been ousted, sometimes violently, to the marginal positions they occupy. In attempting to represent the voices of those so 'othered', this book intends to take us beyond the notion that livelihoods can only be assessed against the yardstick of Western capitalism.

In so doing, *Livelihoods at the Margins* also sets out to further break down one of the ubiquitous dichotomies that dominate mainstream analyses: that drawn between formal and informal sectors of the economy. Not all of those working in regulated employment – like the shopping-mall cleaners Brody writes about in Chapter 6 – escape marginalisation and reap the rewards of global capitalism. Neither are all of those working in the so-called informal sector – which accounts for as much as two-thirds of the workforce in some countries (OSCAL 1996: 5) – marginalised in a conventional sense. The Bolivian fish sellers described by Lazar (this volume, Chapter 11), for example, might operate within the informal sector, but are far from the margins of political power. Marginalisation, all this suggests, is not uniformly experienced, and – like the sectors within which one's livelihood gets categorised – neither is it static over time. The split between the margins and the centre – a division mirroring that between informal and formal sectors of the economy – needs problematising. Not only do livelihood activities on the social boundaries have implications for those in the mainstream and *vice versa*, it is often difficult – as we shall see – to situate them in either one or the other.

Perlman's influential analysis of life in the slums of Rio de Janeiro is useful here. Not only does it help challenge the distinction between formal and informal economies, it also disrupts routinely drawn links between marginality and separateness. Despite their spatial separation from the rest of the city, she argues, squatter settlements are highly integrated with the urban economy, and should be seen as part of the solution to, rather than a symptom of, social deprivation (1976; 1990: 6). Offering free housing and reception centres for migrants, the *favelas* are recast in her work as 'thriving communities inhabited by some of the most energetic, creative, and highly motivated individuals in the entire city' (1988: iv). In contrast to Lewis's (1966) idea that groups marginalised by poverty are also culturally separate and deprived – part of a 'culture of poverty' – Perlman points to the importance of *favela* culture to Brazilian identity more generally. Her claims about the centrality of the slums to the wider economy have subsequently formed a focus of critical discussion, but her thinking on the 'myth of marginality' (1976) remains a useful counterpoint to the assumption that socially excluded people are necessarily a group apart from the mainstream.

Despite the limitations of marginality when placed in direct opposition to notions of the centre or the mainstream, or when it is used to fix groups of people in particular locations, the concept has its uses. Tsing's summary of the utility of using a notion of the margins should resonate with several, if not all, the contributors to this volume. She uses the concept to 'indicate an analytic placement that makes evident both the constraining, oppressive quality of cultural exclusion and the creative potential of rearticulating, enlivening, and rearranging the very social categories that peripheralize a group's existence' (1994: 279). Livelihoods at the margins, it seems to me, speak very effectively to this tension between constraint and creativity.

EMERGING THEMES

This brings us, rather neatly, to consider some of the other themes that recur through the chapters of this book and which suggest wider connections between very disparate livelihoods undertaken in a range of cities across the world. The tension between constraint and creativity highlighted in Tsing's (1994: 279) definition of marginality is akin to that drawn between approaches that favour structure and those that focus on agency. To phrase the problem as a question: are people constrained by their circumstances, their actions socially determined, or do they determine their own circumstances by making choices and decisions? While social deterministic analyses have rightly been criticised for overlooking people's capacities to shape their own lives, the subsequent stress on agency has also come under fire for its tendency to overstate the range of choices people have at their disposal when placed in difficult circumstances.

Elsewhere (Staples 2007) – and again in my contribution to this volume (Chapter 8) – I have attempted to cut through this tension by drawing on Bourdieu's argument that action is constituted through a mixture of individually and collectively embodied constraints – what he calls the 'habitus' – and freedom, within these constraints, to act (Bourdieu 1990: 52ff). Despite the criticism that Bourdieu does not move sufficiently far from social determinism (eg, Comaroff 1985: 5; Farnell 1994: 931; Shilling 1993: 146), I would argue that this approach provides a space in which to consider how marginalised people make meaningful choices – or, to paraphrase Ortner (1995: 190), make their own politics – *without* pushing the structural sources of their marginalisation out of the picture. People embody elements of the social structures that simultaneously oppress and enable them, their actions undertaken in the context of that embodiment. This is not, of course, a new problem: it was, for example, an important concern of the postcolonial Subaltern Studies project in South Asian studies (see, for eg, Guha 1998: ix–xxii), the background against which Scott's influential *Weapons of the Weak* (1990), referred to by several authors in this book, emerged. Nevertheless, it remains an issue that ethnographic analysis of livelihoods is particularly well placed to tackle, as many of the contributions to *Livelihoods at the Margins* illustrate.

Frankland (Chapter 2), Butler (Chapter 3) and Conticini (Chapter 4), for example, all highlight the multi-layered difficulties experienced by urban street-dwellers in, respectively, Uganda, Brazil and Bangladesh, but they also illustrate the ways in which they retain control over their destinies and create fulfilling lives. Agustín (Chapter 7) exposes the logic of migrants working in the sex industry – otherwise homogenised in the literature as the powerless victims of traffickers – who potentially earn more in one day than in several months of hard factory labour. But she does so without glamorising what is often the prosaic nature of the work. Brody (Chapter 6) and Mosse (Chapter 9) both draw on Scott's 'everyday forms of resistance' (1990) – implicitly, in Mosse's case, to show how groups as different as Bangkok cleaners and labourers in western India exercise a range of subtle survival strategies that undermine attempts to label them as supine victims of modernity. Kaiser's work with Sudanese refugees in Uganda

(Chapter 10) similarly shows how, despite the inhospitable conditions in which they find themselves, refugee camp dwellers continue to develop meaningful strategies for their survival. Sen (Chapter 5), who also uses Scott in her analysis, illustrates how the militant slum-dwelling women of her ethnographic description are in some ways the antithesis of conventional representations of oppressed women. Armed and much feared, these right-wing Hindu women 'manipulated their notorious image to threaten factory owners, business men and entrepreneurs within the unorganised sector to acquire legal and illegal jobs and assets' (Sen, this volume, Chapter 5). In short, the cumulative effect of the chapters is to rewrite conventional notions of victimhood – within which marginalised people come to be represented only in terms of their failings – while, precisely because of their ethnographic richness, avoiding the trap of romanticising poverty and resistance (Abu-Lughod 1990; Brown 1996).

Power – and its relation to agency – is never monolithic, as a number of studies have shown. Dube, for example, in his analysis of mission stations in colonial India, demonstrates that colonial authority was never a 'totalized terrain' (2004: 10). Rather, colonial hegemonies, 'dripping with dominance' (*ibid*: 53), in themselves offered the tools by which they might be resisted. To use an alternative metaphor, the more dominant that ideas at the centre become, the more they are prone to seep out to where they might be appropriated, often in unexpected ways, at the margins. The dominant distinction drawn between rural and urban domains, for example – with the former characterised as backward and traditional, and the latter as progressive and modern – might well be used to exclude and stigmatise but, as Lazar shows (this volume, Chapter 11), it is also picked up and used to provide salient markers by which people negotiate their own lives. In the case she describes, distinctions between the city and countryside were invoked not as taken-for-granted distinctions but in order to protect their livelihoods at particular times. In reality – both in Lazar's Bolivian example and elsewhere – the urban and the rural are heavily inter-connected domains, with people, as well as material goods, flowing back and forth between them. As both Mosse (Chapter 9) and Brody (Chapter 6) illustrate, rural livelihoods often rely on urban migration, while marginal urban livelihoods are frequently made bearable through social ties back in the countryside. In the case of refugee settlements, as described by Kaiser (Chapter 10), the distinction between urban and rural to some extent breaks down, the settlement constituting a liminal space that challenges rather than expresses the categories.

Nevertheless, the work represented here undeniably shares a focus on the 'urban': the centres of activity distinguishable from the rural settings within which a number of studies of livelihood have been carried out (eg, Homewood 2005; Ellis 2000), and for which the notion of sustainable livelihoods frameworks was originally devised. Accepting that the urban/rural split should not be overplayed, the chapters of this book also indicate that it is usually within cities that livelihoods at the margins are most clearly pronounced. For the hawker, the beggar, the petty drug dealer and the migrant labourer, the city offers spaces in which to create opportunities that do not exist to the same extent in the countryside. As several chapters attest, urban environments also bring with them distinctive problems. In addition to more restricted access to physical space, migrants to the city also report the fragmentation of extended kinship affinities (cf Sen, Chapter 5) and, with the shift of ethos towards individualism, an increased sense of alienation (cf Butler, Chapter 3). Cities are clearly rich sites for the study of livelihoods, as Stan Frankland's description in the next chapter suggests. He refers to Kampala, but the description could well be applied to several of the other cities we encounter in this book:

> Here, in the 'disorder of development' (Chernoff 2003: 47), the aspirations of 'formal' space merge with the frustrations of the 'informal' into an uncertain and ambiguous cityscape. While the skyline of cranes and neon signifies all the benefits that can accrue from economic development, the streets of the city represent a far more complex picture of the consequences of progress.

The city thus emerges as a centre of transnational flows and cosmopolitanism; as a place where formal and informal spaces merge; and where the head-on collision between economic and industrial development with nationalist fears of cultural erosion takes place.

Another recurring theme is the difficulty – experienced in many different kinds of ways – of looking at marginal livelihoods through the prism of 'development.' While the chapters challenge the traditional (but much contested) notion that 'development' is necessarily an unmitigated force for social good – exposing it as the product of particular worldviews, embedded in particular political structures – they also go beyond that general critique to look at the specific ways in which policy interventions fail, and ask what might be done to rectify this situation. Many of the people encountered in this book, for example, are not only economically marginal but are variously stigmatised as dirty, backward, immoral, criminal and depraved. The development gaze tends to accept these perceptions as unproblematic, with interventions designed to cure people of these negatively ascribed identities rather than changing how they are labelled in the first place by contesting the wider external causes of their stigma. Finding ways around this in order to find appropriate solutions to deprivation are self-evidently complex and, if the examples in this book teach us anything, it is that policy needs to be carefully tailored to each situation. Its practice – as Sen's detailed example of a politically-motivated micro-credit scheme shows so well (Chapter 5) – also needs to be interpreted with due respect to context. Blanket strategies for poverty alleviation tend at best to be ineffectual and, at worst, counterproductive.

However, despite their ethnographic specificity, there are some general findings that emerge through the chapters that might usefully inform policy. For example, the ways in which legal restrictions – often intended to protect the socially excluded – serve as impediments to livelihoods at the margins recur sufficiently often to suggest a more general problem. People struggling to make a living on the streets as hawkers and beggars; refugees in settlements; and workers in the sex industry are all shown here to suffer the consequences of legislation ostensibly there to protect them. Mosse's analysis of the difficulties faced by migrant labourers in western India shows that even when appropriate legislation is in place, its benefits are frequently inaccessible to the marginalised. Exploration of the wider implications of such legislation – and of policy in general – is overdue, and suggests a widespread failing to connect micro-concerns to macro-policy. How can the particular priorities of socially marginalised groups be incorporated into the development-driven focus on countrywide policy? The case studies offered in this book provide policy makers with the kind of raw material vital to making these connections and point the way towards considering that material outside forceful disciplinary and moral narratives. Several chapters also suggest how such approaches might be applied in particular settings.

Further elaboration of these central themes – and more besides – is best undertaken through an overview of the chapters that make up this book and the links between them.

CHAPTER OUTLINES

The chapters in this volume have been organised thematically, in the hope that by placing alongside each other chapters that deal with apparently similar issues, readers will be encouraged to make connections and to reflect back on the material in ways that might not have been likely had the chapters stood alone. That said, there are a number of different ways in which the book could have been ordered, and readers might wish to find their own way in, taking cues from the titles and/or from the summaries below to create a personal ordering based on region or some other factor.

Read chronologically, the first three chapters are linked by the themes of youth and livelihoods on the streets, starting with Stan Frankland's exploration of the livelihoods of the *bayaye*, a pejorative term used to describe the young men who survive on the social boundaries of Uganda's capital city, Kampala. The *bayaye* cluster in groups according to the activities they are engaged in; in the case described, this is selling drugs to the expatriate community. Each group has its own territory and set of loose elective affinities and strategic compliances that bind them together. As Frankland shows, the same demonising mythology that defines them as the 'other' in relation to which positive Ugandan identities are constituted, also provides a unifying identity around which the *bayaye* can organise. From one another they obtain the moral and physical support they need to survive the streets, while from the provider-user relationship with their expatriate clients they find the individual means to escape the hardships that come with such a life. Beyond this, the chapter also offers a particularly evocative account of the wider urban landscape within which the *bayaye* are enmeshed. Kampala is not, of course, every city every time, but many of the points Frankland draws out resonate through the chapters that follow. The chapter also exposes us to an alternative vision of the city to that framed by development discourse: a specifically Ugandan vision that also sees economic development in terms of cultural and spiritual loss.

Udi Butler's chapter likewise deals with youth and street-based livelihoods, drawing on fieldwork with young people who live on the streets of Rio de Janeiro. Here the focus shifts to their emotional motivations and survival strategies that, Butler contends, are encapsulated in the concepts of *revolta* and of freedom, its antidote. *Revolta* roughly translates as 'inner-rage or rebellion' and, Butler argues, is a common experience and organising narrative expressed by many young people on the street. The chapter analyses *revolta* as the embodiment of oppression: the encounter of the individual with a set of social relations that are experienced as repressive, violent, discriminatory or excluding. It also explores the experience and narrative of *revolta*, examining how the 'structural oppression' on which it draws is individually experienced, and how these experiences and narratives may serve to justify certain kinds of practices and the claiming of particular identities. *Revolta*, in this sense, is explored as a form of resistance as well as the consequence of oppression.

Continuing the theme of youth and the streets, Alessandro Conticini's chapter takes a more applied perspective to focus on how children in street situations – the precursors, perhaps, to Frankland's *bayaye* and Butler's 'enraged' youth of Rio's *favelas* – protect and promote their livelihoods in Dhaka city, Bangladesh. Street life here involves a consequential process of adaptation through which newcomers pass from survival strategies to the development of more complex coping strategies typical of well-established street dwellers. Theoretically, the chapter draws on a top-down rights-based approach integrated with a bottom-up sustainable livelihoods framework – an orientation that provides Conticini with a unique perspective on children's priorities and preferences in comparison to their institutional rights. In particular, this approach allowed observation of what street-living children are already doing in terms of managing their poverty to serve as the starting point, later setting their coping dynamics – how they built on their assets – into a broader context of children's rights.

Despite their ethnographic specificity – and the range of approaches to street life outlined in these three opening contributions – more widespread concerns are already beginning to emerge. People who survive on the urban streets might be trapped within the politically powerful and morally negative identities that are imposed on them – depraved, corrupting and dangerous – but they are not the passive, absolutely deprived 'other' that the moral majority simultaneously defines them as. Like the other marginalised groups encountered in this book, these chapters show how street-dwellers across the globe draw imaginatively on an array of resources way beyond material assets in order to get by.

In Chapter 5, the focus shifts from youth to women. Here, Atreyee Sen's emphasis is on low income, working-class women who allied themselves with the Shiv Sena, a Hindu fundamentalist political party, in Mumbai (formerly Bombay), capital of the western Indian state of Maharashtra. The chapter builds on the author's previous research, which traced women's transformation from a submissive support group (the Mahila Aghadi) within a manifestly male movement, to a violent, partially autonomous women's task force. The Aghadi's micro-finance scheme was the first large-scale economic policy for women formulated by the Sena, and the chapter discusses how a micro-credit society created under political patronage was privately intended to provide political and economic gains for the party, despite its publicly stated motive of empowering women with marginal livelihoods. In the process of manipulating genuine socio-economic concerns of its ordinary members, however, the wing also jeopardised the cohesiveness of identities that it had attained through its other mobilisational strategies. Sen's analysis of the ramifications of all this further nuances the discussions of agency and exploitation that have emerged through the preceding chapters, and points to the implications of leaving out those whose work is at or beyond the boundaries of legality from policy-making. It also challenges – in common with the two chapters that follow – stereotypical notions of what it is to be a woman.

Chapter 6 begins an overlapping set of contributions exploring issues of migration while continuing a focus on women's livelihood patterns. Here, Alyson Brody draws on research conducted among rural migrant women who worked as cleaners in a smart shopping mall in central Bangkok. The women were mainly from Isan in the northeast of Thailand, an area commonly associated with extreme poverty and backwardness. The chapter considers the modes of con-trol and discipline evident in the mall, with a specific focus on the role of cleanliness and order in maintaining working relations and identi-ties. It then goes on to look beyond these mechanisms of control to explore how everyday actions of the cleaners served to challenge the apparent primacy of established rules and hierarchies within the mall. In particular, with reference to the women's life stories, Brody suggests that there are limits to women's tolerance in respect of what they were willing to accept at work. Their stories indicated that, even as casual, low-paid workers, they had an implicit sense of their labour rights, even when this was not realised fully as unionised activity. The chapter concludes that those 'in charge' of the cleaners were well aware of what the limits of their tolerance would be and that the boundaries of the acceptable within the workplace could not be imposed. Rather, they were matters of subtle negotiation within the matrices of employer, supervisory staff and cleaners.

Chapter 7 also deals with migration, taking as its focus migrants to western Europe who work in a variety of jobs in the sex industry. Here, Laura Agustín argues that discussion of commercial sex is usu-ally framed as a moral problem, with those selling it classified – like the children Conticini describes (Chapter 4) – as victims without agency. Agustín challenges this moral framework and the assumption that sexual jobs are necessarily a wholly negative experience. Based on ethnographic research conducted in Spain, she reveals the enormous diversity of sexual jobs, many of which cannot usefully be called 'prostitution', in which skills and working conditions vary widely but high wages are the norm. Migrants who sign up for three-week live-in contracts in Spanish sex clubs, for example, may earn €5,000 a month. The chapter also demonstrates, however, that employment in the sex industry is not only about money. The locations she describes are also informal markets for migrants seeking sponsors, lovers and spouses who can help them in the process of becoming 'legal' in Europe. Sex work should, therefore, be understood as complex strategies for getting ahead and not simply as 'work'. Agustín also demonstrates how the traditional focus on marginality and victimisation mask how this huge, unregulated, sector belongs to the 'informal' economy and thus represents significant opportunities for migrant workers.

Like Sen's chapter, Agustín's contribution points very clearly to the twin problems of situating certain groups of people as beyond the pale, and – when they are included in the policy-making process at all – of starting from the assumption that they necessarily want to change their lifestyles and should therefore be treated as victims and helped to change. Policy, as Conticini notes, is too often based on common myths and on what is politically acceptable rather than on evidence: '[T]he truth is that *not* learning from experience characterises the knowledge-creating dynamics of much of the development endeavour' (Conticini, this volume, Chapter 4).

Another form of migration comes under scrutiny in Chapter 8, but a more important reason for placing it here is that, like Agustín's contribution, it attempts to consider a livelihood practice outside the moral discourse within which it is usually constrained. In this case, we are not talking about commercial sex but about begging, a form of interaction that falls betwixt and between the more widely analysed categories of market exchange and of gift giving. It is explored here, in my own contribution, as an embodied practice and as a survival strategy employed by a group of South Indian people affected by leprosy. This group, which regularly migrates to Mumbai in western India from a rural community on the opposite coast, is shown to utilise begging to positive effect, its practice fulfilling the development-defined goals of 'empowerment' and 'self-help' more effectively than most of the non-governmental organization (NGO) projects conceptualised as alternatives to begging. Although begging is technically illegal, for the 'leper beggars' I worked with, it provided a route to self-respect and financial security otherwise denied them. When begging, the bodily signs otherwise associated with social stigma were positively utilised. The chapter thus demonstrates the range of symbolic, political, and socio-religious resources available to leprosy-affected people within the constraints of a begging identity, and concludes by considering the implications of all this for NGOs and State organisations working with leprosy-affected people.

Chapter 9, by David Mosse, extends further our scrutiny of migration, placing the experience of tribal migrant labourers in the cities of western India within the broader context of institutions and agencies of State, trade unions and NGOs, contractors and brokers. The chapter asks how and why those who are mandated to protect those labourers manifestly fail to do so. These are not simply academic questions, but are posed specifically in the context of the author's work as a consultant to the DFID on its efforts to set up a programme to support *adivasi* (tribal) migrant labourers in the western region. The chapter's concern, then, is with hardship and exploitation, and how to contend with it, without denying the positive opportunities urban migration might offer. At the same time, it also sets out to avoid being held captive to powerful disciplinary narratives, within which anthropologists have tied the analysis of migration to narratives of modernity or progress, and environmentalists and developers have linked migration to narratives of decline, de-peasantisation and the creation of 'ecological refugees' or itinerant proletarians. Rather, Mosse argues that migration may index neither transformations of social mobility, nor the erosion of rural ways of living. On the contrary, it may have become the *only* means by which settled, agricultural livelihoods are possible or sustainable.

Chapter 10 concerns itself with *forced* migration, exploring the livelihood chances of refugees – displaced populations living not just figuratively but literally at the margins, shunted to border regions and confined to refugee camps. In the chapter – based on ethnographic fieldwork in a settlement for Sudanese refugees in neighbouring Uganda – Tania Kaiser considers some of the strategies employed by refugees to overcome the multiple obstacles to their social and economic survival. The immediate and most pressing question facing them – one which resonates with the socially demonised groups encountered in previous chapters – is how to get by when many of the economic activities open to them are officially illegal, or involve behaviours that contravene or transform social norms. As Kaiser demonstrates, they do so *not*, as one might expect, because of the legal and institutional structures supposedly put in place to protect and support them, but *despite* these measures. The well-intended 'Self-Reliance Strategy', for example, typically involves the allocation to refugees of inadequate plots of agricultural land, but does not enable them to trade or work freely beyond the boundaries of their refugee settlements. In this sense, the chapter shows that not only do development practices often fail – as we have seen in previous chapters – but that their apparent successes are often more ambiguous than they might initially appear. Refugees who succeed often do so because they transgress social and legal boundaries. Importantly, the chapter also shows that social and economic processes are inextricably intertwined and that understanding the values and priorities of refugee communities with respect to subsistence issues must incorporate an awareness of their socio-cultural ramifications.

The final chapter, by Sian Lazar, explicitly links the micro-practices of marginal occupations with much wider macro concerns, highlighting the connections between informal street traders and national upheavals. El Alto, Bolivia, forms the backdrop to the chapter – an 'informal city' where up to 50% of the economy is derived from commerce in the informal sector, the overwhelming preserve of Aymara-speaking rural-urban migrant women. The chapter examines the ways in which street traders organise themselves collectively in order to interact with local and national governments. Those associations are then affiliated to a citywide federation, which acts as a union, negotiating with and confronting State bodies on their behalf. Using ethnographic work with the leadership of this federation and an association of fish sellers, Lazar explores organisational structures and modes of interaction with the State, and the ethno-cultural position of middle-woman in which the street traders are located – between indigenous producers and consumers – and the implications of these for their political agency. A particular insight of the chapter, suggesting one way of reflecting on the other contributions to this book, is its challenge to conventional notions of marginality: in the case Lazar describes, people are not only constrained by the wider socio-political structures within which they are marginalised, they also play a significant role in shaping and reconstituting them. Her notion of 'in-betweenness' provides a less emphatically negative framework through which to consider livelihoods at the margins.

AND FINALLY …

One of the major aims of this book has been to present the kind of material and analysis of urban livelihoods not produced when one begins with the assumption that there are particular problems to be

resolved through external intervention. That is not, however, to confine the contributions of this volume to what some might consider
arid academic debate. On the contrary, they provide precisely the
kind of data, critique and analysis – unconstrained by perceived
needs of policy – that is needed if policy makers are to find more
workable strategies for engaging with urban marginality. It would be
misguided to presume that ethnographies of marginal livelihoods,
disassociated from the imperatives of constructing politically acceptable policy or the hegemony of 'development', are value-free and
thus present a truer picture of how people live. No research is disin-
terested. Nevertheless, the cumulative drip-drip of accounts from a
range of different perspectives *does* have the potential to change,
sometimes in subtle ways, both political imperatives *and* policy. Such
accounts also enable the micro-concerns of significant numbers of
people across the globe to inform and guide the macro-concerns of
governments and global institutions. This book is intended to be part
of that process.

References

Abu-Lughod, L (1990) 'The romance of resistance: tracing transformations of power
    through Bedouin women', *American Ethnologist*, 17(1) 41–55.
Arce, A (2003) 'Value contestations in development interventions: community develop-
    ment and sustainable livelihoods approaches', *Community Development Journal*,
    38(3) 199–212.
Behrman, J (1993) 'Macroeconomic policies and rural poverty: issues and research
    strategies', in Quibria, M (ed), *Rural Poverty in Asia: Priority Issues and Policy Options*,
    Hong Kong: Oxford University Press, 124–215.
Bourdieu, P (1990) *The Logic of Practice* (translated by Richard Nice), Cambridge: Polity.
Brown, M F (1996) 'On resisting resistance', *Amercian Anthropologist*, (N.S.) 98(4)
    729–735.
Cannon, C (1997) 'The struggle against social exclusion: urban social development in
    France', *IDS Bulletin*, 28(2) 77–85.
Carney, D (1998) 'Implementing the sustainable rural livelihoods approach', in Carney,
    D (ed), *Sustainable Rural Livelihoods: What Contribution Can We Make?* London:
    Department for International Development.
Carney, D, Drinkwater, M, Rusinow, T, Neefjes, K, Wanmali, S and Singh, N (1999)
    Livelihoods Approaches Compared, London: Department for International
    Development.
Chambers, R (1989) 'Editorial introduction: vulnerability, coping and policy', *IDS
    Bulletins*, 20(2) 1–7.
Chernoff, J M (2003) *Hustling is Not Stealing: Stories of an African Bar Girl*, Chicago:
    University of Chicago Press.
Collinson, S (ed) (2003) *Power, Livelihoods and Conflict: Case Studies in Political Economy
    Analysis for Humanitarian Action* (HPG Report 13), Overseas Development Institute:
    London.

Comaroff, J (1985) *Body of Power, Spirit of Resistance: The Culture and History of a South African People*, Chicago: University of Chicago Press.

DFID (1999) 'Introduction', Sustainable Livelihoods guidance sheet 1, Department for International Development, retrieved from www.livelihoods.org (accessed 15 January, 2007).

DFID (2000) 'Uses overview', Sustainable Livelihoods guidance sheet 3, Department for International Development, retrieved from www.livelihoods.org (accessed 15 January, 2007).

DFID (2001) 'Comparing development approaches', Sustainable Livelihoods guidance sheet 6, Department for International Development, retrieved from www.livelihoods.org (accessed 15 January, 2007).

Duany, J (2002) 'The mobile livelihoods of circular migrants between Puerto Rico and the United States', in Sorenson, N N and Olwig, K F (eds), *Work and Migration: Life and Livelihoods in a Globalizing World*, London: Routledge, 161–183.

Dube, S (2004) *Stitches on Time: Colonial Textures and Postcolonial Tangles*, Durham and London: Duke University Press.

Ellis, F (1998) 'Household strategies and rural livelihood diversification', *Journal of Development Studies*, 35(1) 1–38.

Ellis, F (2000) *Rural Livelihoods and Diversity in Developing Countries*, Oxford: Oxford University Press.

Ellis, F (n/d) 'Introduction to the PIP papers', Department for International Development, retrieved from www.livelihoods.org (accessed 15 January, 2007).

Farnell, B M (1994) 'Ethno-graphics and the moving body', *Man*, N.S. 29(4) 929–974.

Fields, G (1994) 'Income distribution in developing economies: conceptual, data and policy issues in broad-based growth', in Quibria, M (ed), *Critical Issues in Asian Development: Theories, Experience and Policies*, Oxford: Oxford University Press for the Asian Development Bank, 75–107.

Guha, R (1998) 'Introduction', in Guha, R (ed), *A Subaltern Studies Reader, 1986–1995*, Delhi: Oxford University Press, ix–xxii.

Grillo, R D (1997) 'Discourses of development: the view from anthropology', in Stirrat, R L and Grillo, R D (eds), *Discourses of Development: Anthropological Perspectives*, Oxford: Berg, 1–34.

Homewood, K (2005) (ed) *Rural Resources and Local Livelihoods in Africa*, Oxford: James Currey.

Lenoir, R (1974) *Les Exclus: Un Franaais sur Dix*, Paris: Editions de Seuil.

Lewis, O (1966) 'The culture of poverty', *Scientific American*, 212(4) 19–25.

Long, N (2000) 'Exploring local/global transformations: a view from anthropology', in Arce, A and Long, N (eds), *Anthropology, Development and Modernities: Exploring Discourses, Counter-Tendencies and Violence*, London: Routledge, 184–201.

Mazumdar, M (1994) 'Urban povery and labour markers', in Pernia E (ed), *Urban Poverty in Asia: A Survey of Critical Issues*, Hong Kong: Oxford University Press, 81–125.

Mills, E and Pernia, E (1994) 'Introduction and overview', in Pernia E (ed), *Urban Poverty in Asia: A Survey of Critical Issues*, Hong Kong: Oxford University Press, 1–51.

Mitlin, D (2005) 'Editorial: Chronic poverty in urban areas', *Environment and Urbanization*, 17(2) 3–10.

Moser, C (1996) *Confronting Crisis: A Comparative Study of Household Responses to Poverty and Vulnerability in Four Poor Urban Communities*, Washington DC: World Bank, Environmentally Sustainable Development Studies and Monographs Series No. 8.

Mosse, D (2005) *Cultivating Development: An Ethnography of Aid Policy and Practice*, London: Pluto Press.

Office of the Special Coordinator for Africa and the Least Developed Countries (OSCAL), Department for Policy Coordination and Sustainable Development (1996) *Informal Sector Development in Africa*, New York: United Nations.

Ortner, S B (1990) 'Resistance and the problem of ethnographic refusal', *Comparative Studies in Society and History*, 37(1) 173–193.

Perlman, J E and Hopkins, E M (1988) *Urban Leadership for the 21st Century: Scaling Up and Reaching Out From The Neighbourhood Level*. The Mega-Cities Project Publication MCP-046 (accessed at www.megacitiesproject.org on 4 April, 2006).

Perlman, J E (1976) *The Myth of Marginality. Urban Poverty and Politics in Rio de Janeiro.* Berkeley: University of California Press.

Perlman, J E (1990) 'A dual strategy for deliberate social change in cities', *Cities*, 7(1) 3–15.

Pernia E (ed) (1994) *Urban Poverty in Asia: A Survey of Critical Issues*, Hong Kong: Oxford University Press (for the Asian Development Bank).

Quibria, M (ed) (1993) *Rural Poverty in Asia: Priority Issues and Policy Options*, Hong Kong: Oxford University Press.

Rakodi, C with Lloyd-Jones, T (eds) (2002) *Urban Livelihoods: A People-Centred Approach to Reducing Poverty*, London: Earthscan Publications Limited.

Scott, J (1990) *Weapons of the Weak. Everyday Forms of Peasant Resistance*, Delhi: Oxford University Press.

Shilling, C (1993) *The Body and Social Theory*, London: Sage.

Sorensøn, N N and Olwig, K F (eds) (2002) *Work and Migration: Life and Livelihoods in a Globalizing World*, London: Routledge.

Staples, J (2007) *Peculiar People, Amazing Lives. Leprosy, Social Exclusion and Community-Making in South India*, Delhi: Orient Longman.

Thomas-Hope, E (2002) 'Transnational livelihoods and identities in return migration to the Caribbean: the case of skilled returnees to Jamaica', in Sorensøn, N N and Olwig, K F (eds), *Work and Migration: Life and Livelihoods in a Globalizing World*, London: Routledge, 187–201.

Tsing, A L (1994) 'From the margins', *Cultural Anthropology*, 9(3) 279–297.

Wallenstein, I (1974) 'The rise and future demise of the world system: concepts for comparative analysis', *Comparative Studies in Society and History*, (XVI) 387–415.

Washbrook, D (1990) 'South Asia, world system and world capitalism', *Journal of Asian Studies*, 49(3) 479–508.

2 No Money, No Life: Surviving on the Streets of Kampala

Stan Frankland

WELCOME TO KAMPALA

There is a moment on the drive into Kampala from the international airport at Entebbe when the road crests a hill and suddenly, a wonderful panorama of the city centre opens out in front of you. What lies before you is a vision of the capital city of Uganda that captures a particular moment in the current phase of globalisation and the postcolonial possibilities of contemporary Africa. Across a valley lies Nakasero Hill, the political and moral centre of the nation-state. The skyline is dominated by skyscrapers, cranes and other signs of modernisation, and, at night, the streets below are bathed in the glow of progress from the neon signs that bejewel them. The buildings of government, the banks, and transnational corporations and agencies do their business on the slopes of the hill. Exclusive houses and hotels, and expensive bars and restaurants provide an aura of cosmopolitan luxury for the urban elite. It is an image of a thriving city symbolising the rehabilitation and regeneration of Uganda that has occurred under the auspices of President Museveni's regime, making visible the nation's desire for opportunity and advancement. Yet, as you get closer, the city spreads out around you and a different image appears. Driving in through the traffic and congestion of the suburbs, the streets and markets are alive with the hustle and bustle typical of many African cities, and of what

Chernoff (2003: 48) calls 'urban poverty in action'. Most of the million-plus people who make their lives in Kampala do so here, away from the skyscrapers, where the dreams of economic possibility are tempered by the urgent actualities of daily life. Here, in the 'disorder of development' (*ibid*: 47), the aspirations of 'formal' space merge with the frustrations of the 'informal' into an uncertain and ambiguous cityscape. While the skyline of cranes and neon signifies all the benefits that can accrue from economic development, the streets of the city present a far more complex picture of the consequences of progress.

As a boundary zone and filtration point for the global flows of economic and cultural capitals, Kampala is by definition a place of constant transformation and contradiction. Mudimbe (1988) has suggested that the resulting social upheaval is recognised within a dichotomising system that contrasts African traditional values with an imported Western culture. The dual role this provides the city as the site of both moral consolidation and behavioural transformation is inherently ambiguous, with a fundamental paradox between the desire for economic development and material gain, and the fear of spiritual loss and cultural decay brought about by globalisation. In this sense, the city is a landscape of fear and desire, a place of attractions and repulsions. As the key conduit for the flows of transnationalism, it is arguably *the* space in which the struggles between indigenisation and homogenisation are paramount, and *the* place where the multicultural competencies of cosmopolitanism are at their highest value in Uganda. Consequently, it is in Kampala that the evidence of transculturation and the acceptance of Otherness are most visible and, as a result, it is also where the revulsion towards certain manifestations of modernity is most pronounced. The city symbolises the moral decay that is an inevitable corollary to such gains; it is both a collecting place for what is good and a receptacle for all that is bad. Through this ongoing dialogic, the cityscape becomes the place in which the ideal character of the modern Ugandan is played out on a daily basis through an array of mythic configurations and symbolic characters, such as the *malaya* (prostitute) and the *muyaye* (street thug),[1] that form the basis for the national debates on morality.

The idea of Kampala as a degenerate city is not new: it lingers on in historical traces that are still etched into the urban landscape. In one of those well-worn clichés so beloved of the travel business, this modern city is often described as a place of colonial origin, lying across the seven hills of Mengo, Old Kampala, Lubaga, Namirembe, Kibuli, Nakasero and Makerere. Such a banal tourist aphorism may seem relatively meaningless, nothing more than the casual mythologisation of a space from a limited semiotic system, with its lazy nod to ancient Rome. Yet it does open up the city to other narratives of the past and other cycles of external influence. The image of the 'seven hills' in particular highlights a historical moment in which the power of British imperialism was inscribed through the architectural dominance of the landscape. Through this identification of the city, previous methods of encountering difference and the idea of an autochthonous 'urban past' are swallowed up within a matrix that conflates colonialism with urbanisation and modernisation. On top of Mengo Hill lie the remains of this 'past' in which goods, fashions, customs and ideas spread from the royal capital of the Baganda out into the rest of the region (Médard 1998, Reid 1999). However, all around are the symbols of external power and permanence that engulfed the pre-colonial 'local'. Directly opposite the royal palace, on Old Kampala, is the site of Lugard's fort built in 1890 as a sign of British political might, military will and long-term intention. Stretched out across nearby hills are the cathedrals and mosques of the great faiths that brought their 'civilising' missions to Uganda, their panoptical obviousness extolling the guiding force of benevolence. Add Makerere University and the diplomatic centre to these structures of dominance and the old colonial skyline creeps back into view. As with postcolonial Kampala, it is an horizon of possibilities, a place of desire. The hills are like skyscrapers, the city a centre for foreign things and the dissemination of colonial ideologies throughout the new nation-state.

Once again, however, this is an uncertain landscape. The hilltop city is a place of transformation that embodies the very structures of change, but down in the valleys, in the 'great amorphous squalid *agglomeration urbaine*' (Hodgkin 1956: 64, emphasis in original), there is a very different sense of change. While the city was critical to the 'civilising mission' of the British, there was a concomitant fear expressed by colonial officers that the changes embodied within the process of urbanisation would have 'an injurious effect on the traditional ways of life of the African population' (Southall and Gutkind 1957: 44). Before World War II, the relatively low numbers of migrants to the city kept such suspicions at a low intensity. However, this situation changed with the increased emphasis on industrialisation and urbanisation that followed the war. Kampala expanded according to urban planning principles derived from Britain, but given a particular colonial twist. Suburban housing estates (eg, Nakawa and Ntinda) were designed to house the increasing African population and maintain a residential segregation between races (Southall and Gutkind 1957: 45–50). Implicit in this planning was a realisation of changing patterns of migration, away from the relatively short-term, circulatory migration of work and return (Middleton 1965), towards a more permanent idea of settlement and new forms of social relationships.

The planning of the new towns in colonial Uganda attempted to impose structure onto the process of development. However, despite this regulation of space, Kampala and the second city of Jinja were 'alien towns' (Evans Larimore 1958) both conceptually and in the perception of the foreign behaviours they provoked. In the same way that the early missionary doctors saw the trading and administrative centres as disseminating points for the spread of invading diseases such as typhoid and syphilis (Foster 1980: 76–78), colonial officers saw in them the less direct, but no less critical, threat of moral contagion. New categorical beings emerged in an attempt to control these 'alien' and transgressive spaces, with the officials and intellectuals of colonialism constructing, for example, a negative stereotype of 'town women' in an effort to control their movement and autonomy (Davis 2000: 28–60). With the filling of colonial towns by migrant men, the first women in the city were those providing sexual services, and they were frequently labelled with the stigma of prostitution (Southall and Gutkind 1957: 90). Through the binary oppositions of married woman/prostitute, and town/country (Davis 2000), the 'proper' place for a 'proper woman' (cf Ogden 1996) was the marital home, preferably in the village. By extending this masculine morality into the praxis of colonialism, the *malaya* became, mythically speaking, the indigenous woman of the frightening city and a menace to be controlled. What is interesting about the *malaya* is that this dangerous figure populates the urban landscapes of Ugandans and 'outsiders' alike, representing a coalescence of shared fears and desires over the 'future' (Frankland 2002: 164–184). She is a clearly recognisable trope within Ugandan literature and remains a key mythic character in a meta-social demonology of urban deviance. But she is not alone in this racialised, gendered and generationally-governed space. Alongside the *malaya* stands her male counterpart, the *muyaye*, another equally mythologised social threat and destroyer of structures. Born out of the dualities of the colonial city, the transgressive male was given mythic shape during the instabilities that followed independence, emerging into the cityscape in the collective form of the *bayaye*: 'ignorant, rough and tough ... [a] declassed, depoliticised group attracted to bourgeois ideology but ambivalent to bourgeois norms and values' (Obbo 1980: 222–223).

MIGRANT MYTHOLOGIES

Not only was there an assumption shared by coloniser and colonised alike that 'the town was not a suitable habitat for a permanent African society' (Obbo 1980: 22), Kampala today still poses extensive behavioural and philosophical problems to both the global and local systems of sociocultural order. As a space of utter uncertainty, Kampala is a shared landscape across both space and time. In response to the conditions of the colonial city, Kampala represents a complex interaction between the mythologisation of Africa by the colonisers and the mythopoetics of the decolonised and postcolonial. For Fanon (1967), the archetypal colonial city was split between the 'Settler's Town' nestled on the hillsides and the 'Native Town' wallowing below. As with Kampala, these were the proximate but separated worlds of the alien Other and the native Self. Through this realisation of difference came an alienated Self and, through the unequal merging of worlds, a perception of loss. The city is placed in contrast to the unchanging certainty of the village, perceived as a space that destabilises 'traditions', fragmenting them with 'centrifugal tendencies' (*ibid*: 180).

Perhaps nothing encapsulates the importance of the village in the Ugandan sense of national Self more than the often repeated phrase from Okot p'Bitek's ([1966]1984: 41) famous poem, *Song of Lawino*: 'the pumpkin in the old homestead must not be uprooted!'. The simple meaning of this Acoli proverb is that old customs should not be discarded without due consideration. Used mainly by elders, it refers to the young and educated Acoli men and the fear that they may abandon their culture for the lure of the white man's world (Heron 1976: 39). Lying behind this fear of loss is the reality of rural-urban migration that developed in the 1920s as a consequence of World War I and the emergence of administrative and trading centres (Obbo 1980: 21). As mentioned above, these were initially temporary relocations that did not break long-term ties to family and community (Middleton 1965: 13). However, certain attitudinal shifts were noted among the returning young men, especially in their responses towards elders and displays of urbanity towards women (Southall 1954). Out of such behaviour and the simple fact that not all young men returned to the village, came the fear of loss of traditional ways, of the 'uprooted pumpkin', in which the rural represented the 'ultimate security against the vicissitudes of urban life' (Obbo 1980: 30). This idea is captured in a passage from Gakwandi's (1997: 79–81) historical novel about one man's odyssey through the political turmoil of

Uganda, in which an older village man chastises a young migrant male as 'an irresponsible wanderer' who has turned his back on his community by seeking work in the 'foreign land' of Kampala.

The greater the levels of rural-urban migration became, and the more people settled in the city, the greater the intensity of this paradox in the practices of everyday life. This sense of loss intensified as the emerging gap between rural 'poverty' and urban 'wealth' grew in significance. An ambiguous myth developed, pitting the notion of the city as a necessary financial evil against the notion of the city as a source of moral corruption. Mukasa (1981: 30) echoes the colonial fears outlined above in his description of Jinja as a 'mechanical town,' which in its conception and development displayed only the interests and characteristics of Uganda's colonial masters and not those of the indigenous population. As a consequence, the supposed immorality of the place, in its many temporal incarnations, is related directly to the growth of the city during the time of colonial rule. The physical and spiritual move away from the village is understood as having the effect of transforming lifestyles by cutting people off from the roots of their 'culture', from the very traditions that gave them a cohesive identity. In the movement to Kampala, the fear is that the seductive qualities of the Other are so overwhelming that they entice one to give up the core beliefs of the Self and become a Westernised African (Obbo 1980: 22).

In another of his works, p'Bitek (1973) wrote that if the aspirations of post-independence African nationalism were ever to be attained, then Africa must rediscover her authentic self. This could only be achieved by Uganda ridding herself of all 'apemanship'; only then would she be able 'to develop a culture of her own' (ibid: vii), and only then would there be an African solution to African problems. To cut oneself off from one's past is to consign oneself to ignorance; to ignore the wisdom of the authentic Self leaves only the option of aping an alien Other. Mazrui (1995: 336) has labelled the postcolonial tension between what was, and what has come to pass, as 'the war of cultures in the African continent'. For him, this 'war' between mythic codes and cultural authenticities is at its fiercest in the struggle between modernisation and re-indigenisation. On the one hand, there is a reduced form of capitalism – lacking the structures of its Western progenitor, it has produced a series of anomalies that include patterns of consumption without techniques of production; urbanisation without industrialisation; materialism without rationality; and greed without discipline. This is a distorted capitalism, a mirage of development that has produced a shallow Westernisation in the social behaviour of Africans. On the other hand, there is a reversal of this trend via a return to authenticity, an original essence, a spirit and substance that can be recovered from within Africa's own history (*ibid*: 350). Such authenticity represents an essential and essentialised heritage in which traditional values are understood as timeless and without change. These values may have been covered over by the detritus of globalisation, but under the surface scree of plastic and neon lie the ways of the 'ancestors', their roots reaching deep into the rich, red soil of Africa (p'Bitek 1984: 41).

In the same way that the emissaries of colonialism imposed a stasis on African history, freezing it within an unchanging world of tribal certainty, so too does p'Bitek. Ranger (1995: 247) has described how European colonialists invented the notion of a traditional Africa of customs and continuity that was 'profoundly conservative – living within age-old rules which did not change'. This image of an eternal Africa ignores the looseness and flexibility of custom and identity in favour of rigid definitions of culture and bounded tribal entities (*ibid*: 247–248). A similar process, using the same colonially-created abstractions as a baseline, is evident in Ugandan exhortations to the past in which the images of Africa, tribe and village are reified. O'Donohue (1995: 69) refers to this idealisation as a 'myth of cultural identity', a myth that 'pretends that the people of Africa are in some way different from the rest of mankind'. It is a myth of exception, 'an Africanist myth of a pure and primal Africa contaminated by a sinful West' (Trewhela 2000: 63). For Ranger (1995: 254), these manipulations of 'invented traditions' can be understood as 'a means of asserting or increasing control' with the social construction of heritage very much a matter of power, of one group attempting to assert authority over another within the fluid networks of an ever-transforming social structure. This is what Coleman (1994: 119) has referred to as 'mythopoeic tradition', the nationalistic interpretations in which positive stereotypes are used as a counter to the negative. As with other myths of nationhood, either inclusive or exclusive, the simple fact that they may well be interpretations, imaginations or inventions is irrelevant as this does not impinge upon the perception of them as being real. What does count is that people believe them to be true and that they are effective in serving practical purposes, in this case, the reification of a sense of 'Ugandanness'. Through the moral values attached to culture-as-tradition, a balance is sought with the economic and technological superiority of the West. A separate, spiritual domain is opened up in which a sense of cultural distinctiveness is fashioned that is 'modern' in the sense of *developed* but, at the same time, non-Western in outlook and origin (cf Chatterjee 1996: 214–215).

Within this context of negation, there is a form of what Billig (1997) has termed 'banal nationalism', the imagining of the community of 'us' in opposition to an equally imagined 'them'. It is this type of deixis – the 'syntax of hegemony' (*ibid*: 87) used by the various broad-casters of modernity – that creates the stereotypes of both normality and deviation. This process of Othering is a highly political and reli-gious 'strategy of extraversion' (Bayart 1993) that accepts certain ele-ments of global culture as being beneficial while rejecting others as detrimental. Through the morality tales of contemporary novelists, the zealous sermonising of religious leaders, the evangelical morality of political rhetoric, and the populist hullabaloo of the media, a sem-blance of national unity is projected that transcends internal differ-ences and enables the imagination of a consensual majority. And it is through this moral community that an idealised set of conditions are created that determine the ways in which the Self and non-Self are defined. In this sense, the city becomes a space of desired conformity, of morally regulated sexualities and expected behaviours.[2] However, as much as this may reflect a broad national consensus, it relies on the negation of transgression through the mythologies of deviance. There is a teratology of dangerous beings, such as the *malaya* and the *bayaye*,[3] who populate a social geography of fear, a space beyond the moral parameters of a dominant patriarchy and 'glocal democracy'.[4] The alien city reappears as a source of contagion where the nation's youth can be infected with foreign behavioural patterns that are extrinsic to the conservative myths of gerontocratic dominance. And it is on the streets of Kampala that the contradiction between the visions of youth and the images of authority are manifested in day-to-day life. It is here that contemporary Ugandans have to deal with the moral dilemmas and 'epistemological ruptures' arising from modern living (Labidi 1996: 75–89), such as the conflict between rural and urban lifestyles and the culture clash between collective beliefs and autonomous practices.

THE MYTH OF YOUTH

The *bayaye* are everywhere in the cities of Uganda, hanging out on every street corner, spots they have occupied for quite a while. For a long time, the rural-urban migration that brought young men to Kampala produced a 'surplus' population, as the number of job seek-ers outweighed the available employment opportunities (Mushanga 1975: 164). With this came a growing number of estranged migrants, alienated from rural home ties (*ibid*: 162) making their livelihoods on the economic fringes of the city. During the years of violence that followed Amin's takeover, the urbanisation of Kampala and the growth of its suburbs continued (Calas 1998), and this growth has only accelerated since President Museveni has taken power. However, even with the economic rehabilitation of the country and the implementation of structuralist economic policies, the 'informal sector' has continued to grow. Indeed, it has been within the *magendo* (parallel) economy that the majority of the urban 'surplus' has found at least partial employment, or what has been referred to as 'disguised' unemployment (Nyakana 1995: 207–208). This particular economy has a long history in Uganda: as a space beyond colonial controls; as the main source of livelihood during the violence perpetrated on the nation by the dictatorships of Amin and Obote; and as either a supplement or necessity for most Ugandans living under Museveni. For the *bayaye*, the *magendo* economy is where they work, earning a living that does not produce a sufficient or regular enough income to survive within the imagination of formal economic parameters. The streets represent a space that is beyond the authority of the State, beyond the rules of the formal economy and out of the grasp of formal development. In this sense, the vibrant street economy that breathes life into the concrete of Kampala is a place for the excluded, those people for whom there is no space within the economic redevelopment of Uganda. They exist beyond the classificatory capabilities and systems of identification necessary for reform; they are structurally invisible.

However, as I have mentioned, those who dwell in this space are given mythic form within the social geography of the city, and are attributed with certain characteristics of deviance. With regard to the *bayaye*, as an exemplar of a marginalised African 'youth' in general, a 'lost generation' (Cruise O'Brien 1996), there is the perception that they are either 'actual or potential criminals' (Nyakana 1995: 208). Their position on the borders of legality is legitimised by a social history that reflects the political turbulence of post-independence Uganda. Because of the vicissitudes of the past, the *bayaye* are unable to participate in the culture of development that surrounds them, the same past having denied them the necessary skills. In broad terms, the successive calamities of war and AIDS, combined with the increased urbanisation, have produced a generation of disenfranchised youth. Family structures have been torn apart and there has been a subsequent loss of adequate parental guidance (*ibid*); the nation's moral fibre has been weakened, resulting in a lack of respect

for the old and for values of traditional decency (Mutibwa 1992: 122).
With insufficient education and an almost total lack of employment
opportunities within the formal economy, the *bayaye* have grown up
surrounded by the needs and temptations of the city, 'devoted to
shady deals, if not outright theft' as a way of getting by (Harmsworth
1987: 98–99). In this explanation, the *bayaye* are recognised as a product of the Self, a logical consequence of profound social upheaval.
However, cast as criminal, their very presence on the streets brings
the constant threat of violence and danger to the norms and values of
the moral majority. They are a classic example of all that youth should
not be, a danger to the Self precisely because of their alienation.

It is within this context that the *bayaye* are incorporated into the
wider debates on 'youth' as constructed discursively across social and
political levels of influence (cf Sinha-Kerkhoff 1999: 117–139). There is
a pervasive perception that the young, as a conservative collective
identity representing the future of the nation, should be deferential,
respectful, subservient and immune to the fashions of the West. But,
parallel to this, there is a 'culture of juvenile derision' (Bayart 1993:
253) that chastises the youth for their weakness, idleness, and failure
to resist the shallow temptations of globalisation. Once again, the loss
of tradition is understood as the moral result of the acquiescence to
external forces of change, rather than a consequence of internal failings. There is a basic feeling that adherence to traditional values is
incompatible with the adoption of foreign practices, and an assumption that to desire the fads and fashions of the West is a product of
ignorance and a cause of degeneracy. As Bayart (*ibid*: 31) has written,
'the constituent hybridisation of cultural invention in the colonial or
postcolonial situation is always a wrench', and it is in the fusions of
bayaye lifestyle that the greatest wrench between the authority of age
and the vitality of youth becomes apparent. It is not the notion of
change itself that creates the moral conundrum, but the means and
methods adopted in managing the lived situation of change; the creative combination of divergent elements from both tradition and
modernity, and from the Self and Other.

An article in the Ugandan daily newspaper *The Monitor*
(09/10/1998: 28) typified the continuing fear of 'apemanship', claiming that 'ubiquitous television in urban areas has lead to a lot of copy-
ing of America's counter-cultures without understanding their
essence'. Within this is a paternalist and patronising critique of
'youth' – those who succumb are derided for their acquiescence to
external influences, but also for their inability to understand fully
what it is that they are emulating. However, in a world where no

viable future is presented and there are no role models to emulate, visions of the Other provide a sense of freedom that cannot be found in the material environment of the Self: 'Rambo becomes an escape valve' (Monga 1996: 95). While the image of Rambo is now somewhat archaic, the assimilation of Western culture by 'youth' becomes a tactic of evasion (Bayart 1993: 254) within an 'informal' system of resistance (Monga 1996: 111) through the active creation of difference. By adopting the guise of the alien, if only in appearance, a visible distinction is drawn between the generations, and even between classes to the extent that they exist in Uganda. This gap is extended through different ways of seeing and age-defined gazes. El-Kenz (1996: 55) suggests that there is a process of 'selective' viewing among African 'youth' in general in which visual cultures are adopted into particularised spheres of reference. There is a specific form of cultural translation, a different method of responding to the external, that conflicts with the dominant motives and values of 'Ugandanness'.

For Monga, the idea of a role model was confined to Rambo and other white action heroes, but the arrival of satellite TV in Uganda has opened up a whole new world of potential for young Africans. One afternoon in 1998, I was sitting in a bar in Fort Portal.[5] The place was empty, but the silence was broken by the TV, tuned to Channel O as usual, beaming in from South Africa an endless stream of American R&B videos. As I sipped my beer, the young barman watched with eager attention as Tupac Shakur rapped his way through one of his releases from beyond the grave. Gazing intently at the screen, he began to assume small body postures that matched Tupac's 'gangsta' poses, his fingers mimicking gestures he saw on the screen. The song faded out and the pseudo-American presenters came on; their clothes, accents and hand movements displaying a similar imitation of 'gangsta' style. As the next video started up, an old man walked into the bar and took the stool next to mine. He looked up at the TV, unimpressed by the spectacle it presented, and asked the barman if it was possible to switch channels to UTV, the State-run terrestrial channel. The barman replied curtly, 'it is not possible'. He continued, gesturing at the TV, 'it's international now', pausing for effect before adding, 'Uganda is out of service'. What this short anecdote emphasises is two very different ways of seeing and listening. The old guy saw uncouth behaviour and heard a displeasing racket, while the young man saw a role model to emulate and heard an attitude of resistance; one saw a degenerate youth and the contamination of tradition while the other saw a rich young black man succeeding against the odds and an external world of opportunities.

In this context, the politics of aesthetics – of how things look and to whom – is inextricably bound up with the dialogic formation of the moral community and the assertion of values. As such, it is possible to say that the same image can provide the raw material for substantially different gazes, and for radically different interpretations of the same event. Tupac is a perfect emblem of this visual dissonance, being an incarnation of a nightmarish future for the dominant generation while, at the same time, presenting a dream of possibility for young men living in a world beyond their control. More than this however, the dream itself opens up the differences between the imaginative possibilities of desire and the assertions of hope. El-Kenz (1996: 55) has suggested that there is a gap between fantasy and reality that 'constitutes the most specific and original feature of the youth of the Third World'. Such a gap exists not only between the Self and Other, but also amongst the multiplicity of Selves, most notably between genders and generations. This is evident in the contrasting values attached to the image of Tupac: for the old man, he was an example of the swamping of 'local culture' and 'loss of self'; for the young man, the dead rapper presented an entirely different conception of the external and of a reimagined Self. Through such differences in the translation and reception of mythologics, and through divergent uses and displays of material objects, the city becomes the centre for contrasting imaginations of modernity (cf Halstead 2002: 273–293). As Weiss (2002: 119) has said in relation to young men in Arusha, Tanzania, 'fantasies are *real* and they are poised … at precisely that intersection of global possibility and local limitation'. For the *bayaye* of Kampala, that intersecting space is a long way from skyscrapers and suburbs: it exists in the turbulence of the streets 'where tomorrow is only a dim prospect, [and] striking it rich is hardly more fantastical than scraping by' (*ibid*: 118–119). It is here that fantasy is brought to life in the city, in a dreamworld that does not match the linear desires of national progress.

DRUGS AND DREAMS

It is difficult to identify a singular young man who embodies the full range of demonic qualities attributed to the *bayaye*. However, within the inequalities of cosmopolitanism and the power relations inherent within the current conditions of existence, it is possible to identify a social space of a 'male-specific oppositional culture' (Abdullah 1999) in which traces of the mythic figure can be identified. If there can be said to be a physical centre to the grey area between legality and illegality in the city, it is in the valley below Nakasero Hill where an unruly complex of markets, *takisi*, and bus parks comprise the nerve systems of street life. In the new *takisi* park, young men cluster in groups according to distinctions in the work they are doing, forming discrete occupational geographies that make up the nodal points in the networks of the urban economy. At the corner of a street overlooking this hub of activity, there are the *boda-boda* (mopeds that take paying passengers) drivers leaning on their bikes, waiting for a pickup. Nearby might be a group of unlicensed hawkers trying to flog anything from razor blades to children's toys. Just on from them may be a group of money changers, a clutch of young men with bundles of bank notes who make their money by breaking down their customer's larger notes into smaller bills for a commission. This is the territorialised world of the *bayaye*, spaced out by different occupations, each with their own variations and crossovers, but each with their own piece of the street. Each individual has wider networks of social relations beyond and along the street, but it is at these congregational points that a loose affinity is created. This 'ownership' of particular spaces is reflected in the young men's assured behaviour, a familiarity of place that enables a self-confidence in attitude, but that also ensures a visibility of labelling.

One such self-demarcated zone is Nakasero market, a popular fruit market in central Kampala that has a long history of young men acting as guides for *bazungu* (white people). Over time, the market has become synonymous with this particular activity. In the years leading up to independence in 1962, it was standard practice for young men to help *bazungu* with their shopping by carrying their baskets and suggesting which stall to go to (cf Hills 1977). This practice still goes on today, although in a more complex form. Simply described, the *bayaye* act as intermediaries between the customer and the vendor, leading the way to the market stalls and the surrounding shops and kiosks. The individual earns his cut, his commission, through either overcharging or receiving tips and gifts in return for his services. This style of street life is not unique to Uganda's *bayaye*. There is a history in Africa of 'pilots', of 'virtual or potential delinquents fending for themselves by stealing, gambling, acting as guides to sightseers, or directing European sailors and soldiers to prostitutes' (Henriques 1962: 380). This style of 'piloting' corresponds closely to the wide range of survival techniques employed by similarly excluded young men across the globe. Generally, the mediating services of these 'entrepreneurs' are associated with the peripheral areas of tourism space (eg, Dahles and Bras 1999), but in Uganda, due in part to the low number of tourists, it occurs at the edges of the expatriate community, a hotch-potch of white Africans, foreign businessmen, development workers and the few tourists.

In response to the standard greeting of 'how's life?', a regular answer from the young men would be either 'surviving' or 'fifty-fifty'. The follow-up would move further along on the same lines: 'life is tough, there is no money around'; 'my pockets are empty'; 'you know how it is ... no money, no life'. Such a life of survival is framed by the constant struggle for access to resources and material things, a continual fight against exclusion from the benefits of modernisation. In this context, what better opportunity for survival than the wealth of the *bazungu*. One of the young men, Bob, explained to me why he first went to Nakasero.[6] His story was fairly typical in the sense that Nakasero provided the best option available to him in a time of crisis. Like most of his colleagues and many Ugandans in general, his personal history was a difficult one. His father, a policeman, had died while he was still at Secondary School and his mother could not afford to pay the fees. As Bob put it, 'the money ran out'. He had no qualifications so it was impossible to get a job. His only option was the street, and Bob chose the market:

> Somebody told me about it ... that if you try at the market you can talk to the white people, you know, then they can give you an offer to continue your studies, but I never got the chance so I just ended up there.

He started out carrying the bags of *bazungu* shoppers and running errands for shopkeepers, gradually carving out a niche for himself within the market. By the time I knew him, he owned his own small house in the 'ghettoes' below the Kibuli mosque and had a long-term partner with whom he had just had his first son. Still based at the market, he continued to make his money as a 'pilot':

> I'm like a market salesman; I know all the prices around. If I bring you to somebody to sell something, he knows that if I don't want to bring you there I can take you somewhere else. So I have to get paid.

His main source of income was, however, the dealing of drugs to *bazungu*, a job shared by most of the 'Nakasero boys'. If it was bag-carrying that defined them in the 'innocence' of colonialism, it is drug-dealing that does so today. Walking through the market, any likely looking punter is greeted by a barrage of propositions: '*muzungu! muzungu!* You want marijuana, *bhangi*? I can get you anything'. It is with this propositional intensity that the hustle begins. Marijuana is the number-one seller, normally as ready-rolled joints called *kikumi* (one hundred), relating directly to their actual street price. For the tourist or casual visitor that price is inflated as much as possible and one *kikumi* could sell for as much as 1,000 *Ush*. Normally, that price would buy a bundle of five loose joints. However, the prices come down and the quality goes up for a regular buyer, partly because the quantities purchased increase, but also because the contact develops from being a random score to a recognisable dealer-user relationship. It is as this point that the tourist ceases to be of importance, and the expat, 'the *muzungu* who stays', becomes the target opportunity. These client relations are closely guarded as they are considerably more profitable than other more straightforward mediations. They also tend to be of greater intimacy than others made with *bazungu* primarily because the illegality of the transaction requires a shared secrecy, a joint complicity that entails a move off the streets. With this move, the relationship is transformed, opening up new potentials and possibilities for the *bayaye* through the extension of their social relations. A number of the Nakasero dealers built wider networks among expatriates through one initial connection, using this relationship as a way to move from Nakasero into the cosmopolitan nightlife of Kampala, a different but more profitable marketplace. It is in this sense that the *muzungu*-as-commodity provides the opportunity to realise, at least in part, the dream of escaping from the street, albeit temporarily.

One of the more successful of the Nakasero *bayaye*, Peter, still carried the shopping bags for one particular expatriate family. I asked him why he continued to do this menial task when he could afford not to bother. Peter replied, 'it is my job'. His rationale was implicit: his job was to maintain a long-standing relationship that he had developed over a number of years, and bag-carrying was a symbol of the value he attached to it. The relationship certainly involved a lot more than postcolonial subservience. Peter would help out with almost anything that he was asked to do, from moving furniture to recovering a stolen mobile phone. He would often be called on his own mobile phone and summoned to assist in a time of crisis. But the most important part of his relationship with this family, and the reason why he did many of the other things, was the pusher-punter arrangement he had with the son. This young expat was a heroin user and it was through the dealing of 'brown sugar' that large sums of money could be made. Through this and his other drug related 'friendships', Peter had been able to buy a house in a relatively comfortable suburb of the city as well as a motorbike, which he used to provide a personal delivery service to his clientele. He still frequented the market to visit his old colleagues, but it was no longer his place of work. Drugs and *bazungu* had enabled him to move beyond the limitations of the street.

Sold in small wraps, *kikete*, which cost between 1,000 and 2,000 *Ush*, and gram bags for 10,000–15,000 *Ush*, heroin is obviously a more expensive commodity than marijuana. However, it is the increased consumption rate by the user that makes the heroin-dealing relationship particularly profitable for the dealer. A 30,000 *Ush* marijuana deal would buy around two pounds in weight, enough to last a heavy user two-to-three months. The three grams of heroin that could be got for the same amount could be used up in a single afternoon. One of the dealers I knew had a heroin client in a regional town who used to come to Kampala every couple of months and buy 50 grams at a time. This is most definitely 'serious money', and as a result the heroin clients are the most fiercely protected of all the provider-user relationships in the market. As such, there is a greater secrecy about them than with other dope deals, and the handover of the drug is infinitely more discrete. Partly because the punter would not want to publicise his addiction, and partly because the dealer would not want others to know his finances, smack is always dealt at a pre-arranged meeting somewhere away from the prying eyes of the law and from the other Nakasero boys – 'if they see too much then they will get jealous; they will try and steal the business'.

The greatest competition lies between the dealers themselves. Peter and Bob had been friends for a long time; they had originally come to the market around the same time, but they no longer spoke to each other and operated from the opposite ends of the same street, each with their own set of acolytes. The source of their argument was a fall-out over a customer; Peter had gone away to Kenya with a white girl and during his absence Bob had started to sell 'brown sugar' to one of Peter's most regular clients. On his return, Peter found out and accused Bob of trying to steal his business and the dispute escalated from there. What is interesting about this fight is the reduction of the *muzungu* to the level of an object that can be possessed, and over which ownership can be claimed. It is at this depth of symbolic consumption that the opportunity the *muzungu* represents is most fully realised. The only comparable situation to this within the range of Nakasero boys' practices is when one of them is able to get a *muzungu* girlfriend. As with the rest of the tourism business in Uganda, sex tourism is not a thriving sector, particularly in the context of female tourist/male host relations, or what Pruitt and LaFont (1995) call 'romance tourism'. However, odd instances of it do occur, and a few of the Nakasero boys, usually the ones who correspond to the familiar global image of the dreadlocked beach-boy, have made the most of their opportunities.

One young man who had a number of white girlfriends, Tom, explained to me why such opportunities arose: '*muzungu* girls don't want to fuck rich Ugandans, they want to love poor Ugandans'. The way to capitalise on this postcolonial guilt was to 'show them you are rich in your heart'. This approach seemed to work for Tom and he had numerous affairs with white women. He was always very careful not to let them know that he was also a drug dealer so as not to spoil his carefully constructed image of the noble poor. This separation of roles was particularly evident when his Ugandan wife had a baby by Caesarean section. As soon as the operation was over, he went straight to his American girlfriend. I pushed him about the morality of going immediately from his wife and newborn child into the arms of his lover and he responded by drawing a clear distinction between the two relationships. With his wife it was 'life and love', whereas with the girlfriend it was 'business, it's survival'. This same pragmatic approach to morally ambiguous situations was also evident in the heroin dealer-user relationship. During my fieldwork, a teenage expat suffered a heroin overdose and nearly died. He was sent abroad to recover, but on his return to Kampala, he went back to Nakasero and the welcoming arms of his dealer. I asked Bob whether he would sell to the young guy if he was in that situation. He replied: 'This is how we live; this is the world. What they ask, that's what we give. How they use it is their business'.

STREET LIFE

As a collective group spatially defined, the Nakasero *bayaye* can be compared to the emergent socialities and uncertain groupings described by Maffesoli (1996). The elective affinity of togetherness breaks down the discursive totality of the generic *bayaye* into a varied collection of diffuse unions (*ibid*: 73) that come about through face-to-face interactions within the different occupational geographies of the city. Within these voluntary and empathetic collectives, togetherness is based on 'proxemics' and 'the foundation of a succession of "we's" which constitutes the very essence of all sociality' (*ibid*: 139). There is competition between particular individuals as well as the temporary affiliations among the young men within the market, but each grouping provides a critical network of mutual support that enhances the prospects of surviving on the streets. And despite the divisions and different loyalties among the Nakasero boys, there is also a broader notion of 'shared sentiment' (*ibid*: 20), a particular way of seeing the world, and a will to live that transcends the squabbles of daily life. Survival is framed within a range of contexts that incorporate the individual *muyaye* within a localised sense of unity, a togetherness born out of physical and philosophical closeness. In the context of the deictic strategies of the nation-state, the 'we's' of the *bayaye* are fundamentally oppositional. The ongoing mythologisation of 'bad' youth within the national debates on morality is counterbalanced by the temporary groupings in which the individual can seek out alternative possibilities of being within specific networks of sociality that, in turn, coalesce with a more widespread notion of street culture and attitude.

The overwhelming tone of the contemporary moral discourse in Uganda concerning the conflict between continuity and change is one of exclusion. Despite the stated political inclusiveness of the President, the rhetoric of his nationalism precludes this potentiality. In Simmel's terms, the stranger can be understood as 'a synthesis of nearness and remoteness' (1950: 407), and, as such, is a danger to the boundaries between 'us' and 'them'. In this sense, the mythic characterisation of the *bayaye* that renders them as strangers within their own land are 'ideological manoeuvres' by which the assumed majority, the imagined community of the nation, is given an essentialist identity (Bhabha 1986: 300). However, this manoeuvre also gives to the *bayaye* their own essentialist identity as a 'them' excluded from the national whole. By living the life expected of them or by being perceived as corresponding to the mythic archetype, such characters devolve their own power as an oppositional example for an alternative method of survival within the frightening city. They become the embodiment of the fear that makes them such a powerful discursive figure and, in so doing, two different, but coterminous formats of 'reverse discourse' (Foucault 1981) come into play.

In a Foucauldian sense, there is a strategy of the marginalised who try to re-inscribe themselves within the centre of culture by taking on the dominant categories as a means of self-justification. The *bayaye* are, in many ways, exactly what one would expect them to be – loud, proud and aggressive – which reinforces the notion of their externality in regard to nationalist rhetoric. While on a Saidian level, 'a certain reverse Orientalism is seen to occur when an African identity is sought in opposition to an "idea" of what is believed to be the West' (Vera 1996: 6), or an identity is sought in opposition to the idea of what is supposed to be the dominant majority. This is the stance of being *bayaye*, of being a different kind of Ugandan altogether. By sticking to their guns, by living life as it comes, the *bayaye* chart a path, haphazard and ill planned at times, through the turbulence of every-day existence in Kampala. Away from the abstractions of myth, there is a sense of strong individual self-reliance, but also a shared sense of togetherness that provides an alternate, if amorphous, belief system that is narrower yet more precise the greater the collective spirit. The more their perception of their shared experience moves from being together through occupation to being together because of lifestyle, then the greater emotional depth of what is shared, and with this sense of security comes a greater self-belief and a stronger awareness of individual power and autonomy.

Notes

[1] The m-/mu- prefix denotes the singular while the ba- prefix indicates the plural. This usage is consistent throughout the text.

[2] For further analysis of this issue, see Davis 2000, Frankland 2002, Ogden 1996, and Wallman 1996.

[3] This urban teratology also includes such 'deviant' figures as street children, beggars, thieves, armed robbers, terrorists/rebels and homosexuals (Frankland 2002: Section 3).

[4] The phrase 'glocal democracy' refers here to the locally specific manifestation of the global concept of democracy. During President Museveni's regime a particularised form of this political ideology has emerged that is commonly referred to, without irony, as 'no-party democracy'.

[5] This chapter is based on 20 months' fieldwork carried out in Uganda during 1997–1999, and a supplemental visit in the summer of 2000.

[6] I have changed all of the names of the 'Nakasero boys' for obvious reasons.

References

Abdullah, I (1999) 'The role of youth in conflicts', unpublished paper presented at a workshop, 'The Role of Youth in conflict prevention in Southern Africa', held in Livingstone, Zambia, 11–16 April 1999.

Bakwesegha, C J (1982) *Profiles of Urban Prostitution. A Case Study from Uganda*, Nairobi: Kenya Literature Bureau.

Bayart, J F (1993) *The State in Africa: Politics of the Belly*, Harper, M et al (trans.), London: Longman.

Bhabha, H K (1986) 'Signs taken for wonders: questions of ambivalence and authority under a tree outside Delhi, May 1817', in Gates, H L Jr (ed), *'Race', Writing and Difference*, Chicago: University of Chicago Press, 163–183.

Billig, M (1997) *Banal Nationalism*, London: Sage Publications.

Calas, B (1998) *Kampala. La Ville et le Violence*, Paris: Karthala.

Chatterjee, P (1996) 'Whose imagined community?', in Balakrishnan, G (ed), *Mapping the Nation*, London: Verso, 214–225.

Chernoff, J M (2003) *Hustling is Not Stealing: Stories of an African Bar Girl*, Chicago: University of Chicago Press.

Coleman, J S (1994) *Nationalism and Development in Africa: Selected Essays*, Sklar, S L (ed), Berkeley and Los Angeles: University of California Press.

Cruise O'Brien, D B (1996) 'A lost generation? Youth identity and state decay in West Africa', in Werbner R and Ranger T (eds), *Postcolonial Identities in Africa*, London: Zed Books, 55–74.

Dahles, H and Bras, K (1999) 'Entrepreneurs in romance: tourism in Indonesia', in *Annals of Tourism Research*, 26(2) 267–293.

Davis, P J (2000) 'On the sexuality of "Town Women" in Kampala', *Africa Today*, 43(3/4) 29–60.

de Certeau, M (1984) *The Practice of Everyday Life*, Rendall, S (trans), Berkeley and Los Angeles: University of California Press.

El-Kenz, A (1996) 'Youth and violence', in Ellis, S (ed), *Africa Now: People, Policies and Institutions*, The Hague: Ministry of Foreign Affairs (DGIS), 42–57.

Evans Larimore, E (1958) *The Alien Town: Patterns of Settlement in Busoga, Uganda. An Essay in Cultural Geography*, University of Chicago, Department of Geography Research Paper No. 55.

Fanon, F (1967) *The Wretched of the Earth*, Farrington, C (trans), Harmondsworth: Penguin.

Foster, W D (1980) *The Early History of Scientific Medicine in Uganda*, Kampala: Uganda Literature Bureau.

Foucault, M (1981) *The History of Sexuality Volume 1*, Hurley, R (trans), London: Penguin Books.

Frankland, S (2002) 'The tainted pearl: stories of war, tourism and development in Uganda', unpublished PhD thesis, School of Oriental and African Studies, University of London.

Gakwandi, A (1997) *Kosiya Kifefe*, Nairobi, Kampala and Dar es Salaam: East African Educational Publishers.

Halstead, N (2002) 'Branding "perfection". Foreign as self; self as "foreign-foreign"', *Journal of Material Culture*, 7(3) 273–293.

Hannerz, U (1980) *Exploring the City. Inquiries Toward an Urban Anthropology*, New York: Columbia University Press.

Harmsworth, W J (1987) 'The Ugandan Family in Transition', in Wiebe, P D and Dodge, C P (eds), *Beyond Crisis. Development Issues in Uganda*, Kampala: Makerere Institute of Social Research/African Studies Association.

Henriques, F (1962) *Prostitution and Society: A Survey. Volume 1, Primitive, Classical and Oriental*, London: MacGibbon and Kee.

Heron, G A (1976) *The Poetry of Okot p'Bitek*, London: Heinemann Educational Books.

Hills, D (1977) *The White Pumpkin*, London: The Quality Book Club and The Travel Book Club, joint edition.

Hodgkin, T (1956) *Nationalism in Colonial Africa*, London: Frederick Muller.

Labidi, L (1996) 'Building public morality', in Ellis, S (ed), *Africa Now: People, Policies and Institutions*, The Hague: Ministry of Foreign Affairs (DGIS), 75-89.

Maffesoli, M (1996) *The Time of the Tribes. The Decline of Individualism in Mass Society*, Smith, D (trans), London: Sage Publications.

Mazrui, A A (1995) 'Is Africa decaying? The view from Uganda', in Hansen, H B and Twaddle, M (eds), *Uganda Now. Between Decay and Development*, London: James Currey, 336–358.

Médard, H (1998) 'Competing for power symbols: urban changes in the capital of Uganda in the 1890s', *Les Cahiers de l'IFRA*, 9, 23–55.

Middleton, J (1965) *The Lugbara of Uganda*, Chicago: Holt, Reinhart and Winston.

Monga, C (1996) *The Anthropology of Anger. Civil Society and Democracy in Africa*, Fleck, L L and Monga, C (trans), Boulder: Lynne Reinner Publishers.

Mudimbe, V Y (1988) *The Invention of Africa. Gnosis, Philosophy, and the Order of Knowledge*, London: James Currey.

Mukasa, A K (1981) *The Residential Housing Pattern of Jinja*, Kampala: Makerere University.

Mushanga, T M (1975) 'Notes on migration in Uganda', in Parkin, D (ed), *Town and Country in Central and Eastern Africa*, London: International African Institute, 159–164.

Mutibwa, P (1992) *Uganda Since Independence. A Story of Unfulfilled Hopes*, London: Hurst and Company.

Nyakana, J B (1995) 'Youth in development: street traders of Kampala City, Uganda', in Okoth, P G et al (eds), *Uganda. A Century of Existence*, Kampala: Fountain Publishers Ltd, 207–219.

Obbo, C (1980) *African Women: Their Struggle for Economic Independence*, London: Zed Press.

O'Donohue, J (1995) 'Africa in labour. The growing pains of a continent, *Journal of African Religion and Philosophy*, 3(1) 1–75.

Ogden, J A (1996) '"Producing" respect: the "proper woman" in postcolonial Kampala', in Werbner R and Ranger T (eds) *Postcolonial Identities in Africa*, London: Zed Books, 165–192.

p'Bitek, O (1973) *Africa's Cultural Revolution*, Nairobi: Macmillan East Africa.

p'Bitek, O (1984) *Song of Lawino and Song of Ocol*, London: Heinemann Educational Books.

Pruitt, D and LaFont, S (1995) 'For love and money: sex tourism in Jamaica', in *Annals of Tourism Research*, 22(2) 422–440.

Ranger, T (1995) 'The invention of tradition in colonial Africa', in Hobsbawm, E and Ranger, T (eds), *The Invention of Tradition*, Cambridge: Cambridge University Press, 211–262.

Reid, R (1999) 'Images of an African ruler: *Kabaka* Mutesa of Buganda, ca.1857–1884', *History in Africa: A Journal of Method*, 26, 269–298.

Simmel, G (1950) 'The stranger', in Wolff, HK (ed and trans), *The Sociology of Georg Simmel*, 402–409, Glencoe, Illinois: Free Press.

Sinha-Kerkhoff, K (1999) 'The experience of globalization: Indian youth and non-consumption', in Fardon, R et al (eds), *Modernity on a Shoestring. Dimensions of Globalization, Consumption and Development in Africa and Beyond*, Leiden: EIDOS (European Inter-university Development Opportunities Study-Group), 117–139.

Southall, A W (1954) 'Alur migrants', in Richards, A (ed), *Economic Development and Tribal Change*, Cambridge: Heffer and Sons.

Southall, A W and Gutkind, P C W (1957) *Townsmen in the Making: Kampala and its Suburbs*, East African Studies No. 9, Kampala: East African Institute of Social Research.

Trewhela, P (2000) 'Mbeki and AIDS in Africa: A Comment', in *The New York Review of Books*, XLVII (16), 63.

Vera, Y (1996) 'Introduction', in *Images of the West*, Harare: Baobab Books, 5–7.

Wallman, S (1996) *Kampala Women Getting By: Wellbeing in the Time of AIDS*, London: James Currey.

Weiss, B (2002) 'Thug realism: inhabiting fantasy in urban Tanzania', *Cultural Anthropology*, 17(1) 93–124.

Embodying Oppression:
Revolta amongst Young People Living on the Streets of Rio de Janeiro

Udi Butler

INTRODUCTION

Revolta – which can be translated as revolt, revulsion or rage – is a common expression amongst youngsters in Rio de Janeiro living on the street and in the *favelas* and peripheries. Though in Portuguese *revolta* is an uncommon word used to describe an emotional state, the term gains particular salience amongst impoverished, disenfranchised urban youth who have appropriated it to refer to cumulative experiences of discrimination and frustration at the conditions of exclusion. The term, as employed by these youngsters, is used to describe episodes of physical, emotional, or symbolic violence which are interpreted as unjust and illegitimate, and to explain certain practices such as going to the street and joining a drug trafficking gang.

If emotions can be understood as 'thinking human bodies', as suggested by recent studies in anthropology, social psychology, and the social sciences more broadly, then in *revolta* the human body is thinking about and responding to oppression (Ekman and Davidson 1994, Leavitt 1996, Rosaldo, Geertz, Levy and Shweder 1984, Shweder 1994). In my own research (Butler 2003) *revolta* emerged as what Paulo Freire, the Brazilian pedagogue, philosopher and activist, refers to as a 'generative theme' representing the most pertinent issues in the speech and life of a community (Shor 1993). The other significant generative theme I came across during fieldwork was 'freedom', referred to by youngsters as a motivating factor for going to the street as well as the key benefits the street offered.

In the case of youngsters living on the streets of Rio, the recurring themes of *revolta* and 'freedom' became crucial to understanding a series of experiences, situations, relationships, interpretations, judgments, processes of identification and life-trajectories. As such, addressing these generative themes is a way of addressing important questions concerning the relationship between the self, experience and society. It becomes a way of facing the challenge of trying to understand individual experiences and trajectories in light of the structural conditions within which lives are lived. *Revolta* thus emerges as a particular way through which these young selves engage with and make sense of the social environment in which they grow up.

There is a pressing reason for being concerned with *revolta* in the case of Rio de Janeiro. A number of youngsters on the street, and an even larger number of youngsters from the *favelas* who have joined the ranks of drug trafficking gangs, often attribute to *revolta* the reasons and motivations for their way of life. Unravelling this emotional experience becomes imperative, given the current levels of violence and insecurity faced by Rio de Janeiro's population. Such unravelling will be attempted here, both in the sense of trying to understand the full significance and emergence of this emotion, as well as in pointing to the actions of those who are on the frontline of a battle being fought not only on a social and political level but also on the level of the emotions, selves and identities.

In this process of unravelling two key questions are posed: can the emotion and the actions associated with *revolta* be seen as a form of resistance or defiance, as a struggle against the conditions of exclusion or alienation? And if so, how successful is this resistance and what role does agency play in it? The following discussion takes up the challenge of trying to integrate these issues of self, personhood, emotions and subjectivity with a critical analysis of oppression, poverty and social structure.

THE ANTHROPOLOGY OF SELF AND EMOTIONS

Interpretivist trends in the social sciences have led many to argue that 'meaning' is a public fact and that personal life also takes shape in cultural terms (Rosaldo 1984). This has implications as far as the emotions are concerned, suggesting that rather than being unproblematically biological and therefore universal, pre-social and private, emotions should instead be considered as socially and symbolically produced and expressed (Leavit 1996). Emotions, Michelle Rosaldo suggests, are no less cultural than beliefs; they are cognitions or interpretations involving body, self and identity (Rosaldo 1984: 141). Rosaldo and others have argued that emotions should not be considered in opposition to thought but rather as 'cognitions implicating the immediate, carnal "me" – as thoughts embodied' (*Ibid* 1984: 138). Emotions, she argues, 'are about the ways in which the social world is one in which *we* are involved' and this involvement depends in turn on what our conceptions of such things as body, affect, and self are (*ibid*: 143). 'Feelings', she continues, 'are not substances to be discovered in our blood but social practices organised by stories that we both enact and tell. They are structured by our forms of understanding' (*ibid*).

Exponents of this interpretivist conception of emotions in anthropology (eg, Leavitt 1996, Rosaldo, Geertz, Levy and Shweder 1984, Shweder 1994) all emphasise the notion of emotions involving the whole 'person', entailing what Richard Shweder calls the 'self-involving stories' which make it possible for us to tell stories about our feelings (Shweder 1994). In these 'emotion stories' ('anger', 'love', or in our case, '*revolta*'), somatic and affective states (eg, tiredness, or in the case of *revolta*, the feelings of tension or withdrawal) come to represent a 'self-involving' state in the world (eg, loss or, as far as *revolta* is concerned, a sense of powerlessness, of being oppressed or belittled) which in turn also involves the formulation of a plan. For *revolta*, as we shall see, this may involve a desire to leave home, or the identification with oppositional figures and practices, such as belonging to a drug trafficking gang, taking drugs or robbing people, as means of regaining power, self-esteem and respect.

The notion of 'emotion stories' appears consistent with how I came to understand the experience of *revolta*. My attention was drawn to this 'generative theme' not only because of the commonality of the episodes it described (abuse in the home, violence and discrimination on the street and in State institutions), but also because of the similarity of the language used, involving standardised tropes for conveying the *revolta* experience, as well as the motivational aspects which lead to or justify certain kinds of behaviour and identities. Indeed, *revolta* appeared as a culturally-available idiom or story found within the broader life-stories told about the youngsters' own trajectories. As a cultural idiom *revolta* is found amongst the youth subculture of the *favelas* and peripheries of large Brazilian cities like Rio and São Paulo, though no doubt analogous terms exist in other parts of the world subject to similar conditions of exclusion and discrimination.[1] This suggests that though these cultural tropes have local and specific manifestations, they point to a more global phenomenon amongst disenfranchised inner-city youths. This idiom of *revolta* is also found in musical forms such as hip-hop (and in Brazilian funk), where the 'emotion story' is given an aesthetic form – rap music – and fed back into youth culture, in turn influencing how particular situations, such as police brutality, are perceived.[2] Yet a significant difference exists between a politicised *revolta* found in such cultural forms (for instance in Brazilian radical rap groups such as Racionais MC and MV Bill) and the emotional story of *revolta* 'on the ground' which almost invariably appears as spontaneous but unreflective rebellion against the conditions of poverty, violence and inequality. We shall return to this discussion further on. For now it is important to emphasise – because some anthropological writing on the emotions tends not to address this – that emotions always emerge out of interactions which a person has with her/himself and with others in the world (Denzin 1984: 48). As we will see with *revolta*, although there are cultural elements in the meanings and identities associated with it, the emotion also refers to specific interactions with others and with 'society'. This issue has been raised in sociology, in particular in the writings of T.H. Marshall who writes about the affective source of class antagonism originating in 'resentment against inequality' (Marshall 1977). For Marshall 'class resentment' arises from three distinct processes, which he characterises as: comparison (based on the perception of inequality); frustration (derived from the inequality of opportunity); and oppression (where persons yielding power act against those who do not have it) (Barbalet 1994). When *revolta* is expressed, these three ingredients of comparison, frustration and oppression can also be discerned. Yet, as we shall see, they do not necessarily derive from a 'class consciousness' or class identity. Those in one's community or even one's home can also be the catalyst for *revolta*.

REVOLTA AT HOME

> I don't like saying bad things about my mother, but when she hit me, she hit me not to teach, to fix or correct me, but to really break me, to leave a mark, right. This made me *revoltado* [enraged] even more and made me choose the street as my home. ...

Boys go to the street, I think, because of a lack of leisure, lack of food, lack of work, and some because of their mothers. Because there are many mothers who like to hit and this ends up provoking the young-ster to *revoltar* [rebel, enrage], making him commit this act that is to go to the street. But if the family cares for the child, gives a good school, good study, the child will never end up on the street, you understand? Because a child without love at home, without care, he will go to the street of course. Or else get into drug trafficking. Because no one likes being treated badly. Everybody wants to live well. Everybody wants to walk around well dressed. That's it.

This was a statement by Nego da Bahia, a young man who lived for a number of years on the street, and it succinctly encapsulates the expe-rience of *revolta* in the home. Describing the movement from home to the street, *revolta* is related to an experience of violence and neglect in the home but also to a lack of resources in the community. As he rightly points out, no one wants to be treated badly, everyone wants to live well; and if the resources for living well and being respected are not found at home, the youngster may turn either to the street or to *comandos*, the drug trafficking gangs who have recruited young-sters into their ranks over the last couple of decades. When violence is not mentioned as a primary reason for leaving home, then forms of neglect or confinement may otherwise be found. Many youngsters, especially girls, referred to a feeling of confinement in the home, of being subject to curfews and rules that were too restrictive, a practice that has become more common in light of the increasing insecurity within the *favelas* and peripheries. Youngsters living on the street also described a sense of 'lack' at home; a lack of economic resources for basics such as food, as well as for engaging with consumer society. But also described was a lack of affection, of a sense of protection and belonging. Though many different reasons were given for leaving home, a common factor running through them was a sense of unful-filled needs or of a 'self' subject to a denigrating, stifling environment.

This is the kind of environment that has been described as 'socially toxic', by James Garbarino (1995), describing the way in which, in some communities in the United States, the social environment in which children grow up has become poisonous to their development. Garbarino identifies the 'risk factors' in children's development – absent fathers, poverty, racism, addiction, poor physical health, edu-cational failure, family violence, and adult emotional problems that impair parenting. This is the context of the 'self-involving' conditions in which the emotional story of *revolta* emerges, giving meaning to lived experiences and situations. The encounter with the world by children and adolescents in this environment can manifest itself by somatic feelings of tension or withdrawal which may come to represent a sense of powerlessness, of being oppressed or belittled. Far from being nurtured, the growth and development of the self is frustrated and may look for satisfaction in practices and identities associated with the idiom of *revolta*. The two most extreme possibilities for children and adolescents growing up within this environment in Rio occur within the *tráfico* – the drug gangs – or the street.

There exist some parallels and significant contrasts between the recruitment of children and adolescents into the drug-trade and the trajectories to or through the street, which are characterised by defiance, escape, protection and autonomy. In many instances such trajectories are described as being motivated by *revolta*. But whereas young recruits to the drug-trade seek to be incorporated into a rigidly hierarchical criminal organisation within the *favela*, youngsters seeking escape leave the *favela* and seek out opportunities in the city. Also, whereas the pull of the drug-trade is a relatively recent phenomena of the last couple of decades, there are records of youngsters living on the streets of Rio dating at least as far back as the end of the 19th century. A consideration of numbers, however rough these may be, is also important here. Rio's *favela* population stands at over one million (20% of the city's total population), about half of whom are under 18, whereas youngsters employed in the drug trafficking gangs number roughly 6,000 (Dowdney 2002: 6). Youngsters living on the streets are less than half this figure, calculated to be between 1,000 and 3,000 (De Souza and Rodrigues 1999, IBASE 1992,). This growing influence of drug trafficking gangs has redrawn the battlelines, the approach and priorities of those working with excluded youngsters in Rio who have come to see the drug trafficking gangs as a more urgent and dangerous issue than life on the street itself.

Starting in the late 1970s and early 1980s, the *comandos* have actively recruited and employed young men and boys from the local communities to act as messengers, look-outs and gunmen (Zaluar 1994). Authors like the Brazilian anthropologist Alba Zaluar have tried to explain this growing fascination that the *comandos* exert upon these youngsters. She considers the swelling number of youth involved in drug trafficking to be the result of a process of degeneration in the 'personal networks of control and socialisation' (1994: 113). With the growth of truancy over the past few years, she argues that schools have failed as a socialising agent and a transmitter of instruction. In the crisis of values that follows, youngsters who become evermore disconnected from such structures create their own values and isolate themselves from the world of adults and their own social class. Here lies a possible reason as to the difference between *revolta* and 'class resentment' (Marshall 1977: 180). Whereas class resentment is described as the affective basis of class conflict, based on a sense of shared class identity including a shared vision of the oppressor, *revolta* appears as a more diffuse and individualistic embodiment of oppression, discrimination and the frustrations associated with poverty and inequality.

This degeneration of socialising institutions, Zaluar believes, is further aggravated by a 'consumerist and a pleasure-seeking ideology' (1994: 116),which stimulates youngsters through a dominant cultural framework propagated through the media, and television in particular, and which values and creates a sense of unlimited individual desire. This new sphere of realisation of self or identities that are forged and legitimised through acts of consumption, has come to redefine what is respectable, acceptable and normal in how we organise our lives and what we aspire to. The sphere of 'self as consumer' is nowhere more clearly visible than in the city, and nowhere is the contrast between the inclusion and exclusion within this sphere more marked than in highly unequal cities like Rio in which disparate socio-economic groups live side-by-side. In this case consumerism – rather than mitigating the source of class resentment by offering different classes the possibility for consumption and alternative identities – has exacerbated the experiences of comparison and frustration for many youngsters. This is a key issue for understanding the emotion story of *revolta* amongst youth who are excluded but who nevertheless have very similar aspirations to the rest of the city's citizens.

GOING TO THE STREET; FREEDOM AND SOLIDARITY

In moving from the home to the street – however unsavoury it may appear from the perspective where home is seen as a place of protection and the street a place of danger – many youngsters feel that they are doing precisely the opposite; moving away from danger towards protection. Some authors have argued that their response could be considered a healthy reaction to circumstances of extreme poverty and violence (Veale, Taylor and Linehan 2000).

Whereas many factors influence the journey from the home to the street, youngsters' perception that they are moving from a space that is restrictive and confining to a place where they can be free to play, work and meet others, is very significant. This is not to deny that structural factors are at work, both in their families and in their communities of origin. Yet the pursuit of independence and freedom, which are recurrent themes in the street-children literature, appear to be crucial motivating factors for taking to the street, either as a place where economic opportunities are found or else as a fun, unsupervised space where boys and girls can meet. This 'ethos of freedom' emerged as one of the central nodes upon which their identity is hinged.

On the street it is possible to obtain money in a variety of ways and there are also many avenues of consumption open to youngsters. It is on the street that consumers meet, and where the shops, restaurants, and parking spaces are located. It is here that youngsters can find something that is absent from their communities of origin, in terms of earning as well as spending money: shining shoes; selling sweets, flowers or peanuts; juggling at the traffic lights; carrying shopping bags at the market; parking cars; or begging and stealing, are some of the ways youngsters can earn money on the street.

While involved in fieldwork in Rio, I worked alongside CIESPI – Centro Internacional de Estudos e Pesquisa sobre a Infância (The International Centre for Research on Childhood) – an action-research NGO (non-governmental organization) affiliated with Pontifícia Universidade Católica (PUC), a University. Together we coordinated a large-scale research project on children living on the street. In the CIESPI research we became aware of this taste for freedom when we asked the question 'what is good on the street?' When a positive response was given, it was almost invariably 'freedom'. 'Freedom' equalled work as the most common motivation for going to the street (Rizzini, Soares, de Carvalho, and Butler 2002). As 15-year old Suzana, interviewed in the CIESPI research, said in response to the same question:

> Freedom. On the street you don't hear what you hear at home all the time. There isn't any rubbing your face in it, sometimes on the street you could be hungry, you know that you are risking your life but even so you know that in a certain way you are free, you can think what you want, you can do what you want, no matter what the circumstance, you can do the things you wish (Rizzini, Soares, de Carvalho, and Butler 2002).

Freedom and *revolta* emerged as the generative themes in the lives of these youngsters. The two terms appeared in a dialectical relationship in their life-trajectories, for whereas *revolta* can be understood as the emotional experience of abuse, belittling and oppression, the possibility of freedom arises as its antidote. Freedom and autonomy can then be understood as both an idealised aspiration that contrasts with the scarcity, conflict and confinement of the home or community, as well as a form of rebellion or resistance to these. The Brazilian anthropologist Maria Gregori suggests that youngsters transpose to something generic like the 'street' many of their childhood aspirations: the longing for protection, care, attention, learning and play. And these needs are somehow met on the street (Gregori 2000: 71).

The downside of this sense of freedom and 'living in the moment', is that it is also often associated with a fatalism common to youngsters employed in the drug-trade; an attitude which believes that death may come at any moment. Such an attitude, which can on occasion represent a reckless disregard for one's own safety, encourages the taking of greater risks and engagement in dangerous situations.

This is not to say that every youngster on the street I talked to spoke of freedom, resistance and autonomy. Many also told me that there was nothing good about being on the street. Also, the element of 'choice' or 'agency' is far from being a homogeneous quality for those youngsters who live on the street. Some clearly had less choice than others about being there, since their family (or more commonly their mothers) had brought them up on the street. Yet, what is significant about freedom, particularly in analysing the emotion of *revolta*, is the way it offers a possibility of escape from the conditions with which *revolta* is associated. Whether this is indeed the case is what I address in the next section.

REVOLTA ON THE STREET

On the street *revolta* appears to grow gradually and becomes more acute with increasing age, though most youngsters can be said to have arrived on the street with at least a little of it. It grows through the cumulative encounters with discrimination and disrespect that tend to occur more often the older one gets, usually peaking during adolescence.

On the street, increasing age and the growth of *revolta* appear to be intrinsically bound. This is not surprising considering that the responses to youth on the street are very different depending on whether the individual in question is a child or an adolescent. The latter find it progressively harder to get by on the street through begging, because people are intimidated by their larger size. This is succinctly conveyed by Aldair, a 17-year old:

Interviewer: These people here on the square, who pass by each day, what do you think they think about you?

Aldair: They must think we are going to rob them ... today I asked for R$1 from a woman, she then held on to her watch and mobile phone, and I said, 'look I am not robbing you, I am asking'.

Interviewer: Do you think that people have a reason to think this way?

Aldair: Yes, because the majority of people here rob, do shitty things, so they get scared (...)

On the street it's good when the person is small, but from 15, 16 years upwards things get even worse, because the guards hit you more, they think that we who are big should pay for the mistakes of the little ones. So they take the bigger ones and hit them, the little ones they only give a little slap and send them away, the big ones they put them in the van and break them. The big ones pay for the little ones ... (Rizzini, Soares, de Carvalho, and Butler 2002).

Getting by on the street as a child is much easier because most people are more willing to give children money or food and in general are more sympathetic, and assume that a younger child is abandoned and in need of protection. As children become adolescents this perception shifts, and adolescents are regarded as more threatening and are associated with crime, or else are taunted to get a job. These reactions by the public may produce a feeling of shame in some cases, particularly among girls, or, as is more often the case, the feeling of *revolta*. And so whereas being a child on the street may in some instances provide a temporary promise of freedom or autonomy and an escape from the violence, confinement and scarcity of the home, coming of age on the street becomes ever more associated with *revolta* – an acute experience of exclusion, discrimination and violence.

This suggests that discrimination is cumulative on the street, that the longer you live there and the older you get, the more likely you are to be seen to have the stigmatising signs of the street. A further example is given by Marta, a 15-year-old girl living on the street, typifying the sense of injustice that is often felt:

Interviewer: The people who are passing here on the street, what do you think they think about you?

Marta: Pickpocket, thief, marginal, bum, glue-sniffer, sometimes you don't even use drugs, or maybe you have used in the past, but it doesn't matter, 'when dust mixes with the crumbs you end up eating it all'. If you are in the middle of a posse of minors sniffing glue, but you don't use, you have used but don't anymore, you are taken as a glue-sniffer, you are taken as the same thing as they are. A lot of times the *revolta* of the street children is society, uncle.

Interviewer: What do you mean?

Marta: Because society doesn't understand our side. I know we are wrong in being on the street, we could look for a shelter, or something, but sometimes society makes us get into drugs more quickly, you know what I mean? There are many people who have never gone through what we have on the street and who think that to say something bad to a minor won't hurt them, but we feel, you know what I mean uncle? We also feel. We are also a person, right uncle, even if we are drug users, or whatever, it doesn't matter what he is or isn't, but he is a person, it is a person for me, and I think that everybody deserves a chance in life, not one, many. You just have to take them (Rizzini, Soares, de Carvalho, and Butler 2002).

Marta's statement clearly points to how the 'self', or the 'person' is involved in the emotional experience of *revolta*. *Revolta* is here associated with a denial of personhood through stigmatising labels such as 'pick-pocket', 'bum' or 'glue-sniffer'. Yet though this symbolic denial of the self is tragic enough, more worrying are the many episodes of violence, in particular those perpetrated by the police (on or off duty) and by private security guards.

The most notorious of these incidents, which provoked international outcry, was specifically aimed at street children, and it occurred in 1993. In what became known as the Candelária Massacre, seven children and one young adult were killed when off-duty policemen opened fire on a group of some 40 children and adolescents sleeping outside the Candelária Church in the heart of Rio's business district. As news of the Candelária murders spread across the globe, followed by a wave of national and international indignation and demands for justice, an opinion survey in Rio showed that close to 20% of Cariocas sided with the vigilantes (Scheper-Hughes and Sargent 1998: 352). That a fifth of Rio's population supported the 'urban cleansing' advocated by the extermination group demonstrates the widespread acceptance of a particular vision of urban space, of the right of only certain kinds of person to be there, and of a stereotype of youngsters on the street, as Marta correctly identified, as marginals and thieves. This vision was aided by media reports throughout the 1980s on the increasing lawlessness of the city. Since the 1980s there has been a dramatic increase in crime levels in Rio and in Brazil's other urban centres, but in the media and in the minds of many of Rio's citizens criminality and the phenomenon of the *'menor de rua'*, the street minor, have become increasingly bound together.

Youngsters on the street today continue to suffer from police brutality and there are still a number of unsolved murders of adolescents each year that point to the work of the police or the *comandos*, a distinction that has become progressively harder to make. I have heard a number of accounts of beatings and death threats on the street, as well as more common incidents of practices that generally fall under the term *esculashar* – to disrespect, belittle or humiliate – at the hands of the police. Such episodes are closely associated with *revolta*. It is not only youngsters on the street who suffer from such police abuse. Youngsters living in the *favelas* are also frequent targets of police brutality, as are youngsters who pass through Rio's criminal justice system. For those who describe their own passages through Rio's notoriously inhumane youth correctional facilities, an extremely common expression is that they come out of them even more *revoltado*.

REVOLTA AND OPPOSITIONAL PRACTICES AND IDENTITIES

Youngsters on the street often used *revolta* to describe both why they leave the abuse or confinement suffered at home, and why some of them give in to 'anti-social' forms of conduct and identities, such as robbery, or using/dealing in drugs. Denied the opportunities for self-actualisation in their homes and their communities, and denied the identity of a 'person' – of being 'like anyone else' on the street – the ensuing feeling of *revolta* may prompt some youngsters to turn to oppositional practices and identities in their search for power, respect and self-esteem.[3] In some cases youngsters have described that they are only doing what is expected of them, since in the eyes of others they are already thieves or drug-users.

Some young adults I talked to, who had lived on the streets for many years, also informed me that this growing *revolta*, which some described through de-personalised, mythic, language – such as a 'black cloud' descending or an 'evil of the street' – is also in part a consequence of the influence of their peers, often individuals who have been on the street longer.

Renato, a 22-year old who is no longer living on the street, spoke to me of this 'black cloud ... growing in his heart' after he had been on the street for some years. Here *revolta* as a sense of social injustice and frustration from consumer culture is clearly present. I ask him what he means by 'black cloud' and he replies:

> Black cloud because I began to feel the *maldade* [nastiness, evil] of the street, I began … to hang out with the bad boys, I began to incorporate myself in them, I began to feel the spirit of the pig that the street has, that the street brings to the inside of the boy, of stealing, threatening people, of sniffing glue, of using drugs, of saying 'ah the cool thing is to put a gun round your waist and take that thing from that kid, the cool thing is for you to slap that little dude because he is white, because he is a mummy's boy and he will shit himself, because I am a bad fucker', excuse my language, 'and I will go and take all he has because if I take it away then his dad will buy him a new one anyway, but I will take it from him because I want to wear designer labels just like him'. So it was like this, I had this black cloud inside of me.

Renato's 'black cloud' incorporates many of the key ingredients of *revolta* that we have discussed. It firstly points to the exclusion from consumer society and its status symbols. Renato's cloud also points to the adoption of oppositional practices, symbols and identities: 'the coolest thing is to put a gun round your waist'. It shows an aspiration to a form of racialised masculinity that is able to instil fear, and perhaps, as a consequence, to acquire respect. Renato's awareness of 'race' was the exception rather than the rule, and it is perhaps related to his love of Brazilian rap music, in particular to black rap artists like Racionais MC, whose song he sang in the documentary film I made.[4] As Renato confides in the film, this song was the one with which he identifies the most; its lyrics, like Racionais MC's other work, are highly political, and concern the oppression and violence faced by afro-descendents in the *favelas* and the lack of opportunities available to them. The awareness of 'race' and politics for those on the street appeared primarily to come from Brazil's blossoming hip-hop culture, but also from the Paulo Freire-inspired street pedagogy evident in the work of street educators and in the shelters and day centres through which many youngsters circulated. Whether the image Renato gave me, of the gun-toting 'bad fucker', is to be taken literally or not I do not know; yet the macho, lawless, autonomous bandit figure, or its more old-fashioned and benign predecessor the *malandro* (the urban trickster), or the drug-dealer belonging to the *comandos*, are personas that appeal to some disenfranchised youngsters in a society that has excluded them from the possibility of attaining status and respect.

UNRAVELLING *REVOLTA*

In this final section I turn to how the phenomenon of *revolta* has been dealt with by those working with youngsters on the street in Rio. Clearly, when one speaks of unravelling *revolta* in terms of practices and policies aimed towards tackling the systemic conditions in which *revolta* emerges, a whole range of actions would have considerable effect. One can envisage, for instance, the positive effects of creating employment opportunities in the communities where such youngsters originate; of improving education and vocational training; of improving housing conditions; of providing opportunities for leisure and mechanisms of family support; of tackling corruption and abuse amongst the police; and of creating broad educational campaigns within Rio as a whole concerning the plight of youngsters living on the street in order to reduce their stigma and situations of abuse. All such measures would undoubtedly have an effect upon the culture of *revolta*. Here, however, I wish to address not the social/political/economic battlefield in which such policies and practices play themselves out, but the battlefield of 'thinking bodies', of subjectivity and self.

Humberto, a young man who had lived for many years on the street, speaks eloquently about his *revolta* as something that built up inside him, causing him to behave in 'street-wise' ways, to hang out with peers on the street robbing and using drugs, using slang and keeping others at bay:

> Before I couldn't open up to anyone because there was a great *revolta* inside me. I could only speak in codes, in slang. So I didn't let anyone get close to me. Afterwards when I began to want to be helped nobody wanted to listen to me, and even so because of my *revolta* being so great, because of the misery in which I lived, I didn't give anyone the opportunity and also I couldn't express myself well. How to ask for help?

Slang, which is characteristically a way of establishing group identity, for Humberto is also a means of protection and defence, of self-concealment. For him and others I spoke to, *revolta* is very often characterised as a withdrawal from the possibility of communication. As Humberto put it: 'How to ask for help?' Considering that the experience of *revolta* is often associated with powerlessness, frustration and being belittled, Humberto's question is poignant. Yet the position he describes, of 'asking for help', of being open to change and wanting a way out of the street or the *comandos*, is one that is struggled with daily by government agencies and NGOs working with such youngsters in Rio.

How do you engage with the vicious cycle of *revolta*? Clearly this depends on how the whole phenomenon is perceived and what its causes and conditions are understood to be. One view which is still influential in guiding State policies, police practices and other State security forces, as well as media representations, holds that impoverished youngsters have no place on the streets of the city centre and should be removed even if by force and taken to shelters, back home or to youth correctional facilities.

Forced removal of youngsters from the street continues as a municipal policy, particularly since 'street children' have become a highly politicised subject and a matter of electoral campaign pledges. Though the white vans of municipal authorities removed 2,209 youngsters from the street in 2002, taking many of them to the city's shelters, these youngsters were very often back on the street a few days later.[5]

In contrast to this view an alternative system has emerged in Brazil since the 1980s, influenced by the work of Paulo Freire, in which persuasion, reasoning, and building trust are central. This new pedagogy involves meeting with youngsters on the street and engaging with them in their world, with their anxieties, hopes and histories, and with the possibility of self-transformation. It is a process I heard referred to on several occasions as 'seduction', meaning that you 'seduce' or 'conquer' the youngster by awakening in him or her the desire to leave the street. This, it goes without saying, can only be achieved through a process of gaining their trust and becoming familiar with their particular situation and desires.

There is clearly a significant contrast between a pedagogical approach and a repressive intervention; between the demand for quick solutions (often endorsed by the media and by the population at large) and an understanding of the phenomenon of children and adolescents on the street, and of *revolta* more broadly, as complex and systemic. The new street pedagogy is well summed-up in a statement made to me by a street educator: 'To take away from the street does not mean to collect and put in a shelter, it means that you create in the subject this internal will, this desire, this motivation to no longer live under the bridge'.

The provocation of this will or desire in the subject to leave the street is achieved through many techniques involving a more play-orientated and reflexive approach to education. The curriculum of day-centres includes activities such as *capoeira* (an Afro-Brazilian martial art-dance developed by slaves), circus activities such as juggling, and football, alongside debates on the rights of children and adolescents. However, the most significant contribution of this form of pedagogy, I believe, lies in the provision of spaces, such as day-centres and shelters, in which the youngster feels respected. These spaces of refuge provide a striking contrast to the space of the street, marked as it is by a constant struggle for survival.

All youngsters with whom I talked who had successfully disengaged from the street described the importance of such spaces for initiating their process of reflection, and in particular the significance of key individuals found there who stimulated their desire to leave the street. A common element in these transformations is a new regard of the self, one that is reappraised as no longer powerless, or fatalistically destined to suffer, but rather as endowed with 'willpower' and a capacity for changing one's life.

Willpower is a crucial ingredient for changing one's life, something I constantly heard from youngsters who made the successful transition away from the street. Willpower is related to a newly-found sense of agency, of taking responsibility for one's actions. As Sandra, a 15-year-old girl who had lived for a number of years on the street put it:

> When I lived on the street I spoke like this: I was born only to suffer, to live like this, but I saw that it wasn't that at all which was happening, that everything was different, we suffer because we want to, right, that's it, that's all.

The transition from a fatalistic assessment of one's life situation to one in which the individual feels empowered is a crucial aspect of Freire's notion of the development of critical consciousness. The former fatalistic attitude narrated by Sandra, which is sometimes associated with *revolta,* can be seen as an example of what Freire termed 'semi-intransitive' consciousness, which he describes as a form of consciousness which does not manage to capture the challenges of the context in which it is situated, or which perceives them distortedly (Freire 1976: 73). Freire characterises this form of consciousness as one in which explanations to problems are sought outside reality, in divine signs or destiny, or in the internalisation of feelings of 'natural inferiority' (*ibid*). As such, actions in this state of consciousness often take a 'magico-defensive' or 'magico-therapeutic' form (*ibid*).

Freire's description of a 'semi-intransitive' mode of thought has a close relationship to what I have been referring to as the emotional story of *revolta.* Yet whereas Freire is describing this phenomenon from the point of view of thought and beliefs, I have been describing it from the point of view of emotions, thinking bodies, self-involving situations and identity. Just as critical consciousness involves a re-evaluation of the conditions of one's life in terms of processes of oppression, so it also involves the transformation of a self that was previously powerless, denigrated and belittled. Youngsters who had successfully disengaged from the street often spoke of a new regard for themselves, of considering themselves to be individuals with plans and ambitions, endowed with talent, beauty or other positive qualities. If life on the street is often characterised by 'living in the moment', by a feeling that death could come at any time, then this self-transformation involves the reinsertion of the individual within a life-project. This life-project is encouraged by the opportunities offered within day-centres, shelters and other organisations. As Sandra related to me, being in the shelter has offered her other paths:

> When I arrived here I couldn't write my name, now I am going into second grade [second year of primary school] ... Here I am in the football team, the netball team, I have extra school tuition, I make jewellery, I go to the psychologist every week and also what I like about this place is that doctors are not lacking, there is a health centre right next door.

The perception of others, or of one's effect on and relationship to others, also undergoes profound changes in this process of self-transformation. Whereas we saw how abuse, discrimination and the disrespect of others contributed to *revolta*, many youngsters described the transformative effect of entering an environment within some shelters and day-centres which was characterised by the care, love and respect of others. This had repercussions not only on how they came to see themselves, as we saw above, but also on how they began to relate to others. This shift, then, had repercussions on their relationships with the families they left behind, and many reported re-establishing family relations in the course of their transformation. Clearly the process of being more reflective, being more critically conscious, also entails an emotional transformation of the self. As some of these youngsters came to perceive the world and their position in it differently, so was there an ensuing change in their thinking, perceptive bodies in the way in which they felt themselves to be in the world.

CONCLUDING REMARKS

In this chapter I have suggested how issues of self, personhood, emotions and subjectivity can be integrated with a critical analysis of oppression, poverty and social exclusion. I have tried to do this through *revolta*, an emotion story I often heard that encompasses a particular understanding of the world and a set of actions and identities that may be subsequently adopted. I have not been arguing that *revolta* can be understood in a reductive way as the sole cause of why young-sters go to the street or join the *comandos*. Instead my point is that a number of disenfranchised youngsters living in the *favelas* and periph-eries of Rio perceive, express and react to the conditions of oppression and powerlessness through the idiom of *revolta*. This is an idiom that is circulated through the networks of youth sub-cultures of the *favelas* and peripheries and is also expressed in popular cultural forms such as rap music. The emotion story of *revolta* helps a number of young-sters to interpret somatic feelings and social interactions in which the self is considered powerless, frustrated, belittled, denigrated or other-wise denied the conditions for actualisation. *Revolta* commonly refers to situations of interaction with an other, who may be a family mem-ber, step-parent, police or a passerby on the street, or a generalised conception of 'society' or the 'moral order'.

Revolta not only provides an interpretive framework for represent-ing the conditions of marginality, violence and exclusion but also makes available practices and symbolic resources for identification with which some youngsters engage in their search for respect and self-esteem. As I have tried to describe here, the 'alienation' many of these youngsters experience stems from the impossibility of attaining respect or a desirable sense of self within a society in which valued selves have become intrinsically bound to an acute consumerism.

Going back to the question posed at the beginning of whether *revolta* should be seen as a form of resistance or defiance against the conditions of exclusion or alienation, in one sense the answer is clearly yes. Yet the practices associated with *revolta* on the ground, rather than their more critical exposition by some rap artists, are rarely politicised, nor do they incorporate what Freire would have called a critical consciousness. Instead they are resistances or rebel-lions confined by what Calhoun, in the context of identity politics, termed the 'resources of experience and ability, culture and social organisation' (Calhoun 1994: 28). Equally, contrasted to the experi-ence of 'class resentment' addressed by Marshall (1977) or the politi-cised articulation of *revolta* in some forms of rap music, on the ground *revolta* often appears as individualistic or individualised. More often than not, it refers to an experience that the individual goes through in his or her own life trajectory, rather than an emotion of a class or group. Though the practices associated with *revolta* are anything but complacent, and show an aspiration to move away from conditions of poverty and exclusion, it is far from obvious that this movement is positive as far as the individual's life trajectory is concerned.

Admittedly, some youngsters who have passed through the street (like Sandra, whom I quoted in the last section) describe the way in which this experience caused them to grow, transform themselves and access a whole range of NGO-resources – such as vocational training – which they would not have otherwise had. But more frequent are cases in which life on the street or in the *comandos* damages the individual and contributes to the downfall of the community. As far as most individuals are concerned, living on the street or engaging in crime and drug dealing introduces youngsters to a high-risk life in which the possibilities for violence, death or imprisonment are never distant, an attitude they themselves often fatalistically acknowledge. A number of children and adolescents perish on the streets, killed in accidents, by drugs overdose, or by diseases such as AIDS. And a number of youngsters who grow up on the streets are murdered by extermination groups – comprised of off-duty police and security guards – or from the drug *comandos*. For youngsters engaged with the *comandos* themselves, fatality rates have been compared to those inflicted in war zones (Dowdney 2002).

The Freirean-inspired pedagogy practiced by a number of NGOs and agencies in Rio is clearly not infallible and, for personal reasons, many individuals who transit through these spaces do not undergo the process of self-transformation that I have described here. It is virtually impossible to say with any certainty what happens to adolescents who have lived on the street once they come of age, since no quantitative and very little qualitative information is available. Some may find shelter returning to their families, with partners, or in rented or owned accommodations in the *favelas* and peripheries. These luckier young people often become engaged in Rio's informal labour market, doing odd jobs such as selling goods on the streets as *camelôs* (street-hawkers). For many others who remain on the street, however, their trajectories are less clear. For these individuals, adult life on the street invariably proves a lot harder than in the past. No longer can they rely on the generosity of passersby, who are ever more wary of their size and what is perceived as their increasingly threatening presence. Past the age of 18, they can no longer rely on NGOs or the law to protect them and many pass through the penal system and into Rio's notoriously inhumane jails.

As far as the *favela* communities are concerned, the growing strength of the *comandos* has not only taken the lives of many of its sons, from frequent battles with rival gangs and with the police, but has also served to further alienate the *favela* from the rest of the city, which has increasingly come to identify these communities with crime and violence. On a social and cultural level the continuation of the conditions of exclusion, violence and discrimination encourage the proliferation of this 'emotion story' and idiom of *revolta*, ensuring its replication amongst subsequent generations of youngsters.

In order to disrupt the ongoing cycle of *revolta* it is clearly necessary to have the political will to implement policies that can remedy the problems of social exclusion, police abuse and inequality. But what is also required, as street educators and others working on the ground emphasise, is an engagement with 'thinking bodies' and 'selves' for the disembodiment of *revolta*.

Notes

[1] For instance see Philippe Bourgois' (1996) work on drug dealing in East Harlem and James Vigil's work on the *barrio* gangs of Los Angeles (1988).

[2] Whereas cultural forms such as hip hop and funk may be consumed by this subculture, other more general aesthetic representations can also be found, particularly in cinema. In Brazil a number of fiction films and documentaries have addressed this 'emotion story' of *revolta*, for instance in fiction: Hector Babenco's *Pixote* (1980), Fernando Meirelles *Cidade de Deus* (2002), and in documentaries: João Moreira Salles and Katia Lund's *Notícias de Uma Guerra Particular* (1999), and José Padilha and Felipe Lacerda's *Onibus 174* (2002).

[3] 'Being like anyone else' was a recurring aspiration from youngsters on the street regarding their desire to be considered as a 'normal person', as Erving Goffman has noted, this is a common aspiration of those who are stigmatised (1990 [1963]:17).

[4] *Coming of Age on the Streets of Rio* (2002). Udi Mandel Butler (Brazil), 55min.

[5] Figures quoted in *O Globo* newspaper 27 October, 2002.

References

Barbalet, J (1994) 'Citizenship, class inequality and resentment', in Turner, B (ed) *Citizenship and Social Theory*, London: Sage.

Bourgois, P (1996) *In Search of Respect: Selling Crack in El Barrio*, Cambridge: Cambridge University Press.

Butler, U (2003) 'Coming of age on the streets of Rio', unpublished PhD thesis, Goldsmiths College, University of London.

Calhoun, C (ed) (1994) *Social Theory and the Politics of Identity*, Oxford: Blackwell.

Denzin, N (1984) *On Understanding Emotions*, San Francisco: Jossey-Bass.

De Souza, D and Rodrigues, J (1999) *Perfis e mapeamento de população de rua do Rio de Janeiro: padrões de sociabilidade e funcões sócio-espaciais de usos da rua*, FAPERJ/UERJ: Rio de Janeiro.

Dowdney, L (2002) 'Child combatants in organised armed violence: a study of children and adolescents involved in territorial drug faction disputes in Rio de Janeiro', report presented to ISER/Viva Rio: Rio de Janeiro.

Ekman, P and Davidson, R (1994) (eds) *The Nature of Emotions*, Oxford University Press: New York.

Freire, P (1976) *Ação Cultural Para Liberdade*, Rio de Janeiro: Editora Paz e Terra.

Freire, P (1993 [1970]) *Pedagogy of the Oppressed*, London: Penguin.

Garbarino, J (1995) *Raising Children in a Socially Toxic Environment*, San Francisco: Jossey-Bass.

Geertz, C (1984) '"From the native's point of view" on the nature of anthropological understanding', in Shweder, R and Levine, R (eds), *Culture Theory: Essays on Mind, Self, and Emotion*, Cambridge: Cambridge University Press.

Goffman, E (1990 [1963]) *Stigma: Notes on the Management of Spoiled Identity*, London: Penguin.

Gregori, M F (2000) *Viração: Experiencias de Meninos nas Ruas*, São Paulo: Companhia Das Letras.

IBASE (1992) *Levantamento de Meninas e Meninos nas Ruas do Rio de Janeiro*, Cadernos do IBASE, Projeto 'Se Essa Rua Fosse Minha'/FASE/IBASE/IDAC/IDEC: Rio de Janeiro

Leavitt, J (1996) 'Meaning and feeling in the anthropology of emotions', *American Ethnologist*, 23(3) 514–539.

Levy, R (1984) 'Emotion, knowing and culture', in Shweder, R and Levine, R (eds), *Culture Theory: Essays on Mind, Self, and Emotion*. Cambridge: Cambridge University Press.

Marshall, T H (1977) *Class, Citizenship & Social Development*, Chicago: University of Chicago Press.

Rizzini, I, Soares, A, de Carvalho, A and Butler, U M (2002) 'Crianças e adolescentes em situação de rua na cidade do Rio de Janeiro: Tecendo suas histórias', unpublished report, CESPI/Terre des hommes/Rede Rio Criança.

Rosaldo, M (1984) 'Towards an anthropology of self and feeling', in Shweder, R and Levine, R (eds), *Culture Theory: Essays on Mind, Self, and Emotion*, Cambridge: Cambridge University Press.

Scheper-Hughes, N and Sargent, C (eds) (1998) *Small Wars: The Cultural Politics of Childhood*, Berkeley and Los Angeles: University of California Press.

Shor, I (1993) 'Education is politics: Paulo Freire's critical pedagogy', in McLaren, P and Leonard, P (eds), *Paulo Freire: A Critical Encounter*, London: Routledge.

Shweder, R and Levine, R (eds) (1984) *Culture Theory: Essays on Mind, Self, and Emotion*, Cambridge: Cambridge University Press.

Shweder, R (1994) '"You're not sick, you're just in love". Emotion as an interpretative system', in Ekman, P and Davidson, R (eds), *The Nature of Emotions*, New York: Oxford University Press.

Veale, A, Taylor, M and Linehan, C (2000) 'Psychological perspectives of "abandoned" and "abandoning" street children', in Panter-Brick, C and Smith, M (eds), *Abandoned Children*, Cambridge: Cambridge University Press.

Vigil, J (1988) *Barrio Gangs: Street Life and Identity in Southern California*, Austin: University of Texas Press.

Zaluar, A (1994) *Condomino do Diabo*, Rio de Janeiro: Editora Revan.

Filmography

Cidade de Deus (2002), Fernando Meirelles (Brazil), 124min.

Coming of Age on the Streets of Rio (2002), Udi Mandel Butler (Brazil), 55min.

Notícias de Uma Guerra Particular [*News of a private war*](1999) João Moreira Salles and Katia Lund (Brazil), 57min.

Onibus 174 (2002), José Padilha and Felipe Lacerda (Brazil), 128min.

Pixote (1980), Hector Babenco (Brazil), 127min.

4 Children on the Streets of Dhaka and their Coping Strategies

Alessandro Conticini

People think we don't have anything because we live on the street.

They don't see the many things we can have even if living here.
You can say I am poor but I'm not a *kangali* (destitute). NGOs give us
what they want without asking us what is important for us. But we could
not live without certain things we value as important and we do what we
can to get them.

– Fumala, a 17 year-old-girl

INTRODUCTION

This chapter investigates what children in street situations in Dhaka
value as important and how they protect and promote their livelihoods when living on the street.[1] It argues that despite the assumption
of mainstream society, policy makers and NGOs (non-governmental
organizations), these children are not destitute. They have dynamic
portfolios of assets and show complex coping strategies generally
managed as a group. When considering policy implications, this chapter argues that to be effective, sustainable and respectful, intervention
has to abandon a focus on children's deprivations often fostered by a
strict application of child-rights theories. On the contrary, a more systematic investigation of initiatives for improving the lives of children
living on the street should guide interventions on how to help them to
strengthen their assets, rather than to create substitutes for them.

Children living in street situations are one of the most painful reminders of the shortfalls of current interventions to reduce poverty and vulnerability at a time of unprecedented economic growth and global well-being.[2] Deprived children, as well as the other 'perennial losers who … in the aggressive restaging of the new world order are … categories of "superfluous" people' (Scheper-Hughes and Sargent 1998: 3), have easily fallen through the net of planned interventions. The growing number of street-living children in both developing (Panter-Brick 2002) and economically advanced countries (Bradbury, Jenkins et al 2000) is clear proof of the inadequacy of policy and social action to contain and prevent this phenomenon.

This chapter intends to deepen our understanding of the main assets of children living on the streets of Dhaka, and of how these children promote, protect and secure their livelihoods.[3] It focuses on what children in street situations have and what they value as important in their experiences of street life. To gain a thorough understanding of life on the street in order to guide policy and action, it is vital to consider children's personal efforts to improve their lives and their prospects. These efforts include a complex use of both individual and collective coping strategies for increasing and 'accumulating' skills, knowledge expertise, experiences and social networks (see, eg, Wood 2003).

Newspaper articles and NGO accounts of the atrocities of street life can easily overwhelm one with despair, anger and a feeling of injustice. Children in street situations, however, do not wait for outsiders to change their lives. They are not passive recipients of intervention (Ennew 1994). On the contrary, they are engaged in carving greater autonomy and rights for themselves (Bourgois 1995), and their personal agency allows the development of versatile and resilient behaviours (Felsman 1989; Panter-Brick 2002). Yet this complicated process whereby children are tailoring a new social and political space for themselves is riddled with contradictory outcomes and painful experiences.

Children's active opposition to the many shortfalls they face on a daily basis is a useful reminder that even if they are perceived as 'waiting children' by adults (Qvortrup 2004), this often unchallenged perspective does not account for children's ingenuity. As Fumala explains, there are 'things' that are important for street-living children, and they actively protect and promote these 'things' using every means available to them. These efforts tend to be ignored or underestimated by development practitioners because they are responding to 'non-conventional logic' (*ibid* 1994). Policymakers and social workers do not recognise these children's assets and wrongly perceive them as destitute street scavengers.

Non-material assets of children in street situations – such as feelings of affection, trust among friends and protective security – create what Chawla (2002) defines as the 'cultural richness' of street life. This corroborates the recent thesis that children's perception of well-being is influenced more by their social relationships than the material assets available (Harpham 2003). These children are extremely careful in making a distinction between their condition of material poverty, and the richness of their social relationships and complexities of their livelihoods on the street. They deeply value their sense of independence and personal control (Moore, Canter et al 1995). Many of them make sense out of their situation through having pride in their coping strategies, while others value their social networks, sharing resources, mutuality and the social care which they gain by interacting with those in similar predicaments (Kelletta and Moore 2003).

From a policy perspective, this chapter argues that promoting child development – in its widest sense – must start from considering what matters to children, and must be consistent with their own livelihood strategies and efforts. Effective action for poverty reduction begins with strengthening what poor people have already started to put in place, namely, building on their strengths while considering the specific opportunities and constraints that each social environment presents (Moser 1998; Rakodi 2002).

This will help to foster interventions directed at building on beneficiaries' own solutions rather than merely introducing substitutes for them (Moser and Norton 2001). Intervention disrespectful of what children are already doing for themselves is likely to fail, resulting in a marked difference between what the children receive and what they value as important. The conventional focus of interventions upon children's deprivations risks diverting attention from the political-economic structural forces and cultural imperatives that generate poverty, thus tackling the symptoms instead of the causes.

PERCEPTIONS OF POVERTY AND INTERVENTION: THE PROBLEM

Unni and Rani (2003) argue that there is a growing awareness that the goal of development is increasingly concerned with promoting social justice rather than reducing material (especially economic) poverty. Material-needs satisfaction is still presented as the most powerful solution in supporting the multiple deprivations of poor people, suggesting that a wide gap remains between the theoretical recognition of the multi-faceted nature of poverty (Hulme and Shepherd 2003) and the prevailing strategies adopted by most poverty reduction programmes. As Clarke and Sison (2003) have shown, this gap is mainly due to the often enormous difference between the mainstream society and poor people's perceptions of what poverty is, how it affects life and how it can effectively be tackled. A part of the recurrent failures in development efforts is due to preconceived narratives that actors in development projects have about development processes (Roe 1991). These narratives tend to prevail even in the face of research demonstrating their falsehood (Leach and Mearns 1996; Rudqvist and Christoplos et al 2000) because they are easily presented, explained and taught, satisfying the principle of blueprint development (Roe 1991; 1999). Blueprint approaches to development are those in which dominant narratives are literally transferred to other contexts and used to inform parties about what to do. As in any approach based on faith rather than evidence, the advocates are convinced that they already know all the answers. Failures only indicate the need for more dedication to applying the 'right' steps (Hjorth 2003: 384).

In the context of street-living and working children, policy makers and practitioners are often tempted to rely on 'received wisdom' (Leach and Mearns 1996; Rudqvist and Christoplos et al 2000) without questioning the content of this wisdom. As argued by Boyden et al, 'common myths are called up to substitute for hard evidence and justify what has been decided' (1998: 331) as a mutually convenient consensus between governments, groups and international and national institutions. Scant attention is thus paid to systematic research on priorities, expectations and desires expressed by the children, or to the effects of intervention over their life's course.

When applied to children in street situations in Dhaka, this chapter substantially validates the observations made by White (1999) when she argues that in Bangladesh we need to be much more critical about presenting bland statements of common interest between the State, civil society and NGOs vis á vis the expressed needs of the poor. As in other countries, in Bangladesh many types of programmes seek to assist children in street situations, but they often start from unchallenged and narrow assumptions. In particular, they assume these children are lacking everything, and that the livelihood strategies they have been developing on the street are not useful for their 'rehabilitation'. In this respect, the prevailing perception is that children in street situations are deprived in all aspects of their lives. Policymakers, social workers and NGOs make provision for what they think these children lack, often in the form of free meal programmes, night shelters, schooling and clothes distribution.

The shortfalls of such programmes in providing children with a better life, the increasing number of youngsters who prefer to live on the street rather than attending rehabilitation and reintegration activities, the reluctance of many children to change their lives, and the despair of many social workers are clear evidence that this approach is, at best, questionable.

As Dordick (1997) explains, homelessness encourages a process in which personal relationships are mobilised in trying to produce what the physical environment fails to provide: a safe and secure place to live. Yet, while the development literature is replete with 'lessons' and 'learning from experience', the truth is that not learning from experience characterises the knowledge-creating dynamics of much of the development endeavour (Bond and Hulme 1999; Hjorth 2003), and interventions on street-dwellers are no exception.

Whilst a lack of money and material assets are problems for the urban poor, the nature of social relationships both within low-income settlements (including the streets) and between excluded categories of urban people and mainstream society, is important in understanding the processes that perpetuate poverty and exclusion (Mitlin 2003). As explained in this chapter, children in street situations are able to develop, promote and protect their livelihood assets when living on the street. Understanding and strengthening the assets of the poor has substantial implications for their empowerment (Moser 1998). When extended further, this perspective leads to the understanding of urban poor communities and marginalised subcultures (such as children in street situations) no longer as simply people in need of social welfare, but as leading partners in processes to improve their communities and as contributors to the overall well-being of the city (Shubert 1996; Riggio 2002).

METHODOLOGY

By definition, marginalised, urban subcultures have experienced economic, social and cultural segregation from mainstream society. In addition, before taking up street life, children in street situations have experienced a number of psychological, physical and often sexual traumas inflicted by adults – often trusted members of the household or community (Conticini and Hulme 2004). These emotional shocks generated by adults are likely to compound their suspicion towards members of mainstream society. Most street-living children mistrust adults and they will not reveal their intimate street experiences to a stranger with a survey instrument, no matter how sensitive the interviewer may be (see also Bourgois 1995). How can we expect that a stigmatised group of street-dwellers will provide accurate data through impersonal surveys on their coping strategies when, in most cases, those very coping strategies are a cause of their discrimination.

Studies of excluded subcultures can only obtain reliable data by establishing long-term relationships of trust with the observed group. Being on the street often implies that children have built self-protecting walls against adults. The researcher must crush this wall of suspicion, mistrust and fear to truly get to know the children's world. As Paulo Freire argues: 'We must wait for the magic moment when the child's hostility has been overcome. Be patient and wait for the pleasure of that moment when the child discloses the mystery of his existence' (UNICEF 1987: 13).

It would be wrong to value the trust-building process only in terms of gathering reliable data. When conducting research with children in street situations a trust relationship is also a matter of respect and love, showing that researchers care for those children beyond the purpose of their research.

This chapter draws on one year of field research in Dhaka I conducted beginning in August 2002. A total of 62 boys and 31 girls took part in the research, covering participants working and living in four main sites with a high degree of economic activity (a market, train and bus stations and a river port). Most of the children were not permanently involved in any rehabilitation or reintegration programmes at the time of the research, but a majority (65%) had previously been enrolled in NGO activities.

My research is based on a constructivist paradigm of investigation, focusing on children's livelihoods. The theory of sustainable livelihoods is a particularly powerful conceptual framework when applied to child development because it allows us to identify what children (in this case, children in street situations) have, rather than what they do not have. It also allows policies to strengthen children's own inventive solutions, rather than substitute or undermine what they are already doing. It brings out what they seek, and manage, to achieve and the process of securing livelihoods instead of what they are lacking.

The main methods used were ethnographic observation of participants, playing activities, in-depth interviews, daily activity schedules and group discussions. Additionally, eight boys and eight girls volunteered as members for two advisory groups responsible for reviewing all parts of the field research process, implementing some of the interviews, facilitating group discussions and suggesting changes in the research process. Towards the end of field research, a semi-structured questionnaire was utilized to triangulate qualitative data that had been collected and to add a quantitative dimension to the analysis. Eighty children participated in the semi-structured questionnaires, 37 boys and 43 girls. The majority of the children involved in the questionnaire had already participated in earlier phases of the research. This meant there was a trust relationship between interviewer and children, making data more reliable than that collected through a one-off questionnaire (Ennew and Milne, 1996).

A constructivist approach to inquiry assumes that children and their relationships are dynamic across individuals, context and time. Consequently, efforts have to be directed to understand how the worlds of children operate, describing and analysing the contextualised social phenomena observed (Hatch 1995; Greig and Taylor 1999) starting from participants' perspectives (Denzin and Lincoln 1998), and by assuming a role of 'passionate participant' to the process of knowledge creation (Lincoln 1993).

WHEN CHILDREN ARE PERCEIVED AS DESTITUTE

The government agency Appropriate Resources for Improving Street Children's Environment (ARISE), reports that there are 500,000 children living on the street of Bangladesh, of which 75% are in Dhaka (ARISE 2001). This figure is horrific enough, but many NGOs believe the real number is almost twice as high (see, for instance, CSKS 2002). In Bangladesh, as in many other countries, the prevailing perception of mainstream society towards these children is that they live in absolute deprivation, based on the clothes they wear as well as their low levels of cash, material resources, and savings. Society stigmatises Bangladeshi street living children using the term *kangali* (destitute). As expressed by Arif (a 15 year-old-boy):

> They [mainstream society] call us *kangali* and they say to us: 'What are you doing on the street? Go back home, find yourself a good job, don't dishonour your family' ... But we are not *kangali* ... we are working for a living and we also do many other good things.

According to Harriss-White (2002), destitution refers to the complete or near complete absence of assets or control over owned assets.

Moreover, destitution is conceived as an individual phenomenon because, arguably, when a person is destitute he/she does not have any social support and his/her social safety nets have already collapsed. As pinpointed by Devereux (2003), the strength of Harriss-White's definition is in combining the notion of economic destitution ('having almost nothing') with the notion of social and political destitution ('being almost nothing'). Thus, these children are perceived as incapable of meeting their minimum subsistence needs, with no access to productive assets, and dependent on public and/or private transfers.[4]

In addition, the use of the word *kangali* often implies not only the attributes of deprivation, but also the condition of being depraved. The street's dust and mud are conceived as visual representations of a competing world dominated by illicit activities and deviances, by immorality and sins. This determines a portrayal in which these children are depicted as 'an unacceptable phenomenon of human degradation' (ARISE 2001).

WHAT IS IMPORTANT IN YOUR DAILY LIFE?

To challenge the assumption that street-living children are destitutes, the present study investigated their livelihoods starting from a simple question: 'What is important in your daily life?' In answering this question, children often directed the researcher's attention to their coping strategies and the way they develop, protect and promote what they think is important in their street living.

When the children were allowed to present what is important in their street life using their own words, eight assets were identified by them as most important: (1) a feeling of love and trusted friends; (2) cooperation; (3) money (including savings, remittances, debt and credit); (4) working and playing activities; (5) food; (6) education; (7) health status; and (8) use of space. Children also presented a further asset: 'A feeling of security'. However, this last category, indicated by the children as an asset in itself, is not an independent variable but a dependent one, and its development is arguably a direct consequence of the management of all the previous assets (Conticini 2004). In the following, then, a brief insight into each asset is provided, according to gender differences and stages of street adaptation.

A feeling of love and trusted friends

A feeling of love and trusted friends are the prime assets presented by children when talking about their life on the street. This contrasts widely with the perception they give to mainstream society, because, as an NGO director explained it to me: 'emotional support, sentimentality and affection can weaken the nature of children and reduce their survival skills.'

Children stressed that the wealth of their life is highly dependent on social processes of interactions, including sharing of affection and trust. Supportive social networks are not only perceived as important during periods of particular crises but are a fundamental component of improving the quality of every activity they undertake (see also Moser 1998). The group of peers progressively assumes a central role in providing both emotional and physical security for the children. The group appears as a mainly open, informal, partially democratic structure in Bangladeshi streets, where membership is largely voluntary and is based on trust, reciprocity, convenience and care for each other. As observed in other studies (Beazley 2003; Bourgois 1995; Rizzini and Butler 2003), the group enables children to develop both a feeling of belonging and a collective identity, providing the primary space for identity creation. Children participate in group activities while maintaining their own independence, but they also learn how to adapt their personal needs to the necessities of the group and how to use personal skills for the benefit of friends. The emotional interaction of the child with trusted friends is a means of sharing worries and alleviating sorrow. Group members usually have common experiences which are the basis for understanding their respective problems and listening to each other.

There is a complex system of mutual support which allows for an intense exchange of money, information and goods among children belonging to the same group. Moreover, the distribution of common assets among the group is likely to give priority to those more in need than others.

Love and friends are what make children feel at home on the street. According to Shoel (a 13-year-old boy): 'Home is not where you sleep but is where you feel loved' and the feeling of being part of a street group can be so emotionally deep that some children simply refuse to accept opportunities to leave the street for fear of losing their friends. Children are more likely to leave the street when this process is a planned strategy that involves friends and peers. When they make this attempt alone, they usually develop a feeling of betrayal and social injustice, eventually returning to the streets because their friends are still there. The same result is often seen when NGOs try to help a single child and ignore the strength of social ties established by the child with his/her group of friends. This is likely to raise the probability of unsuccessful reintegration through NGOs pro-grammes, and is perceived by the children as an intervention disre-spectful of children's efforts in building up alternative social relationships.

When talking about affection, children also mentioned their sexual activities. These were characterised by girls as an attempt to fulfil their need to be loved and their desire to be accepted by mainstream society. In contrast, boys were less inclined to refer to sexual activities as a way of sharing affection, preferring to describe them as a 'game', a 'means of income' and a 'source of pleasure'. In addition, while it is easier for boys to satisfy their need for affection through relationships with peers, girls were likely to look for affection through relationships with adults. Girls explained their preference for adult men as partners by saying that boys in street situations were unstable in their affections and not faithful. Adult men were perceived as wiser and more likely to provide lasting relationships. Boys reported they had little interest in forming stable relationships. This, in turn, affected children's self-esteem. While boys were less subject to depression following the breakdown of rela-tionships, girls were more prone to deep emotional distress.

Cooperation

The cooperation between children in street situations is an important form of socialisation and a means of increasing knowledge and skills. While a strict utilitarian approach would argue that children cooper-ate with peers only to achieve personal gains and to access opportu-nities that are unavailable otherwise, evidence from qualitative interviews suggests that this vision is narrow and incomplete. Children's reciprocal solidarity cannot be exclusively reduced to self-ishness but should also take into account values of reciprocity, altru-ism and benevolence – solidarity indeed.

As argued when explaining the rationale for children moving to the street (Conticini and Hulme 2004), children pay more attention to the development of social relationships than to the maximization of economic opportunities. On the other hand, supportive social net-works can improve children's access to better economic opportuni-ties. For example, well-established children in street situations help newcomers gain access to work opportunities. Older children often have stronger social connections, making it relatively easy for them to find better-paid and more secure jobs. In a number of cases, estab-lished children tried to convince their employers to give the same opportunity to their younger friends.

Nevertheless, in a number of cases, regression of cooperative activities after a long experience of street life was observed, leading to progressive isolation of the child from their peer group. Some children excluded themselves from the group because they became extremely suspicious about everything and everyone, even showing depressive and paranoid attitudes. On the other hand, the group actively expelled those children who were reluctant to abandon activities considered immoral or which did not conform to the group's values.

Money

When talking about 'money' children mentioned a number of financial activities ranging from cash management to savings, from remittances to credit and debt. Far from having a simplistic hand-to-mouth existence, these children displayed a complex series of strategies in managing their finances, including bartering.

Many children never had direct access to cash before arriving on the street. Consequently, they progressively learned how to manage their cash and allocate their expenses (Hickey 2000). After an initial period of street life, children learn how to take advantage of various job opportunities through the social networks they build. Their access to the urban informal labour market can double their income earning capacity compared to what they could earn in rural areas. However, such a direct comparison is difficult given the different costs of living and the higher taxes/bribes children pay in urban areas. The majority of children interviewed reported a daily income ranging from 40 to 70 *Taka*, but this varied greatly according to the job.[5] For instance, children involved in the sex market were likely to earn from 150 to 400 *Taka* per night, while beggars often reported earning less than 30 *Taka* per day. Well-established porters reported a salary between 50 to 70 *Taka* per day while newcomer porters did not earn more than 30. These differences in earned income were significant because of the taxes/bribes that street children have to pay. These taxes/bribes are usually levied by *mastaans* (mafia members), *matabbars* (community leaders), police, guards, and station senior staff (see also Kabir 2002). Girls are subjected to higher taxes than boys even when performing the same work. This is due to the dominant culture downgrading women to the position of second-class citizens (Monsoor 2002), thereby increasing their exposure to higher exploitation. In a number of cases, taxes paid by girls could easily reach 50 to 60% of their income. Those paid by boys were usually between 30 and 50% but varied according to the nature of work, the connections the child had, and the workplace.

During the early phases of street life, children tend to have very low levels of savings due to the scarcity of work and the lack of access to safe places to deposit their money. Once the child starts to build trust relationships with social workers or street agents, he/she is likely to start a saving process, however irregular. Tables 4.1 and 4.2 present children's saving capacity in the week prior to interview and their total amount of savings deposited anywhere.

'Money-guards' (Rutherford 2000) were friends, elder brothers/sisters, shopkeepers, social workers, NGOs, protectors and relatives. As insurance for reducing the risk of losing all their savings, it was common to find children depositing their money with two or three people at the same time. Money-guards were often chosen according to their reputation, accessibility and emotional proximity to the child. They were also chosen because of kinship linkages or because other friends were doing the same. Above all, mutual trust was the main factor involved in choosing a money-guard.

Table 4.1

Children's Daily Saving Capacity

Number surveyed: 80 children

	Very little or no savings	Less than 30 Taka per day	Between 30 and 100 Taka per day	Between 100 and 200 Taka per day	Don't Know
Percentage of Children	35%	27%	20%	8%	10%

Source: Author's survey.

Table 4.2

Total of Deposited Savings

Number surveyed: 80 children

	No Savings Deposited	Between 0 and 500 Taka	Between 500 and 800 Taka	Between 800 and 1500 Taka	More than 1500 Taka	Don't Know
Percentage of Children	15%	28%	26%	10%	9%	12%

Source: Author's survey.

With the exception of sex work, girls have access to fewer remunerative income-generating activities than boys and this correspondingly affects their capacity to save. Nevertheless, when the same earning capacity was reported, girls showed a tendency to save more than boys. This caution was explained by Jhinu Rani's (an eight-year-old-girl's) statement that 'girls never know what Allah reserves for them the next day'.

In contrast, when children are 'addicted' to street life – meaning they cannot conceive of themselves out of the street – they do not save and tend to spend all their earnings, living on a day-by-day basis. This is due to a number of factors. In particular, if they are involved in illicit activities, they tend to consider their earnings as *papyer pisa* (money of sin); that is, not worth saving. Other factors include their declining health status after living on the street for a considerable length of time (Masud Ali, Mustaque Ali et al 1997). Finally, lack of personal and property security can lead to a fatalistic approach to life and can reduce their capacity for planning. In addition, self-destructive attitudes manifested by children 'addicted' to street life augment their spending on drugs, alcohol and commercial sex.

Strong mutual and support networks lead to an increased incidence of lending and borrowing money between friends. Short-term loans from group members and *mastaans* are common and it is rare to find children who run away after having accumulated a considerable debt. They do not often compromise the support of peers or trusted people in exchange for accumulating lump-sums. Arguably, they understand that the most important asset they can have is social support, and they will not risk losing it by assuming harmful behaviour. However, when a child does not spontaneously pay back a debt he or she will find it increasingly hard to get access to further credit and, eventually, will be excluded by the social network (see also Swart 1990).

Remittances to their original household are also an important aspect of financial management. Particularly at the beginning of their street life some children will send a considerable part of their savings home and in many cases this money represents an important source of additional income for the family. Remittances from working children can contribute up to the 34% of household income (Salway, Rahman et al 1998). The money is sent to the household through trusted people (such as kin) living in the town who periodically return to the rural areas. In some cases remittances were used as a form of informal 'health insurance' and when seriously sick some children would return home to get medical treatment. Other reasons for sending money were mainly linked to a feeling of guilt for having left their household and a sense of responsiblity to contribute to the household's income, especially when there were younger siblings in the family. This attitude gradually fades the longer the child stays on the street, and their savings begin to be channelled into plans for opening a 'business' out of the street or starting up his or her own family.

Working and playing activities

Children in street situations perform a number of jobs in the informal city market. In a recent study presented by Rahman (1996) on the child labour situation of children in Bangladesh, out of 301 economic activities commonly undertaken by street living children, girls had access to only 11 of them and these were nearly all jobs that required no substantial acquisition of skills. The informal labour market on the street only operates through a system of references (Khan 2000), leaving children little choice but to accept patronage in order to gain access to income-generating activities.

Many children worked in excess of 10 hours per day but this varied considerably according to the job performed. The majority were self-employed and worked mostly during the day. Working conditions were generally poor and unhealthy: many experienced excessive dust and dirt. New opportunities, curiosity and a high degree of insecurity in their jobs made children highly mobile in their employments. As confirmed by other studies (Karmaker, Hilaluddin et al 1994), this high level of mobility was increased by the practices of physical punishment and beatings in the workplace.

Despite long working hours, participant children valued playtime as a very important part of their daily activities: 'Playing! Here (on the street) everything can become a game when you also know how to play with the danger' (Ratnha, a 14-year-old girl). As Vogel and Mello (1991) observed, on the street there is no right time for doing anything, leading to a feeling of space-and-time freedom inconceivable to home-living children. Furthermore, their bodies are also used in any manner they please, such as in sexual activity and drug consumption which, in many cases, are deemed game activities.

Leisure time for boys includes going to the movies, hanging around with friends, sitting and watching street life, meeting people, playing video games and visiting girls. Even the movement of daily life on the streets can be an adventure in itself (Edensor 1998: 209). Girls are less mobile during play activities and tend to spend their leisure time playing and chatting with friends in the neighbourhood. The very possibility of talking on the street is seen as a form of freedom, especially if compared to *purdah*, the experience of being confined to the home. As Mukta (a 16-year-old girl) said: 'Now I do believe the street is a public place where not only men have the right to stay. We (*girls*) are entitled too'. Holidays are also valued as important opportunities for the fulfilment of children's curiosity to travel to other cities or even to other countries:

> I have ridden the Chittagong Express to Cox's Bazar Beach, I have taken the Buriganga River's Ferry and swum in the Bengal Bay, and never paid for a ticket. I went to Mumbai twice and I visited some friends in Sylhet ... while many people here have never left Dhaka for more than two days (Shafique, a 15-year-old boy).

Children's curiosity, relative freedom of movement and capacity to 'make friends', make them experts in finding their way around, and gives them the opportunity to take advantage of what is available in different places. This ability to use the street and public space as a playground is a direct challenge to the image of the street as only a 'painful experience ... of deviance and contestation' (Daly 1998: 111) commonly reported when describing homelessness.

Food

While many NGOs focus interventions on ensuring health and education for children in street situations, food was generally deemed to be more important by children. In many cases nearly 50% of children's available income is spent on food. As they gain access to better-paid jobs, they tend to increase the quantity and quality of food consumption for themselves and their peers. Sharing food is an important part of children's socialisation on the street. It does not matter how much is available: there is always a bite for a friend.

Children in street situations reported having at least two meals per day, frequently three. The nutritional value of these meals varies considerably from day-to-day. Rice, *chapati*, *ruti*, pulses, eggs, fish and vegetables are the main ingredients of their daily diet. In addition, for children undertaking heavy physical work and in better-paid jobs, meat is also important for 'feeling stronger and looking prettier'. As reported by a health professional from a local NGO, children in street situations are more likely to meet their daily dietary requirements than the majority of slum and rural children. They eat more and better than their counterparts in slums and rural areas due to their greater access to income-generating activities, direct control over their earnings and a broader range of choice in the city's market.

On the other hand, basic requirements for a balanced diet and norms of hygiene are still far from being met on the street. There is evidence suggesting that these children are at risk of nutritional disorders such as deficiencies of Vitamin A, iodine and iron. These deficiencies lower their resistance to infections and increase morbidity rates, as well as causing night blindness, impairment of physical and mental development, anaemia and micronutrient malnutrition. Newcomers are particularly exposed to hunger, but their situation progressively improves as their knowledge of opportunities and available social networks increases.

Health status

According to the World Health Organisation, health includes not only physical but also mental well-being, thus implying the importance of children's self-esteem. Reports on the topic include diarrhoea, physical injuries, anorexia, stomach and respiratory infections, skin diseases and sexually transmitted diseases as among the most common health problems affecting children in street situations (Ahmed and Adeeb 1998; Das Gupta 2000). These observations were confirmed by heath workers from NGOs and are compatible with the symptoms presented by children in describing their most common diseases. Tetanus, measles, typhoid and diphtheria are also cited in a number of cases (Islam 1990). Many diseases are waterborne, and safe drinking-water and latrines are luxuries only a few have access to. Overall, the children participating in the survey reported being sick on an average of two-to-three days over the previous month and the people they went to for health care included friends, trusted adults, relatives or household members, traditional doctors, social workers, and doctors from NGO clinics. Further, as the health officer for a local NGO reported:

> If we compare the health status of these children in their first period of street life with the health status of established children in street situations, we will notice a gradual betterment in the first years. However, when the child stays on the street for very long periods, his or her health conditions progressively worsen, even taking into account such self-destructive behaviours as self-mutilation, use of drugs and non-protected sex activities.

A recent United Nations Children's Fund (UNICEF) study reports that the amount paid for heath care among disadvantaged adolescents ranked below addictive substances and alongside entertainment and toiletries (Kabir 2002). Treatments were often sought from traditional or unqualified practitioners, with only one child out of four consulting qualified doctors. Gaining access to hospitals and clinics is a major problem presented by children speaking about health status. They reported that 'doctors say, "what do you want here? You are a 'dirty *kangali'*, go back to where you come from"'.

Overall, children's access to medical treatment is hampered by six main obstacles: (1) discrimination between 'deserving' and 'non-deserving' poor in delivering medical assistance (see also Hossain and Moore 2001); (2) cost of treatment; (3) locations difficult to reach; (4) lack of awareness of their medical needs; (5) lack of awareness of medical facilities available (Masud Ali, Mustaque Ali et al. 1997); and (6) bureaucracy of health-care structures. Access to NGO clinics is easier and children have sometimes gained access to hospitals through these clinics. Still, the cost of treatment remains a problem, especially for a sick child. However, through the mutual support of peers the child may be able to buy the needed medicines and recover for a while.

When considering the sexual behaviour of these children, this study found an overall high exposure to sexually transmitted diseases and HIV due to the general lack of knowledge of protective measures and the threats associated with unprotected sex. From the semi-structured questionnaire, 70% of children said they were sexually active but only one child out of four had heard about HIV or AIDS. Amongst those, only one-third had any idea about the effects of becoming HIV positive or how HIV is communicated. Amongst sexually active children, only a minority reported having ever used condoms, and no child used them regularly. Especially in the case of sex workers, the children could not impose the use of condoms because of the lack of bargaining power with clients.

A common feature reported when describing children's mental health is their lack of self-esteem when living on the street (ARISE 2001; Husain 2000). My analysis suggests that this element, however important, cannot be generalised because it varies greatly according to children's personal characteristics together with children's life cycle and experiences. As previously mentioned, the children's phase of street adaptation plays an important role in determining their self-perception and esteem. This leads some children to define themselves as good children; some to define themselves as good children but growing up in a bad environment; and some to define themselves as bad children in a bad environment.

The problem was finally compounded by the general perception mainstream society has of street life. As previously argued, Bangladeshi

society views the children's condition of economic poverty as a manifestation of moral degradation, and in many cases the children themselves are blamed for their living status. This, in turn, could have a
negative impact on children's self-esteem. However important, these
elements do not create an overall rule of negative self-esteem, and their
shared experiences with peers was a very important component in raising the children's self-esteem.

A key comparative issue is whether the discourse on self-esteem
suggests differences between street-living and home-living children.
There are not sufficient data to present a comprehensive answer to
this question. However, a few initial observations can be presented. In
particular, if we look at the number of suicides as an extreme indicator of very low levels of self-esteem, we might observe that
'Bangladesh has a high rate of suicides especially among home-living
adolescent boys and girls, and young married women'.[6] Moneera, a
16-year-old girl, argued that when children took their own lives in
order to escape violence imposed on them by adults – often their own
relatives – their deaths 'should not be considered as suicides but as
homicides by adults.'

In contrast, no cases of suicide have been reported by children in
street situations or by social workers. Even children 'addicted to street
life', characterised by high levels of depression and a negative self-
image, do not seem to consider suicide as an option. They might con-
sciously adopt behaviours that are likely to hamper their future
survival, but participant children have never referred to these behaviours from a perspective of suicide.

Conversely, when referring to young people's aspirations for the
future as an indicator of self-esteem, this study found evidence that
children growing up on the streets have highly varied aspirations, but
that a number of them may have more limited aspirations than non-
street living children. Arguably, in a context of insecurity and disap-
pointment, low expectations can be considered a psychological coping
strategy (Harper and Marcus et al 2003). As Narayan, Chambers et al
(2000) have observed, in some cases children learn to restrict their
ambitions, moderating their aspirations according to the environment
in which they grow up.

Education

Nearly all children in street situations have numeracy skills, but
many remain illiterate. Many reported having no access to what they
considered 'important education', which they described as technical

or vocational courses, and both boys and girls recognised the importance of attending classes. However, some children going to NGO-sponsored classes did express concern about the lack of relevance of what they were studying to their lives, work and future plans. Indeed the quality of education and access to relevant curricula were both points of concern.

Some 80% of children participating in the semi-structured questionnaire reported having attended street education programmes, but 50% did not stay for more than one year. Children in street situations usually have access to informal school programmes run by NGOs. These are lessons of two or three hours organised daily in the open-air, where recreational activities can be combined with formal classes. Among children currently attending street classes, the majority reported regular or semi-regular attendance, usually a couple of hours per day. School attendance for girls was higher and more constant than for boys. This is probably due to the fewer working options available to girls on the street.

The most common reasons for dropping out or not regularly attending classes included lack of interest; work commitments; not having friends among the other classmates; being tired from the previous day or night's work; and fear of being subjected to unwanted medical treatments (ie, blood samples taken by injection). Another reason cited for dropping out was the rejection by social workers of children who did not regularly attend classes. Moreover, school attendance gradually decreases according to the length of street life for both boys and girls. Children who do not get involved in reintegration programmes run by NGOs are extremely likely to drop out from open-air schools, preferring work or playtime hours to education hours. Arguably, educational activities are a suitable entry point for building a trust relationship between the social worker and the child, and for giving willing and 'deserving' children the possibility to move upward to increasingly supportive reintegration programmes. However, when NGOs fail in getting the child more involved, then education starts to be perceived as a waste of time both by the child and also, partially, by the social workers who consider him/her 'beyond assistance because of the child's unwillingness to change his/her life'.[7]

Use of space

As recently expressed by Holloway and Valentine (2000), 'place' is of paramount importance in what they call 'the new social studies of childhood'. The concept of place combines the social and spatial aspects of the children's lives (Young 2003). Children's feeling of belonging is created by developing social interactions which are context-based (time and space), and their attachment to specific areas of the city is mediated by personal feelings and experiences (see also Beazley 2003). Consequently, children's heterogeneity is reinforced by the different meanings they attribute to different places according to the experiences they had there, and on their phase of street adaptation.

Children in street situations live in public areas with little or no possibility of gaining access to private space. Despite its characteristic of being 'public', this does not equate to being 'free'. In fact, public space is subject to extensive regulations and control by a number of players such as police, *mastaans*, shop owners and other influential people. Groups controlling such places display attitudes towards children ranging from repression and taxation for the activities taking place there, to tolerance and promotion of such activities.

Bangladeshi children in street situations have shown a high capacity for adapting the space available to them to their necessities. This same ability to travel around the city, country or to other countries is a source of personal pride. As reported by Rahaman Khan (a 14-year-old boy):

> Here on the street we are free ... Being free means that you can go where you want and you can bet with your friends that you will go to places where it is nearly impossible to go ... I meet people (*and*) ... I discover new things. I can go where poor people cannot go.

During the process of street adaptation, children's relationship with place changes according to their capacity to transform unknown and dangerous spaces into 'home territories'. This occurs when they reduce the complexities of encounters, maximising those with people already known and reducing encounters with unknown people (Lofland 1985). For children who succeed, urban space becomes progressively safer to explore, easier to understand and more predictable (Karsten 2003). On the contrary, those who do not succeed are trapped within a space which they constantly perceive as dangerous and alienating.

The use of space has also a gender dimension for street-living children in Bangladesh. Girls were comparatively less mobile than boys and while boys were often willing to explore and to colonise new areas, girls were more reluctant to do so, feeling more protected in known places with known people. Because of this, the size of social networks and controlled territories are generally wider for boys.

CONCLUSIONS AND POLICY IMPLICATIONS

When reviewing the characteristics of successful programmes for poverty reduction in urban areas, Mitlin (2003) stressed that to be effective, intervention should have a strong emphasis on consolidating and developing poor people's assets. Programmes rarely address a single type of asset. Rather each strategy tends to support a set of processes that are mutually reinforcing.

The failure of many of the ongoing programmes to provide children living on the street with a better life can be explained by their lack of consideration of what matters to children. These programmes tend to underestimate the importance of the coping strategies children cooperatively develop during their period of street life. Development practitioners' approach is too often oriented toward implementing a cocktail of standardised interventions that are not relevant to children's expressed needs, desires and aspirations, resulting in a number of proposed services that don't fit children's interests and don't acknowledge what they value as important.

Through answering the question 'What is important in your daily life?' the children have presented their priorities. They actively establish strategies for protecting their livelihood and promoting a starting point for attaining increased well-being. Although material-needs satisfaction is an important element in children's lives, their perception of well-being is highly dependent on the quality of social relationships and affectivity they build with peers.

The material poverty of children in street situations is juxtaposed with the complexity of the social relations they build in order to access emotional and protective security, as well as income-generating activities, food security, health and education. This ingenuity in finding suitable and logical solutions to the shortfalls in their living situations deserves to be presented as 'cultural richness' (Chawla 2002). Street-living children have more assets than we think, but far fewer than they need and to which they have a right. To admit that a remarkable number of children are resourceful in difficult circumstances implies neither that a dangerous environment is favourable, nor that the children should be expected to tolerate adversities (Boyden 2003). However, the focus on children's livelihood strategies does bring into question the inevitability of a life of destitution for these street-dwellers.

When a child-rights framework is applied in a relatively purist top-down fashion with no local framework of understanding, it risks focusing on deprivations more than achievements. In particular, when turning our attention to unfulfilled rights, we usually focus on the gap between what should be in a 'perfect' world and what is in the real world, missing the value of the achievements accomplished or the coping strategies put in place by poor people. A child-rights framework of this sort is likely to stress children's deprivations because the living conditions of these children are compared to the ideal and standardised child presented in the Convention on the Rights of the Child (UNICEF 1989). Such an approach is more concerned with negatively evaluating how desperate things are, rather than positively considering what is possible, starting with the observed situation, the improvements already achieved by beneficiaries over time, and the pursuit of their expressed preferences.

What is missing is an evaluation of what beneficiaries are already doing for themselves. For social change to take place it is necessary to understand the environment and opportunities that exist in each social and political context. This is where the theory of sustainable livelihoods becomes an important counterpart. It can bring a more bottom-up perspective to the child-rights approach and enable the creation of a comprehensive conceptual framework that fosters sustainable development – which, while trying to reach universal goals, is built upon local opportunities for action and beneficiaries' strengths.

Finally, this study has not fully dealt with two areas in which more research is needed. First of all, much of children's livelihood management depends on their patterns of adaptation to street life. These patterns will, in turn, have different outcomes over children's lifecourses.[8] This chapter has neglected this aspect of the analysis, leaving to future work the responsibility to consider in greater detail the implication these patterns have for children's present and future lives, and for creating multiple options for what we might call the 'consequences' of street life for children. Secondly, the relationship between the micro-level study and the wider environment and social structure has only briefly been touched upon. Issues such as gender, inter-generational transmission of poverty, religious identity, class, political context and market dynamics, for instance, do play a role in shaping the findings of the presented research. While all these elements have been considered throughout the study, perhaps a deeper and more robust analysis of the social contexts in Bangladesh and how they relate to street culture is important to further contextualise the research findings.

Notes

[1] An initial version of this chapter appeared in *Environment and Urbanization*, Special Issue on Chronic Poverty, 17(2) 69–82, 2005.

[2] 'Children in street situations' is a term that has been preferred to the commonly used expression 'street children'. There are a number of reasons for choosing the former expression over the latter. Arguably, when referring to those children as 'street children', we implicitly associate the negative characteristics of the street environment to their childhood, conceptualising them as belonging to the street and assuming an approach which is both offensive (Dallape 1996) and incomplete (Aptekar 1988). Further, 'street children' is a static definition unable to recognise the capacity of these children to move among different social environments (Lucchini 1996).

[3] Drèze and Sen (1991) distinguish between a 'protective' and a 'promotive' aspect of managing livelihoods to attain security. The former aspect focuses on mechanisms to prevent a sharp decline in income, whereas the latter deals with public action to raise persistently low incomes.

[4] See Dasgupta (1993: viii) who sees destitution as 'an extreme condition of ill-being' or 'extreme commodity deprivation', which results in a failure to meet a 'basic minimum living standard' or 'basic physiological needs'.

[5] At the time of interview, 1 US$ = 58 *Taka*.

[6] Information provided by the former Chief of UNICEF Child Protection Section, February 2003. Triangulation of this information is partially conditioned by no study having been found on the issue, and by the practice of police officers hiding suspected cases of suicides through the reporting of 'death for accidental reasons'.

[7] Interview with a street educator, January 2003.

[8] A number of publications produced by the BASIS Collaborative Research Support Program, for instance, seek to deepen our understanding of the importance of time and cycles in understanding poor people's assets (see www.basis.wisc.edu)(accessed 29 January, 2007).

References

Ahmed, S and Adeeb, A M (1998) *Methods and Techniques of Street Education and Substance Abuse Prevention Among Street Children*, Dhaka: Aparajeyo-Bangladesh and Childhope-Asia.

Aptekar, L (1988) *Street Children of Cali*, Durham: Duke University Press.

ARISE (2001) *Baseline Survey of Street Children in Six Divisional Cities of Bangladesh*, Dhaka: Department of Social Services, Ministry of Social Welfare, Government of Bangladesh.

Beazley, H (2003) 'The construction and protection of individual and collective identities by street children and youth in Indonesia', *Children, Youth and Environments*, 13(1) retrived from http://colorado.edu/journals/cye (accessed 29 January, 2007).

Bond, R and Hulme, D (1999) 'Process approaches to development: theory and Sri Lankan practice', *World Development*, 27(8) 1339–1358.

Bourgois, P (1995) *In Search of Respect: Selling Crack in El Barrio*, Cambridge: Cambridge University Press.

Boyden, J (2003) 'Children under fire: challenging assumptions about children's resilience' *Children, Youth and Environment*, 13(1) retrieved from http://colorado.edu/journals/cye (accessed 29 January, 2007).

Boyden, J, and Ling, B et al (1998) *What Works for Working Children*, Florence: Rädda Barnen (Swedish Save the Children Fund).

Bradbury, B and Jenkins, S P et al (2000) *Child Poverty Dynamics in Seven Nations*, Florence: United Nations Children's Fund.

Chawla, L E (2002) *Growing Up in an Urbanising World*, Paris: Earthscan-UNESCO.

Clarke, G and Sison, M (2003) 'Voices from the top of the pile: elite perceptions of poverty and the poor in the Philippines', *Development and Change*, 34(2) 215–242.

Conticini, A (2004) 'We are the kings: the children of Dhaka's streets', unpublished PhD thesis, Institute for Development Policy and Management, University of Manchester.

Conticini, A and Hulme, D (2004) 'Escaping violence, seeking freedom: why children in Bangladesh migrate to the street', unpublished paper.

CSKS (2002) *Street Kids*, Dhaka: Chinnamul Shishu Kishore Sangstha

Dallape, F (1996) 'Urban children, a challenge and an opportunity', *Childhood, Global Journal of Child Research*, 3(2) 283–294.

Daly, G (1998) 'Homelessness and the street: observation from Britain, Canada and the United States,' in Fyfe, N (ed), *Images of the Street*, London: Routledge.

Das Gupta, A (2000) *Baseline Survey on Street Children of Dhaka City*, Dhaka: World Vision.

Dasgupta, P (1993) *An Inquiry into Well-Being and Destitution*, Oxford: Clarendon Press.

Denzin, N and Lincoln, S Y (eds) (1998) *The Landscape of Qualitative Research*, London: Sage.

Devereux, S (2003) *Conceptualising Destitution*, Brighton: Institute of Development Studies.

Dordick, G A (1997) *Something Left to Lose: Personal Relations and Survival Among New York's Homeless*, Philadelphia: Temple University Press.

Drèze, J and Sen, A K (1991) 'Public action for social security: foundations and strategy', in Ahmad, E, Drèze, J, Sen, H J and Sen, A K (eds), *Social Security in Developing Countries*, Oxford: Clarendon Press, 1–40.

Edensor, T (1998) 'The culture of the indian street', in Fyfe, N (ed), *Images of the Street*, London: Routledge, 205–221.

Ennew, J (1994) 'Parentless friends: a cross-cultural examination of networks among street children and street youth', in Nestman, F and Hurrelman, K (eds), *Social Networks and Social Support in Childhood and Adolescence*, Berlin: de Gruyter, 409–425.

Ennew, J and Milne, B (1996) *Methods of Research With Street and Working Children: An Annotated Bibliography*, Stockholm: Radda Barnen.

Felsman, K J (1989) 'Resiliency in context: children coping in extreme circumstances', in Dugan, T and Coles, R (eds), *Child in Our Times: Studies in the Development of Resiliency*, New York: Brunner/Mazel.

Greig, A and Taylor, J (1999) *Doing Research With Children*, London: Sage.

Harper, C, and Marcus R et al (2003) 'Enduring poverty and the conditions of childhood: lifecourse and intergenerational poverty transmissions', *World Development*, 31(3), 535–554.

Harpham, T (2003) 'Measuring Social Capital of Children', Young Lives, Working Paper No. 4, retrieved from www.savethechildren.org.uk/younglives/data/publications (accessed 29 January, 2007).

Harriss-White, B (2002) 'A note on destitution', unpublished paper presented at the Dissemination Workshop of the NCAER/QEH/DFID on Poverty: Alternative Realities, New Delhi.

Hatch, J A (ed) (1995) *Qualitative Research in Early Childhood Settings*, Westport: Praeger.

Hickey, S (2000) *Street Children and Urban Poverty in Lusaka, Zambia: Vulnerable, Excluded and Empowered?* Cambridge: Africa Studies Association.

Hjorth, P (2003) 'Knowledge development and management for urban poverty allevia-
tion', *Habitat International*, 27(3) 381–392.
Holloway, S and Valentine G (2000) 'Children's geographies and the new social studies
of childhood', in Holloway, S and Valentine, G (eds), *Children's Geographies: Playing,
Living, Learning*, London: Routledge.
Hossain, N and Moore, M (2001) 'Arguing for the poor: elites and poverty in developing
countries', Sussex: IDS Working Paper.
Hulme, D and Shepherd, A (2003) 'Conceptualising Chronic Poverty', *World Development*,
31(3) 403–424.
Husain, S (2000) *Breaking the Cycle. Working Children in Bangladesh*, Dhaka: World Bank
and Government of Bangladesh.
Islam, N (1990) *The Urban Poor in Bangladesh: Comprehensive Summary Report*, Dhaka:
Centre for Urban Studies.
Kabir, R (2002) *Adolescent Boys in Bangladesh*, Dhaka: United Nations Children's Fund.
Karmaker, R and Hilaluddin, M et al (1994) *Child Workers in Informal Sector: A Dhaka
City Scenario*, Dhaka: SC Sweden.
Karsten, L (2003) 'Children's use of public space: the gendered world of the playground',
Childhood, 10(4), 457–473.
Kelletta, P and Moore, J (2003) 'Routes to home: homelessness and home-making in
contrasting societies', *Habitat International*, 27, 123–141.
Khan, I A (2000) 'Making the urban poor stay in town: mobilizing social capital
resources', *Discourse: A Journal of Policy Studies*, 4(1) 21–41.
Leach, M and Mearns, R (eds) (1996) *The Lie of the Land: Challenging Received Wisdom on
the African Environment*, Oxford: Heinemann.
Lincoln, Y S (1993) 'I and thou: method and voice in research with the silenced', in
McLaughlin, D and Tierney, W G (eds), *Naming Silenced Lives: Personal Narratives and
the Process of Educational Change*, New York: Routledge, 29–47.
Lofland, L (1985) *A World of Strangers: Order and Action in Urban Public Life*, Illinois:
Waveland Press.
Lucchini, R (1996) 'The street and its image', *Childhood, Global Journal of Child Research*,
3(2) 235–246.
Masud Ali, A K M and Mustaque Ali A K M, et al (1997) *Misplaced Childhood: A Short
Study on the Street Child Prostitutes in Dhaka City*, Dhaka: INCIDIN.
Mitlin, D (2003) 'Addressing urban poverty through strengthening assets', *Habitat
International*, 27, 393–406.
Monsoor, T (2002) *From Patriarchy to Gender Equity: Family Law and its Impact on Women
in Bangladesh*, Dhaka: The University Press Limited.
Moore, J and Canter, D et al (1995), *The Faces of Homelessness in London*, Aldershot:
Dartmouth.
Moser, C (1998) 'The asset vulnerability framework: reassessing urban poverty reduc-
tion strategies', *World Development*, 26(1) 1–19.
Moser, C and Norton, A (2001) *To Claim our Rights: Livelihoods Security, Human Rights, and
Sustainable Development*, London: ODI, retrieved from www.odi.org.uk/pppg/
activities/concepts_analysis/rightsinaction/Publications (accessed 29 January, 2007).
Narayan, D and Chambers, R et al (2000) *Crying Out For Change*, Washington DC: World
Bank.
Panter-Brick, C (2002) 'Street children, human rights and public health', *Annual Review
of Anthropology*, 31, 147–171.
Qvortrup, J (1994) 'A next solidarity contract: the significance of a demographic balance
for the welfare of both children and the elderly', in Qvortrup, J, Bardy, M et al (eds),
Childhood Matters: Social Theory, Practice and Politics, Aldershot: Averbury.

Qvortrup, J (2004) 'The Waiting Child', *Childhood*, 11(3) 267–273.

Rahman, W (1996) *Rapid Assessment of Child Labour Situation in Bangladesh*, Dhaka: United Nations Children's Fund International Labour Office.

Rakodi, C (2002) 'A livelihoods approach. Conceptual issues and definitions,' in Rakodi, C and Lloyd-Jones, T (eds), *Urban Livelihoods. A People Centred Approach to Reduce Poverty*, London: Earthscan Publications, 3–22.

Riggio, E (2002) 'Child friendly cities: good governance in the best interest of the child', *Environment and Urbanization*, 14(2) 45–58.

Rizzini, I and Butler, U M (2003) 'Life trajectories of children and adolescents living on the streets of Rio de Janeiro', *Children, Youth and Environments*, 13(1) retrieved from http://colorado.edu/journals/cye (accessed 29 January, 2007).

Roe, E M (1991) 'Development narratives, or making the best of blueprint development', *World Development*, 19(4) 287–300.

Roe, E M (1999) *Except Africa. Remaking Development, Rethinking Power*, London: Transaction.

Rudqvist, A and Christoplos I, et al (2000) *Poverty Reduction, Sustainability, and Learning*, Stockholm: Sida.

Rutherford, S (2000) *The Poor and their Money*, New Delhi: Oxford University Press.

Salway, S and Rahman, A et al (1998) 'Urban livelihoods study: preliminary findings from the quantitative panel study', Dhaka: unpublished draft.

Scheper-Hughes, N and Sargent, C (1998) *Small Wars: the Cultural Politics of Childhood*, Berkeley and Los Angeles: University of California Press.

Shubert, C (1996) *Building Partnerships for Urban Poverty Alleviation: Community Based Programmes in Asia*, Kuala Lumpur: UNCHS Habitat.

Swart, J (1990) *Malunde: The Street Children of Hillbrow*, Johannesburg: Witwatersrand University Press.

UNICEF (1987) *Paulo Freire and the Street Educators: an Analytical Approach*, New York: United Nations Children's Fund.

UNICEF (1989), Convention on the Rights of the Child, www.unicef.org/crc (accessed 29 January, 2007).

Unni, J and Rani, U (2003) 'Social protection for informal workers in India: insecurities, instruments and institutional mechanisms', *Development and Change*, 34(1) 127–161.

Vogel, A and Mello, M S (1991) 'Da casa a rua: a cidade como fascinio e descaminho', in Fausto, A and Cervini, R (eds), *O Trabalho e a Rua: Crianças e Adolescentes no Brasil Urbano dos Anos 80*, San Paulo: Cortez Editora, 135–150.

White, S (1999) 'NGOs, civil society, and the state in Bangladesh: the politics of representing the poor', *Development and Change*, 30, 307–326.

Wood, G (2003) 'Staying secure, staying poor: the "Faustian bargain"', *World Development*, 31(3) 455–471.

Young, L (2003) 'The "place" of street children in Kampala, Uganda: marginalisation, resistance, and the acceptance in the urban environment', *Environment and Planning: Society and Space*, 21(5) 607–627.

Hindu Nationalism and Failing Development Goals: Micro-Finance, Women and Illegal Livelihoods in the Bombay Slums

Atreyee Sen

INTRODUCTION

In Maharashtra, 'identity politics' and 'empowerment' cannot be explained in western terms, these ideas are specific to each culture. The Shiv Sena Mahila Aghadi wants to give a unique platform, emotional and economic, to the Sena women. There is insecurity amongst common women irrespective of status, caste and poverty. The credit scheme has been developed to provide insurance to poor women, especially in the unorganised sector. The Marathi women are also the daughters of the soil. Hardworking and often the sole breadwinners in the family, they need financial security.

> – *Poonam, Brahmin, middle class, a doctor and*
> *chief architect of the Shiv Sena micro-credit scheme.*

Yes, all that talk about 'economic empowerment' for women is there. But credit societies will bring many slum women into the Aghadi. The *angutha chhaap* (an illiterate person who signs with a thumb imprint) women have no idea about managing finances. If we help them make savings and get them loans, we buy their loyalty for a long time. We needed a sustainable scheme exclusively for mobilising women.

> – *Srilata, Maratha, head of local Aghadi in the*
> *party's office in the Mahim slums, Bombay*

The riotous Shiv Sena movement in Maharashtra, western India, swerved from violent regionalist politics into pan-Indian Hindu nationalism (or *Hindutva*) in the 1980s. In a desperate bid to emulate national level party politics and also to appease its growing bank of highly militant women supporters, the Shiv Sena (literally, king Shivaji's army) 'allowed' women leaders to form an autonomous wing. The wing came to be known as the Mahila Aghadi, the Women's Front, which drew its primary membership from the expansive slums of Bombay. The anti-minority, anti-State activities of these rabidly pro-Hindutva Aghadi 'warriors' attained a certain momentum, but only came into the limelight after they participated visibly in the communal riots that took place in Bombay between December 1992 and January 1993. The Sena orchestrated large-scale riots after Muslims in Bombay publicly protested the organised destruction of a mosque by Hindu nationalists in north India.

Since then, the Mahila Aghadi has gained in reputation as an independent, militant women's task force. While the senior leadership emerged from among middle and upper class women, the Aghadi sustained itself by appointing a strong local-level female leadership from among the slum-dwellers. The patrolling of urban ghettos by criminalised Aghadi women led to the creation and dissemination of a culture of female militancy, which I have described in detail elsewhere (Sen 2003). These organised groups of lower-class women, leaders and cadres, played into a politics of urban fear: they manipulated their notorious image to threaten factory owners, businessmen and entrepreneurs in order to acquire legal and illegal jobs and assets. Several slum women supplemented their legal incomes with 'soft' illegal activities such as trading in stolen goods or selling marijuana. Others inherited 'hard' gun-running and narcotics businesses from their husbands; the men were often arrested or killed in gang wars or police shoot-outs. Over time, the Aghadi members came to control a range of profitable economic transactions in Bombay, in the process partially moving away from positions of subordination to occupy roles that allowed them to exercise male authority and power.

The female cadres experienced and, over time, expressed a need to expand and retain a definite position within the party, and the Aghadi put more and more emphasis on developing organisational strategies. Small, *ad hoc* schemes offering practical benefits to women were developed, such as the mother-and-child monthly health camps and public toilets for women. However, these short-term schemes – mainly for the benefit of poor women – and the Aghadi's system of securing economic and social justice for 'oppressed women', did not lessen insecurities about creating a future for the women's wing. Informal channels of social intervention, often based on brutal terror tactics, seemed to provide temporary relief to slum women.

In an attempt to further consolidate its base, the Aghadi took the initiative to develop and implement a micro-credit scheme, organis- ing loans and savings for poor women. This project went on to become the first long-term, large-scale economic policy for women formulated by the Shiv Sena. Even though the credit project was imagined to be part of a developmental nationalism, it sprang from the immediate concerns of the Aghadi leaders to create prolonged emotional and economic dependencies amongst the members. It became a new strategy for mass-based action that could help the women's wing occupy a key position in the slums, and consequently play a more central role within the Shiv Sena. The term 'micro-credit' evidently suggests the predominance of 'debt' or lending, while 'micro-finance' signifies a more pervasive set of financial services related to low-scale economic activities (Nair 1998). However, most leaders described the scheme as a 'micro-credit' society, and so I have also (mainly) used this term.

The primary focus of this chapter is to uncover the complex rela- tionship between right-wing vigilante activities, illegal livelihoods, and the flow of credit among women activists. I will show how a micro-credit society created under political patronage can be devised to provide crucial political and economic gains for a party. I argue that the Aghadi's agenda to make the wing indispensable within the movement took the emphasis away from ideal forms of women's empowerment as envisioned within development ideologies.

Rahman (1999), while studying the Grameen Bank in Bangladesh, deftly uses Scott's concepts of 'public' and 'hidden' transcripts (Scott 1990: 4–7) to explore the functioning of micro-credit societies. Appropriating Rahman's use of these dual concepts and applying them to decipher motives behind financial services initiated by right- wing women, I analyse various voices that remain critical to the for- mation of the Sena micro-credit society. Using the term 'public transcript', Rahman (1999) refers to the philosophy behind micro- credit and its official objective to decrease women's vulnerability in the labour market. Such a public transcript in the context of the Aghadi's policies involved the strategies of more elite planners, who wanted to give women access to credit and improve their economic conditions. The scheme was also expected to organise women into co- dependent groups for raising their collective consciousness and strengthening their solidarity.

The hidden transcript, developed 'offstage', is what 'informants often expressed or discussed in a safe context, ie, within their own group or with persons whom they trust' (Rahman 1999: 68). This chapter will further uncover the covert schemes of grass-roots *shakha* leaders who were given the responsibility to implement the project. These lower-class Aghadi leaders wanted to harness the legal and illegal money floating around in the slums, which often went into the hands of moneylenders and other informal credit suppliers. Financial exchanges being the primary concern of slum women, the Aghadi slum leadership felt that channeling money into a savings society would create crucial long-term economic dependencies in the leader-cadre-member relationship. 'If the Aghadi women possessed each other's money, they could never leave the organisation,' explained Priya, an Aghadi *shakha* leader. Rather than offering women real exposure to mainstream development, the Aghadi leaders attempted to create a pool of resources which could fund the wing's sporadic militant activities, demonstrations or picketing. In the same context of hidden transcripts, I also discuss the benefits as well as the resentment the scheme generated after it was formally launched.

The Aghadi tried to pursue political goals within the context of a development scheme; it was most unlikely to achieve the official objectives of micro-credit. Since the Sena women had right-wing loyalties and had remained involved in illegal trade, they also carried the burden of isolation from mainstream development projects, which offered their services to 'the good poor'. This chapter argues that the manipulation of genuine socio-economic concerns of ordinary members of right-wing women's groups could jeopardise a cohesiveness of identities attained through other organisational strategies. The data forms a small part of my larger research on gender and conflict in India. As such, I restrict myself here to analysis of the discourse around the women's micro-credit scheme, rather than its long-term practice. I have changed the names of the Aghadi women to protect their identities.

DEVELOPMENT IDEOLOGIES AND THE SENA SCHEME: PUBLIC TRANSCRIPT

In this section I will discuss the official designs and implementation policies developed by the chief architect of the scheme, Poonam, and some of her associates in the party. I will show how right-wing women leaders used jargons of social purpose to project their cooperative schemes as extensive development projects. The senior leader-

ship was keen to overcome their widespread image as 'women hooli-
gans', and be regarded as a serious and sophisticated source of
women's empowerment.

Policymaker Poonam: background

The all-party leaders, men and women, were unable to locate an Aghadi
leader who had the political maturity to develop and implement a complex economic scheme. Even the chief of the Mahila Aghadi, Meena, had
risen from the ranks and was accused of lacking the 'intellectual capacity' for foresight. It seemed essential to employ a competent policymaker since the project was intended to represent the moderate face of
the Sena women. The party decided to recruit a new member, who had
prolonged experience in formulating official policies. The Sena turned to
Poonam, a renowned women's activist and also an overt sympathiser of
the 'sons-of-the-soil' movement in Maharashtra.

Poonam began her career as a traveling doctor who offered her
services to rural women in Maharashtra. Over time, she realised that
groups of healthy village women would regularly visit her clinic to
gossip and exchange stories about their daily tribulation. This experience motivated Poonam to work closely with non-governmental
organisations (NGOs) and other women's associations. She said, 'I
worked towards getting women to share a common platform and air
their grievances.' In her personal life, however, Poonam felt a growing disillusionment with what she described as 'radical feminism'.
Her grievances were compounded when her 'activist friends' pressured her to terminate a pregnancy, since an addition to the family
could hinder her social work. She decided to 'set aside their warn-
ings' and went ahead to deliver a daughter, who later became a
source of inspiration. According to Poonam, 'I was afraid to join the
Sena because of its notorious reputation. But the Sena upholds family
values along with social service for women. That's why I was drawn
to the party. Radical feminism is so wrong.' Thus, Poonam, who had
proclaimed her conformity to family traditions and had been working
successfully on projects for women, was well-positioned to be formally incorporated into the Sena leadership.

Poonam felt her greatest success story was the implementation of a
micro-credit scheme for quake-affected women in Latur. In 1993, an
earthquake destroyed several villages in the Latur and Osmanabad
districts of Maharashtra; hundreds of homeless women were left without any support.[1] Poonam said she 'visited the affected villages and
concluded that most women could be classified under 22 professional

groups: potters, weavers, tailors, etc. I persuaded the women in each group to work in cooperation with each other.'

After news of the earthquake broke, national funding agencies and banks were willing to offer financial aid. However, they lacked close contact with rural women and were unable to extend funds effectively.[2] Poonam claimed that she approached the top brass of these financial bodies and helped them develop a unified approach towards women's rehabilitation. She managed to mobilise small loans for each of the 22 professional groups, and urged the quake-affected women to also contribute from their meagre resources. With this cash pool, the rural women bought machinery and raw material to start businesses. Later, Poonam located companies interested in marketing the finished products and assisted them in establishing links with women manufacturers. 'The women were able to repay their loans within a few years. It was very tiring but a great success,' she said, assessing her past achievements with micro-credit.

Most scholars argue that an isolated experiment with micro-credit in rural areas needs to be observed critically. Pearson (1998), for example, in discussing the mobilisation of rural women around a credit scheme, points out that coordination of women's professional activities – pooling of work and making women's enterprises profitable – requires massive organisational skills. It can only be developed after years of experience. Even though Poonam did not have any prior knowledge of organising credit societies, her media-aided and self-propagated success stories had given her prominence. Since the Aghadi retained a political mission to refurbish its image before the media and the public, Poonam's 'reputation' as an accomplished maker of women's economic policies made her a suitable candidate for the Sena camp.

The party requested Poonam to formulate a micro-credit scheme for slum women in Bombay, and a special position was created to accommodate her into the Sena. Poonam's task was to replicate her project from Latur and make it workable in the Sena slums. Could it work? Nair's research (1998) on women and micro-credit argues that poor rural and urban women may be equally drawn into a collective because of their continuing financial anxieties. However, the author explicitly argues that the political and social implications of economic policies on women's lives and work, along with strategies for their survival and empowerment, may dramatically shift with a change in focus from rural to urban women on the fringes. While flopping into a cushioned chair in her air-conditioned office, which had two life-size photographs of the belligerent Sena supremo Bal Thackeray on the walls, Poonam told me: 'It is not going to be an easy experiment. Imposing a policy from a rural onto an urban setting has many obstacles. This new project required more research and analysis, but it is a challenge.'

The challenge: the scheme and empowerment 'objectives' of affluent leaders

According to Poonam, the Sena scheme would remain similar to that implemented in Latur. In Bombay, however:

> ...slum women will be asked to pay the local Aghadi leader a minimum of Rs 10 per week. Since the amount is really small, most women should not feel the pinch. If I had said Rs 40 per month, most of the women would have backed away. The *shakha* [local party] leader will open local bank accounts in the names of the women who had entrusted her with the money. She could also keep the passbooks to ensure that all the women are regularly giving money. That way, the slum women would have savings, interest growing on them and not feel the difference in a big way. And the same leader could also get loans from the bank against the accounts whenever the women need it, individually or as a professional group. The women leaders would merely act as links between the bank and the poor women. There is no profit in it for them. The scheme will ensure an ease with which participants can borrow funds, rather than travel far to seek loans. It will be marked by the absence of complex transactions.

Since the slums in Bombay had no rotating or non-rotating savings group, they offered a fertile ground for a savings programme, she insisted.

According to Poonam, her target groups for initial implementation of the scheme were women employees or entrepreneurs, who had greater earning capacity than housewives. Though the scheme would be open to all women, she wanted to focus primarily on women whose propensity to save and reinvest a part of their income was higher.

> Poonam: There is a feminisation of the labour force and the flow of credit to this section of people would enable them to adopt improved techniques of production.
>
> A: What kind of techniques?
>
> P: Like a woman who pounded gram seeds into flour will make a profit if she took a loan and acquired a machine, instead of using the traditional manual grinding system.
>
> A: That means she may also require an electricity connection in her house... the electric supplies in [a particular slum] are all illegal and the

women always complain how the use of heavy machinery leads to power failure ... and...

P: (interrupting) This is only the start. I don't have all the answers yet.

Some scholars, like Deshpande and Deshpande (1998) and Gothoskar (1997), have asked pertinent questions in the context of the rapid feminisation of the labour force in Bombay. Did the phenomenon indicate an increase in female participation rate relative to men or did it mean the substitution of men by women in certain areas of work? I asked Poonam what exactly did *she* understand as 'feminisation' of labour. Poonam changed the subject and brushed aside my question, but it appeared that the creator of the credit scheme had fragmented ideas about women workers in the slums.

'Employed' women in the Bombay slums invariably performed low-skill, manual jobs (such as vending and hawking) which put them in a weak position in the labour market. An income did not increase their bargaining power at home or at work (Shah, Gothoskar et al 1994: WS–47). Poonam had planned to advise women to enhance their already existing professional skills and develop new ones. This could be achieved 'when women would gather to address their financial grievances during the micro-credit society meets.' She was convinced that poor women's openness to professional re-skilling, in order to survive in a male-dominated workforce, would improve their financial status, especially within the family. Since a large section of the women targeted were involved in small businesses, Poonam anticipated that her credit society would enhance their entrepreneurial capacity, which in turn would lead to their 'empowerment'. As she put it: 'An active credit market needs an abundant supply of loans. This in turn would stimulate savings.'

If this policy turned out to be successful, Poonam would address the fears of unemployed women about the unorganised sector. She and her fellow leaders concluded that most educated women were keen to seek jobs and avoid the risks in running businesses. Poonam said, 'The permanency in the flow of income attracts women, but in Bombay, securing a steady job, especially for a woman, is very difficult.' If educated or illiterate unemployed women see other businesswomen making a profit through the micro-credit scheme, they may be willing to invest their energies in entrepreneurship. 'This would lead to the utilisation of entrepreneurial capacity,' Poonam concluded.

Meena, the Aghadi chief, felt a lasting financial policy would integrate women into the development process. 'We do not want to tell women that we are a charity; that we will give you money and not expect you to return it,' she said. Both Poonam and Meena felt the micro-credit scheme was important because it economically empowered the women to take control of their own fund management in addition to their domestic and professional needs, and also to return the loans over time. Meena said, 'We need to unite the women but if women rely solely on informal markets, they will continue to remain outside the economic mainstream.' Women's integration into the mainstream could be achieved through their involvement with an efficient credit system, but it also required a suitable economic policy. Since Meena did not want to leave the Sena women at the mercy of 'unpredictable political events', she felt the scheme would offer a more secure future for women. This was in keeping with the Aghadi's efforts to increase its credibility as a women's social service wing, which remained (partially) independent of party politics and the Sena's Hindu nationalist agenda.

Poonam asserted that the participation of women in designing and implementing this scheme would develop their personal skills and political maturity. She wanted to allow all 224 Shiv Sena offices scattered across Bombay to carry out their own 'need assessment programmes' so that women, under the guidance of the *shakha* leader, could make the scheme flexible enough to suit their local demands. In what was described as a 'successful experiment,' *shakha* leader Aparna invited female small entrepreneurs in her area to form a committee. She became the group president and allotted the duties of treasurers and collectors to the slum women. According to Aparna, 'Women's tasks so far have been right-wing vigilantism. But this was exciting because they were into policy-making exclusively for women.' Aparna seemed content that the first batches of Sena women to join the scheme were 'enjoying' their involvement with the project. Whether it would enhance their self-confidence was a more complex question that could be evaluated in the future. Yet, the formation of a women's entrepreneurial credit committee was seen as 'fashionable' in the slums. This also fulfilled the Aghadi's aim to perk up its dwindling image. A woman fruit-vendor, who had never reflected upon her professional status, told me how she felt 'smart' to be addressed as an 'entrepreneur' and member of a 'woman's board'.

Senior leaders like Surekha stressed timeliness in granting loans. Most women in small business sectors had varied loan demands because of the seasonality of their production. Surekha reflected:

> The women in my area are bangle-makers or candle manufacturers. All illegal businesses you know. The women make the stuff in the slums and the products get sold under a big manufacturer's name. The

demand peaks during festivals. During that period, women should get adequate loans so that they can maximise their profits.

Another senior Aghadi leader, Rina, blamed slum men for reduced savings in many households. Men's habits and preferences (such as smoking and drinking) were influenced by upper-class lifestyles, while women remained more concerned with food security in the family, Rina generalised. Since the Sena upholds the value of the community over the individual, its members should not be tempted to waste money on selfish exercises. 'If all the women have savings and successful businesses, it would reduce competition. When women get more united, it is better for the struggle,' she said. Since Rina, like other senior leaders I encountered, was conspicuously wealthier than the women we were discussing, I felt conscious of a contradiction in her position. I asked whether she curtailed expenditure for 'the struggle' and set an example for her cadres. She responded:

> Of course, the economically active members will contribute more to the general welfare of the community. I have offered a portion of my savings to the Aghadi scheme so that larger interests can be collected on my account, which in turn can be recycled within poorer Aghadi women as loans.

Through her support to area-specific need assessment programmes, Poonam tried to show that she would consider the problems of local creditors while expanding her scheme. Her lack of field knowledge about the viability of her scheme revealed Poonam's inexperience at working with aggressive, right-wing women. Though she seemed quite distanced from the operations of local slum economies, Poonam claimed that she was not 'in conflict' with *shakha* leaders. Most *shakha* leaders, who worked closely within the existential uncertainties of slum worlds, thought otherwise.

SHAKHA LEADERS TESTING THE WATERS: HIDDEN TRANSCRIPT

Even though Poonam's policies appeared to be elitist and ideological, the Aghadi presented them as pragmatic to the academy. The right-wing leaders also sent out detailed pamphlets to the media; this intrigued most reporters of newspapers and television channels, as micro-credit societies were usually conceptualised under the secular aegis of 'development'.

While working in the slums, I realised that grass-roots leaders resented their marked absence from the limelight even though they were the real players, making Poonam's policies practicable for implementation. In this section, I will discuss how the local leadership manipulated this scheme developed by 'richer leaders' to achieve political goals closer to home. This was significant because in the year that I spent with the Aghadi, the differences between the elite and the grass-roots leadership were suppressed through negotiation and informal interaction. With the launching of the scheme, the hierarchy within the Aghadi became conspicuous and the front's agenda for religious and political consensus got diffused. However, the local leaders tried to keep this splitting of interests at the level of implementation under wraps.

Implementing the scheme: Objectives of local leaders

Most of the *shakha* chiefs had worked intimately with the local women and, unlike senior leaders, had unwavering authority over them. The grassroots leadership remained convinced that they could administer savings and credit on a personal basis. According to *shakha* leader Suparna, 'her' women would not trust anyone else with their financial secrets.

> Here individual relationships count, otherwise the efforts to form 'policies' would go to waste. I know women need money to invest in businesses, that includes illegal ones. If I am in charge of the savings group, the women will not be afraid to talk to me … because I know … and I will not tell.

The local leaders remained confident that no other political party or social service organisation would be able to initiate a credit project on such a grand scale. Because of pre-existing community support, the Aghadi had a ready infrastructure to launch the scheme. Since the slum leaders had controlled women's support groups, such as gender justice-delivering squads, they had gained substantial local knowledge about the distribution of wealth according to different criteria like income and age groups, as well as economic sectors. Said Juthikatai, 'No NGO has more detailed information on household composition and budgets, their legal and illegal financial inflows and outflows. We don't need graphs. It's in our heads.'

To almost all the local-level Sena leaders, 'grand ideas about empowerment' held little meaning for marginalised women struggling to make a livelihood at the periphery of a global city. The *shakha* chiefs furtively chided senior leaders for wasting time debating the aims of the scheme. They felt the primary concern should be to make the meaning and operation of a micro-credit scheme *comprehensible* to poor, slum women. Most *shakha* leaders, thus, creatively improvised on the implementation policies.

Shakha leader Surabi launched a poster campaign to convince the illiterate and semi-literate slum women in her constituency about the benefits of the scheme, which she said would reduce misunderstanding. The posters also helped to draw out deeper social conflicts, which apparently 'shocked' the Sena leaders. During one such meeting to discuss the operation of the scheme, Surabi displayed a poster, which was split into two parts. The first part, with a large red X marked across it, showed a moneylender reclining before his vault. The other section of the poster showed a Sena woman in a saffron sari standing between a shabbily-dressed slum woman and a big bank. There was a large green check-mark over the second section. This poster motivated the women to ask questions about the validity of the Sena scheme. Surabi found anguished women – who apparently had been forced to grant sexual favours to local moneylenders – spitting on the first half of the poster.

A SHIV SENA MICRO-CREDIT SCHEME POSTER

Even though Surabi tried to point out the awareness-raising potential of these posters, this particular poster represented one of the most crucial unstated objectives of the *shakha* leaders in launching the scheme. The poster split the world of informal financial exchanges into two parts. It clearly reflected the women leaders' insistence on transference of monetary dependencies from the moneylender (red X-mark), to the Aghadi (green check-mark). This was in keeping with the wing's political aim to create and manipulate long-term financial dependencies between the leaders and the cadres. The poster was an obvious attempt to discourage slum women – depicted first in a sub-servient position before a menacing moneylender, and then on an equal footing with Aghadi leaders – from using informal sources of credit. It was trying to convince poor women that the Sena leaders would prove more reliable in handling their resources. The poster also markedly deviated from pictorial representations of nonpolitical credit-schemes. The latter usually highlighted a group participatory approach and showed poor women sitting together to discuss financial questions. The aim was to do away with intermediaries, not shift them elsewhere. The Sena poster tried to show that the leaders had no self-interest in collecting money since they were merely liaising between money-holders and the inaccessible world of banks. The *shakha* leaders were also advocating that they wanted one-to-one monetary transactions; the money should come to their hands directly. Since these leaders had served the interests of women in the slums for a prolonged period of time, they were apparently not as distrusted as the moneylenders. The visual contrast between the moneylender's safe, and the bank in the background, also underscored the more profitable choice of keeping money in a formal institution where it could collect interest, and be returned safely to the women over time.

'The women are curious about posters … it's more interesting than dull discussions,' summed up Surabi. I felt she feigned innocence about the exploitative relationship between slum women and moneylenders; most *shakha* leaders had meticulous knowledge of forced or voluntary socio-economic exchanges carried out in their locality. However, she threatened to launch a tirade against 'corrupt safe-owners', knowing well that diverting finances towards her own scheme would give her political stability in the long run.

I had a chance to visit a jeweller who was also the local moneylender. He claimed that slum women came to him for financial assistance but he preferred 'to give money to men, because they are more likely to return it. It is also easier to threaten the money out of men without police intervention.' His reluctance to offer loans to women indicated that their chances of procuring funds, even through informal channels, were remote. If there were other credit systems operating in the slums, the Sena women with their criminal backgrounds were unlikely candidates. Thus, the Aghadi project tried to gain in popularity by claiming to save poor women from sustained exploitation and offering them alternative financial structures.

Beneath this facade, the *shakha* leaders became candid with me about their underlying reasons for taking up the project. There was hope from all quarters that the credit groups would lead to more women supporters, and that mass participation to boost the savings programme would lead to greater bonding within the front. The local leaders were strikingly unconcerned about women's integration into 'the national mainstream'; to them, the scheme was another strategy to ensure further the loyalty of local women. According to *shakha* leader, Trisha, 'I don't understand such talk. There is talk about "vocational training to expand intermediary functions"… I don't understand. What I know is that my women need money and if I get it for them, they will stay with me.'

What 'Trisha's women' did enjoy, however, was carrying out economic activities without intervention, since their financial interests often collided with male members of the party. The credit society would provide a ready cash pool, which could be mobilised to meet urgencies *within* the Aghadi. The project allowed the creation of very small deposits, and the individual cash accounts taken in totality made it possible to accumulate lump sums in the bank. These sums of money could be easily withdrawn and used whenever there was a need for the local Aghadi branches to flex their muscles. Sandhya, *shakha* leader, said:

> On a smaller scale, if we need to hold a protest *morcha* [march] small amounts of cash can be obtained through door-to-door collection. But if it is for a bigger cause, like a proper street battle, then we need to quickly accumulate a large sum. Then money in the bank helps.

The activities of the credit group, therefore, were combined with the other organised, militaristic functions of the Aghadi, and the strategy to pool resources also reinforced the Aghadi's purpose to remain in a state of readiness for 'communal war'. Large amounts of money flowed into the party through the Sena's extortion racket and through various 'sympathetic' business houses in Bombay (Hansen 2002); the women were aware that a dent in their accounts due to a massive withdrawal could be replaced over time. 'The women just want some independence … political and economic,' Trisha concluded.

WHY JOIN THE SCHEME, WHY STAY AWAY: CREATING DIVISIONS

According to Kabeer (1998), conflicting ideas arise over the impact of micro-credit societies on women's empowerment because programme evaluations are based on differing models of power, especially in the context of gender relations. None of them examine the impact from the perspective of the impoverished women themselves. In this section, I will highlight the reasons offered by the Sena cadres to determine their level of involvement with the credit project. The women were not simply passive recipients of directives, and were keen to judge whether they would truly benefit from the scheme. The Aghadi members attained a cohesiveness of religious and gender identities that was largely based on the suppression of economic disparities. I will show how the micro-credit society is likely to fragment the Aghadi's unified image along professional and power hierarchy.

WHY JOIN THE SCHEME?

Observing the success of other pro-Hindu cooperatives for women

The success of a few women's cooperatives proved that trade unions did not have the resources to appropriately serve the economic interests of women workers (Carr et al 1996; Rose 1992). For example, the Annapurna home canteen movement, or the Lijjat *papad* (poppadom) factory on the fringes of Bombay, became profitmaking organisations by persuading women to combine their resources, start businesses and locate efficient markets in food services (Shah, Gothoskar, et al 1994). The Aghadi, which had a well-developed base in Maharashtra for several decades, had done its homework about the achievements of cooperatives in urban areas. This was demonstrated further by Aghadi leader Neena's insistence on escorting me to the Lijjat *Papad* factory to meet the employees there. The labour in the factory, like the Sena women, was comprised of migrant, Maharashtrian women. 'See how organised they are. They remain tied by financial interests,' said Neena. I also discovered that most women's lending organisations were compelled to accumulate their capital independently, because the banking system provided few low-interest loans for the urban poor.

Claiming to be 'inspired' by these successful movements, the Aghadi proposed to operate its credit society independent of State machinery. Even though the wing based its strategies on the ideal features of other specialised savings groups, the Aghadi was unwilling to coordinate with other parties. 'The Sena agenda is different and so is the target group.' This line was parroted by most leaders who debated the launch of the scheme. This aversion to State intervention had potential benefits for the Aghadi, as experiences of State-run credit groups in other regions had proved to be humiliating for women. According to Basu (1998), for example, another Hindu nationalist organisation, the Bharatiya Janata Party (BJP) successfully ran a State programme for women in Rajasthan. The project was initially considered to be progressive and 'stole the thunder' of the more secular Congress Party, which was trying to implement parallel pan-Indian women's programmes (*ibid* 1998: 169). A report on State-controlled women's development plans in Rajasthan stated that when women 'volunteers' of the programmes initiated by the BJP decided to be unionised, they were asked to leave (EPW 1994: 3187). In the Sena camp, the women created their own gender policies and could not be sent back to their homes through State intervention. The new scheme was not intended to *initiate* women into the world of 'collective consciousness'. In their own opinion, the Sena women already shared a deep bond, and the scheme would only *increase* their camaraderie. However, the women were also eager to establish a long-term rapport with bank officials, so that the two parties could grant and obtain mutual favours. The Sena project was to remain autonomous from men and the State; something the women felt would be invaluable for sustaining the programme.

Rural securities, low investment and credit sourcing

To the 'ordinary' Sena members, 'economic empowerment' was an abstract concept with no capacity to motivate poor, illiterate women. Some Sena women were enthusiastic to join the credit society because they wanted to recreate social securities lost in the city slums. Aghadi member Suparna reminisces: 'In the village, the women would marry their savings and help the needy.' Personal savings remained scattered in the slums and there was nostalgia for economic and emotional associations. The scheme could bring about a collectivisation of women's labour, finances and trust, and village women would 'once again wash together and work together', albeit within an urban setting.

Even the enormous task of supervising the credit union seemed peculiarly straightforward to the Aghadi members. This was primarily because the costs involved in mobilising personal savings were nonexistent. Reinke (1998), in his study of small enterprise foundations in South Africa, argued that solidarity was an expensive input for financial services production, since the costs of group formation and interaction often outweigh the benefits of high repayment. This problem remained outside the periphery of the Aghadi scheme, as the women's wing had already created social capital in the slums. The *shakha* provided a place for routine meetings. There were no infrastructure costs for arranging group sessions, nor the high transaction costs associated with increased membership that often alarm microfinance groups. Also, private funds came into the party from various external sources, so the fear of economic nonsustainability was absent. Even though the Aghadi women acted as nonprofit financial intermediaries, if they were compelled to invest their own funds to set up the society they would have been displeased. 'There is no cost in door-to-door cash collection. Energy cost is no cost,' said Malini.

A section of slum women complained about their alienation from formal financial institutions. The negligence towards small-savers on the part of post offices (POs) and banks, as well as the unsympathetic attitude of their staff members, encouraged women to consider the benefits of the Sena project. 'We prefer to save in jars at home,' said Sharmila. She was semi-literate, and along with her fellow Aghadi cadre Shilpa, could articulate the need for savings groups which operated in favour of 'women, migrants and illiterate people.'

The primary handicap for women seemed to be the dearth of trained PO personnel who could promote savings in a dynamic way. According to Sharmila, 'The staffers have no patience to listen to my troubles. And I have no time to repeat. They are rude, so the women stay away from them.' There were no PO policies adapted to the needs of women with small savings. Shilpa was a young bride who had been married into the slums of Bombay and she liked to send gifts home to her siblings during festivals. She said: 'I would try to tell the staff about my problems. They would impatiently grab my hand, dab it in ink and stamp on a paper, without explaining anything to me. Where did my money go? Will I get it back before *diwali* (a festival)? I knew nothing.' Along with these difficulties, the slum women also faced the inefficiency of the public distribution system in Bombay, which could not meet the demands of poor women for subsidised credit.

The women found commercial banks to be image-driven toward high-profile clients. They complained: 'Their customer service was in English'; 'they had high operating costs' and 'they were too profit-oriented'. Shilpa said: 'Some of the Sena women, we earn more than the "smart" women who have accounts in these fancy banks. But for them "background" is important.' This expression of bitterness alluded to the large amounts of money in the slums that were under the control of the Sena women.

Banks, it seems, have a history of discrimination against poor women. Most banks were reluctant to let women open accounts for themselves or for their minor children. They rarely extended credit to women, especially if they were employed in independent businesses (Shah et al 1994), due to their incapacity to offer substantial securities against loans. While filling in a form, loan applicants had to disclose their profession, annual income and assets. The legal officer from the bank would then assess the value and legality of the income and assets declared. According to Sharmila, 'Some of our sources of funds and assets are *khufia* (illegal). How can we declare them?' Shilpa and Sharmila were contented that Sena leaders would get them bank accounts and loans without requiring them to enter the premises of these intimidating institutions. '*Apunko paisa milega* (We will get the loans) ... no talk, no tax.' The women slapped each other on the back and laughed aloud while saying the last four words in English.

The complex processes of savings mobilisation launched by formal financial institutions had demoralised women in the slums. The local women leaders, who were from similar social backgrounds as women like Shilpa and Sharmila, raised hopes by offering simple monetary services to poor women. Even though the senior leaders were trying to envisage the credit scheme as a development project and the *shakha* leaders were trying to gain political permanence in the slums, a number of cadres were rallying around the Sena scheme because it promised them practical financial advantages.

WHY RESIST THE SCHEME?

No provisions to repay existing loans; 'Just want to live it up now'

Despite a general acceptance of the scheme, there were Sena women who remained sceptical of its purported successes. These women felt the credit scheme was not pragmatic enough to fit into financial cycles of poverty. In the following paragraphs I will draw out the voices of Sena cadres who resisted the scheme, even though they were otherwise loyal to the party's policies. Consequently, the project could fail as a mobilisational strategy, and the divisive potential of the scheme could undermine the Aghadi's proud solidarity. Opposition to the project further suggested the difficulties of working towards a development goal within a politically mobilised group.

Kherua, a *khanawali* (food supplier) who migrated into the Bhayander slums after marriage, said:

> I want to return to the village home one day. I always send money to my family there. I do not keep money in banks here. I do not want to grow roots in dirty urban slums. I visit my village to oversee things. Working women incur many costs. All the women I work with are repaying various loans. From where will I get extra money for the Sena scheme? If they buy off our earlier loans to moneylenders I would understand. But they are not doing that.

Subha, a sales girl from a second generation of slum women, said:

> My family is at loggerheads with the extended family in the village. We are, thus, a smaller unit. I am working, so we have some extra cash. We prefer to spend the money on small luxuries. My parents fear less for the future, including that of the girl children. We sisters are both earning. We have become detached from traditional codes of marriage and property, which were costly. Investment in jewellery, cattle, land; distrust in

currency assets – those days are gone. Now it's a different ballgame alto-gether. Whatever money we have we spend it on goods. Who knows what will happen in the future? We do not save at all. I just want to live it up now. I do not want to give up my money for uncertain schemes to make my future secure. I may not even be able to retrieve it then.

The voices of Kherua and Subha reflect patterns of savings and invest-ment in individual households driven by various attitudes towards the uncertainties of poverty. According to Montgomery, the poverty-reduction potential of micro-credit schemes is commonly perceived as 'a promotional process through which poor households can graduate out of poverty' (1996: 292). This graduation can be achieved by break-ing the vicious circle of low-investment\low-income\low-investment, through the introduction of capital in the form of credit to generate productive incomes. However, the author himself describes this model of poverty, and its emphasis on credit as the solution, as possibly 'sim-plistic' (*ibid*). Within the Sena's grand scheme, created by elite policy-makers, the condition of poverty was assumed to be stagnant and stable. The leadership remained indifferent to the opinions of women like Kherua and Subha, which highlight the 'emotional' yet resilient characteristics of a life of poverty. Kherua, who wanted to return to her roots, and Subha, who wanted to enjoy her life in the slums, were appeased when the Aghadi wrested financial benefits *for* them (by get-ting them jobs and business contracts in the city). But if the political party were to demand money *from* them, be it for investment or sav-ings, the women were willing to rebel.

Use of force as terror

Even when Sena cadres responded adversely to incentives for joining the scheme, the Aghadi leaders made it clear that they were likely to use force to secure repayment for their investments. Some of them rationalised this as 'an extra push' to make the women realise the value of the scheme. As Radhatai justified it:

> Some of the slum women were sceptical of the Aghadi's adult educa-tion programmes. They went for it because they were afraid of social sanctions in the form of ostracism or even physical abuse. They knew the reputation of the Aghadi. But later they began to appreciate the ben-efits. They could write letters to relatives. The children or the village postman would read it aloud to them. The same logic applies while forcing women to join the credit programme. They are likely to realise the profitability of the project after a while.

The use of force was also considered necessary to recover dues from creditors; it would reassure women that their money would not be squandered. Aparna felt, 'The Sena women are famous law-enforcers. This new task of ensuring that women follow the scheme's rules will not be difficult.' She had taken the initiative to appoint a team of credit collectors who would 'punish' women who were irregular with depositing their monthly savings, or in their loan repayments. This specialised task force was given the freedom to threaten, and at times, assault women defaulters.

The *shakha* chiefs were further willing to use force to vehemently ward off external forces hindering the implementation of the scheme. The leaders were aware that large amounts of public money would be involved, yet remained unclear about legislation for financial institutions. All the leaders addressed these uncertainties with hostility typical of the Aghadi. Juthika, a leader, asked, 'Who will interfere with or wind up anything launched by the Aghadi? They have any fear to save their lives or not?' According to Nair (2000), several micro-finance institutions operated outside the legal structure, surviving on gaps and loopholes within the system. This did not affect the functioning of the programmes. So, circumscribing legalities may not hamper the 'success' of the Sena micro-credit scheme, but aggression against debtors could critically affect its expansion.

Using violence to ensure investment and repayment was not exclusive to a militant women's front. According to the Bangladesh Rural and Agricultural Committee's (BRAC's) own research studies (1998), members of women's cooperatives often demolished the houses of defaulters. Most slum women were skeptical of forced repayment policies. Some of them speculated that they would not be able to repay loans on time, primarily because of fluctuating cash flow in their homes. The violence used by women to run local justice systems and extortion rackets, a unifying force within the Aghadi, was viewed with terror once the Sena women imagined themselves to be on the receiving end. The more docile Aghadi cadres, who felt powerful and protected as members of a martial organisation, were also apprehensive of relapsing into vulnerability. These uncertainties, in my understanding and in the opinion of women opposing the scheme, would generate infighting and jeopardise the bonhomie within the Aghadi.

Was repayment discipline imperative for the implementation of a micro-credit programme? Rahman (1999) observed that peer-group pressure for timely repayment did not lead to borrower empowerment, as originally envisaged by the Grameen Bank. Monitoring defaulters often lead to what is described as the 'institutionalisation of suspicion' (Fuglesang and Chandler 1993). Pressure to attend adult literacy programmes was radically different from the use of violence to collect savings, the latter being linked to questions of surviving poverty as well as to injuring slum women. Hostility was likely to erode mutual trust and increase women's isolation within the slums. If outstanding debts coincided with other eventualities (such as floods or forced evacuations), even small repayments could become a liability for the poor. Forced collection of money at such times would diffuse Poonam's ivory-tower vision of reducing the cycles of poverty among Sena women.

Creating economic divisions

According to Nair (1998: 532), enterprises that fall under the purview of poor women's entrepreneurship could at most be called 'pre-enterprises' that cater to the basic needs of low income consumers and are characterised by simple products, low prices, local markets and dependence on informal credit. She saw a beneficial link between micro-credit groups and women's pre-enterprises, as they offered solutions to many of the problems that pervade the informal system of moneylending (Nair 1998).

During my fieldwork, I realised that the *shakha* leaders knew well that pre-enterprises run by poor Sena women did not generate adequate income. Targeting women small entrepreneurs would not rake in enough savings to even *initiate* a credit scheme. So the local leaders sought out relatively affluent women who controlled the flow of income in their households. This target group consisted of women who were heads of their households; widows, women abandoned by brothers/husbands and often, unwed mothers. In the case of single mothers, the Sena leaders approached 'uncontroversial' women, on whom traditional sanctions had faded over time. The leaders also pressured unmarried women, and older women living among kinsmen, usually with no hope of marriage, to join the scheme. The scheme was also thrown open to housewives with the authority to withhold a part of the family income for saving. The association with the Sena had inverted gender equations in some measure. Even though men were persuaded to give up certain privileges (eg, controlling women's mobility), women workers were still not the sole financial decision-makers. 'Even though some women are the only source of family livelihood, they may have husbands or male guardians to whom they hand over their earnings,' snorted Rina, a *shakha* leader. So for the local leaders, it was important to locate

groups of women who managed their own finances and could contribute to the initiation of the society.

This is, once again, not unique to the Sena scheme. Osmani (1998),
in an analysis of the Grameen Bank, points out that women with
greater initial bargaining power would come forward to join credit
programmes because they already had the autonomy and self-confidence to defy cultural norms. He argued that by a life-cycle effect,
older women often had fewer restrictions on mobility, in addition to
freedom from domination within the family and greater all-round
awareness (*ibid*). In the case of the Sena, however, women of all ages
had achieved a degree of independence by associating with the militaristic activities of the Aghadi. So the women who came forward initially to join the credit programme had already experienced financial
and social autonomy. But female small entrepreneurs or housewives
with no income also formed a bulk of the Aghadi membership. This
section of women felt 'left out', even before the launch of the scheme,
'since the *shakha* leaders visited richer houses to discuss the project'.

The Aghadi scheme would also extend loans to women with illegal
sources of income, which in turn lead to increased supplies of 'black
money' and reinforcement of criminal activities in the slums.
Transparency in account details during society meetings would
clearly demarcate women with illegal sources of income from those
who did not enter prohibited professions. This was another juncture
at which the aims of a political movement could clash with the objectives of a development project. The Sena women previously chose to
ignore monetary rivalries for the common causes of the Aghadi; but
the possibility that women with illegitimate sources of funds could
benefit more from the scheme had already created resentment in the
Sena camp. The poorer women, merely 'sulking' at this point, felt the
scheme would highlight the economic differences between Aghadi
members. Contrary to the aims of launching credit schemes, this project once implemented could prove divisive for slum women.

CONCLUSION

As Mayoux (1998: 40) points out, women in the same context can have
different attitudes towards the same programme and can also be
affected differently by it; thus 'programme evaluation cannot be
described as an exact science'. The duration of the Sena programme
was important in order to study the real socioeconomic and cultural
implications of micro-credit for the members.

During the formulation of the scheme, the *shakha* leaders felt confident that the pre-existing Aghadi infrastructure would make the implementation of the scheme non-problematic. According to Montgomery (1996: 291), the ideal of peer groups based on social collateral relies on groups that 'screen and self-select their own members to form relatively homogenous groups in micro-finance'. Such semi-autonomous solidarity groups also help to break cycles stemming from the more qualitative dimensions of poverty, such as alienation and helplessness (Chambers 1988). The Aghadi was a peer group, which through years of militant activism had successfully broken cycles of isolation in the slums. On the one hand, the ability of ordinary members to play influential roles, transparency in legal and illegal accounts, and the absence of formal application processes could allow poor women to feel involved in the new scheme. On the other, strict enforcement laws and visible class differences could push women back into seclusion and poverty. The Aghadi would end up pulling down what had taken years to build.

Even if Aghadi solidarity suffered, would the implementation of the scheme really 'empower' the forced or voluntary members? Khandker (1998) felt that the measure of any micro-credit programme evaluation lay in attempting to increase the bargaining power for women through increased access to credit resources and consciousness-promoting training. Poonam felt her programme was meeting these developmental objectives, since it was designed to facilitate the flow of resources within a community. However, this was only in keeping with the positive dimensions of development planning; other experiences presented a mixed picture about the rates of success of micro-credit societies in empowering women. Sinha and Hashmi, for example, show that participation in Grameen Bank and BRAC is positively associated with women's level of empowerment, defined flexibly as a function of their physical and economic mobility, involvement in household decisions, legal awareness and participation in political campaigning (Hashemi, Schuler Riley 1996; Sinha 1998).

However, a number of studies have appeared in recent years – in various regional contexts – which attempt to critically analyse the effects of micro-finance on empowering poor women, and assess whether or not it leads to an increased productivity and purchasing power. For example, Chavan and Ramakumar (2002) observed that the methodology of the Grameen Bank contributed to considerable disempowerment of poor women. In order to maintain repayment schedules, the women entered a loan-recycling process, which intensified their debt liability and increased intra-household tensions (*ibid* 2002: 961). According to Kabeer, offering loans to women to increase their domestic productivity simply upturns the feminist notion of redistribution of home-based responsibilities, a structural feature of gendered power relations (Kabeer 1994, 2000). Other critics, notably Goetz and Sengupta (1996), argue that . repayment problems with men are more difficult to resolve, so women become softer targets of micro-credit programmes. The Sena women were vulnerable to all these various conditions. The implementation of a micro-credit scheme within a cohesive women's group did not necessarily promise an end to their suppressive gender roles. Even though the Sena women had long been exiled from development projects because of their overt right-wing loyalties, it was actually their affiliation with 'an extremist political party' that had helped them acquire more visible domestic and public roles.

The Aghadi policymakers were concerned with building a more sophisticated image for the women's front. They were eager to erase their negative image as religious trouble-makers by entering the serious world of development projects. But this was in sharp contrast to the interests of the *shakha* leaders, who were implementing the scheme in order to reinforce their violent, militaristic activities. The *shakha* leaders wanted to erode the market niche of moneylenders by keeping money floating around the slums within the party. One intention was to create long-term interdependencies within the Aghadi by allowing leaders and members to control financial resources in each others' homes. This strategy reflects the underlying power relations which moneylending often relies on. But for the *shakha* leaders, an independent pool of resources also meant the wing could organise and develop its militaristic functions without monetary restraints. More funds meant greater violence. While the policymakers were trying to suppress the aggressive dimension of the Aghadi by implementing this scheme, the *shakha* leaders were planning to use the same scheme to underline it. The scheme exposes the hierarchies that exist among elite and local Aghadi leaders, consequently revealing the conflicts between political and developmental goals.

The Aghadi grassroot-level leaders, however, remained somewhat hopeful about the transformative potential of intervention, for women and for the wing. By offering support to an illegal businesswoman who would not be able to secure a loan otherwise, the leaders attempted to fulfill a poor woman's aspiration to build a more stable future. And this woman would also remain with the Aghadi in the future. For the local Aghadi leaders and members, 'their' women were not faceless neutral figures on a micro-finance programme sheet. All the women in the slums, whether in legal or illegal businesses, were 'real' women, and they had hope that the micro-credit institution would bring about what Mosely (2000) described as a reconfirmation of the power of collective action. According to Poonam, the grand architect of the scheme, 'The credit scheme is only to open the minds of the women ... it is a means and not an end in itself.'

I often wondered whether this Aghadi micro-credit scheme would turn out to be another experimental 'development' intervention, which could easily be withdrawn in the face of challenges to it. The policymakers and the local leadership did not seem to anticipate an organised form of resistance to the scheme; they were accustomed to unconditional loyalty from the Sena cadres. But there were emerging hierarchies and growing resentments which would make the implementation of a development scheme in a political context grossly convoluted. Some grassroots leaders like Trisha felt that low incomes, lack of price stability and fear of inflation could pose a real threat to the implementation of the scheme. As a resolution, she was willing to offer economic sops to women investors. She said, 'I have to promise illegal ration cards and a jump in bank queues for loans.' Temporary unlawful sops were unlikely to help women rise above poverty, and prolonged lack of financial options for slum women was likely to result in their investments furthering the activities of a right-wing women's organisation. The Aghadi's scheme, thus, brings out different shades of a lopsided developmental nationalism, which should have serious implications for poverty-alleviation policy research in the future.

Notes

[1] Government of Maharashtra Records, 1993.
[2] Source: The Maharashtra Earthquake Rehabilitation Programme (June 1994–1998).

References

Basu, A (1998) 'Hindu women's activism in India and the questions it raises', in Jeffrey, P and Basu, A (eds), *Appropriating Gender: Women's Activism and Politicised Religion in South Asia*, London: Routledge.

Chavan, P and Ramakumar, R (2002) 'Micro-credit and rural poverty: an analysis of empirical evidence', *Economic and Political Weekly*, March 9.

Chambers, R (1988) *Poverty in India: Research and Reality*, Sussex: Institute of Development Studies, Discussion Paper No. 241.

Carr, M, Chen, M and Jhabvala, R (1996) *Speaking Out: Women's Economic Empowerment in South Asia*, London: IT Publications on behalf of Aga Khan Foundation and United Nations Development Fund for Women.

Deshpande, S, Standing, G and Deshpande, L (1998) *Labour Flexibility in a Third World Metropolis: A Case Study of Bombay*, New Delhi: Indian Society of Labour Economics.

(EPW) *Economic and Political Weekly* (1994) Report on 'The state's role in women's empowerment: for better or for worse'.

Fuglesang, A and Chandler, D (1993) *Participation as Process – Process as Growth: What We Can Learn from Grameen Bank, Bangladesh*, Dhaka: Grameen Trust.

Goetz, A-M and Sengupta, R (1996) 'Who takes credit? gender, power and control over loan use in rural credit programmes in Bangladesh', *World Development*, 24(1) 45–53.

Gothoskar, S (1997) *Struggles of Women at Work*, New Delhi: Vikas.

Hansen, T (2002) *Wages of Violence: Identity in Post Colonial Bombay*, Princeton: Princeton University Press.

Hashemi, S M, Schuler, S R and Priley, A (1996) 'Credit programmes and women's empowerment in Bangladesh', *World Development*, 24(4) 635–53.

Kabeer, N (1994) *Reversed Realities: Gender Hierarchies in Development Thought*, London: Verso.

Kabeer, N (1998) *'Money can't buy me love'?: re-evaluating gender, credit and empowerment in rural Bangladesh*, Institute of Development Studies Discussion Paper 363.

Kabeer, N (2000) *The Power to Choose: Bangladeshi Women and Labour Market Decisions in London and Dhaka*, London: Verso.

Khandker, S R (1998) *Fighting Poverty With Micro Credit: Experience in Bangladesh*, New York: OUP for the World Bank.

Mayoux, L (1998) 'Participatory learning for women's empowerment in microfinance programmes: negotiating complexity, conflict and change', *IDS Bulletin*, 29(4) 39–50.

Montgomery, R (1996) 'Disciplining or protecting the poor? Avoiding the social costs of peer pressure in micro-credit schemes', *Journal of International Development*, 8(2) 289–305.

Mosely, P (2000) 'The microfinance experience of poor countries: lessons for banks in India', in Basu, K and Jindal, K (eds), *Microfinance: Emerging Challenges*, New Delhi: Tata McGraw Hill.

Nair, T S (1998) 'Meeting the micro credit needs of the poor: issues in focus', *Indian Journal of Labour Economics*, July–September, 531–538.

Nair, T S (2000) 'Rural financial intermediation through commercial banks: a review of recent trends', *Economic and Political Weekly*, 35(5) 299–306.

Osmani, L N K (1998) 'Impact of credit on the relative well-being of women: evidence from the Grameen Bank', *IDS Bulletin*, 29(4) 31–38.

Pearson, R (1998) *Feminist Visions of Development Gender Analysis and Policy*, New York: Routledge.

Rahman, A (1999) 'Micro credit intitiatives for equitable and sustainable development: who pays', *World Development*, 27(1) 67–82.

Reinke, J (1998) 'Does solidarity pay? The case of small enterprise foundation in South Africa', *Development and Change*, 29(3) 553–576.

Rose, K (1992) *Where Women are Leaders: The SEWA Movement in India*, London: Zed.

Scott, J C (1985) *Weapons of the Weak: Everyday Forms of Peasant Resistance*, London: Yale University Press.

Scott, J C (1990) *Domination and the Arts of Resistance: Hidden Transcripts*, New Haven: Yale University Press.

Sen, A (2003) 'Women and communal violence in India: a countervictimology', unpublished PhD thesis, School of Oriental and African Studies, University of London.

Shah N, Gothoskar, S, Gandhi, N and Chhacchi, A (1994) 'Structural adjustment, feminisation of labour force and organisational strategies', *Economic and Political Weekly*, April 30, WS 39–48.

Sinha, S (1998) 'Introduction and overview', *IDS Bulletin*, 29(4) 1–10.

6 Keeping it Clean: Discipline, Control and Everyday Politics in a Bangkok Shopping Mall

Alyson Brody

INTRODUCTION

People employed in the Thai janitorial sector have remained largely invisible and voiceless in the existing literature on labour and migration, despite the fact that the sector is a major employer of rural migrants into Bangkok.[1] This is partly an effect of the invisible, undervalued nature of domestic work. It is also a function of the way in which rural\urban migration in Thailand has been framed largely in terms of prostitution. While the issue of prostitution is highly significant, there are nonetheless other sectors, such as the garment and service industries, that have not received the same amount of attention but employ many migrant women. This chapter aims to redress the balance in the literature. It is based on research I conducted between 1999 and 2000 with a group of migrant women working as cleaners in a Bangkok shopping mall, who came mainly from rural northeastern Thailand, the poorest region of the country and the most significant supplier of migrant workers to Bangkok.

The chapter starts by discussing some of the ways in which notions of civilisation and progress are translated through the material effects that produce and control bodies in space and time. Specifically, it shows how uniformity, docility and hierarchies play an important role in constructing meanings in the modern Thai workforce, and how these played out in the space of the shopping mall. I present ways in which

the regulation of time, space and bodies reinforces perceived differences between 'undisciplined' rural and 'disciplined' urban lifestyles.
The chapter first historicises these issues, then considers their relevance
in the locus of the mall. I then consider how the cleaners found ways to
reclaim themselves against the threat of uniformity and control by
means of indirect forms of agency forged through everyday strategies
in and around the workplace. These strategies could fall into the category of 'everyday resistance' (Scott 1990), which can ultimately have
more collective significance than explicit protests (Turton 1984). These
forms of resilience or resistance target specific aspects of working practices, rather than aiming at the company that employed the women, or
being fuelled by what are conventionally considered political ideas. My
work responds to Escobar's criticism of the common assumption in
development and human rights discourse that 'a "survival strategy"
cannot simultaneously be a political strategy' (1995: 187). The chapter
highlights the important, productive roles played by the migrant
women I knew – and indeed by many Thai women from rural and
urban areas – as well as the sense of responsibility that can transcend
feelings of revulsion for 'dirty', low-status work like cleaning toilets. I
show how the women I knew were often guided by a strong sense of
integrity, pragmatism and pride, which enabled them to gain some
degree of personal satisfaction from their work, and which were
embedded in personal and cultural meanings. However, these principles also imposed limits on their willingness to tolerate certain terms
and conditions of work.

PARADIGMS OF PROGRESS: THE HISTORICAL
SIGNIFICANCE OF DISCIPLINE

In 2004, Thailand's Prime Minister, the millionaire Thaksin
Shinawatra, was angling to enhance Thailand's role in the global
arena by buying Liverpool football club. Such an apparently incon-
gruous action, coming from a country so far away from Liverpool, has
precedents elsewhere in Thailand's past. This is a nation that has been
in a constant process of self-definition since the beginning of the 20th
century. It has moved through various phases of national affirmation
that share an important tenet – the desire not only to be 'civilised'
(*sivilai*) but to be *seen as* civilised. Over the years, what it means to be
civilised has gone through various incarnations. During the fading
years of French and British colonial rule in the countries surrounding
Thailand, civilisation in this never-colonised country meant demon-

strating how westernised Thais could be. This included compulsory hat-wearing, and was marked by King Mongkut's foray into Western science, thus effectively spurning 'folk' beliefs.[2] From the 1950s, civilisation was subsumed under the term 'development', entailing the restructuring of the agricultural sector and industrialisation of the economy. More recently development has been equated with globalisation – a desire to launch Thailand as an internationally respected player in industry, finance and technology. In the period of slow recovery following the 1997 economic crash that originated in Thailand, Thaksin's gesture can be seen as a symbol of Thailand's global rebirth.

Central to this overriding narrative of civilisation is an evolutionary undercurrent which posits Thailand on a linear trajectory starting from forest dwellers, through rural existence to urban modernity, and exemplified in the metropolis of Bangkok. The influential writer Rajadhon, whose work has been widely read in schools and other institutions, reinforced perceptions of civilization as a process in which societies move from simplicity to complexity. He explains that civilization is based on rules for behaviour, especially 'qualities of neatness and order' (1972: 14). The effect of such assumptions is the placement of Bangkok at the pinnacle of society, with rural areas lagging behind and in need of education in proper manners and speech and, above all, cleanliness and order a point to which I later return. The region of Isan, in particular, is placed at the tail-end of this trajectory, with its customs and language linked to the less-developed Lao nation, patronisingly referred to as Thailand's 'little brother'. This characterisation is bound up in old rivalries and a brief period of colonisation by the Siamese over the Lao kingdom in the mid-17th century (see Evans 1999, and Ngaosyvathnn and Ngaosyvathnn 1994).

How this official version of progress plays out in reality belies the simplicity of the message. Although official government propaganda gives the impression that rural Thailand and its farmers are rapidly becoming anachronisms, half of Thailand's population still live and work in rural areas, and the vast majority of those are farmers, mostly working their own land. I have argued elsewhere (Brody 2003) that the endurance of the rural sector signals an alternative vision of Thailand, its people and its future. It also enables the Thais who farm the land to root themselves literally in their country's soil.

Why is this background important for understanding the subject of migrant cleaners working in a Bangkok shopping mall? I argue that the mall is a microcosm of the complex intersection of realities and issues that pervade contemporary Thailand. Those employed to clean, the act of cleaning itself, and the employment structures that encompass them, reveal much about influential narratives of development and its underlying contradictions. Above all, these topics communicate ways in which poor, rural migrant women make sense of various conflicting possibilities and create spaces for themselves.

FROM THE FARM TO BANGKOK: SHIFTING PATTERNS OF MIGRATION IN THAILAND

For anyone spending a certain amount of time in Bangkok, it soon becomes clear that many of the crowded city's residents and/or workers are from 'upcountry' (*tang jangwat*). At *Songkran*, the Thai New Year, Bangkok becomes noticeably quieter as its migrants return to their villages for annual celebrations. Migration has been an integral aspect of Thai society from the mid-19th century, when peasants were encouraged to appropriate and cultivate plots of land (see Phongpaichit and Baker 1995: Chapter 1). Since the 1950s, the 'new frontier' has been the cash economy offered by city-based industrialisation and the demand for cheap and readily available labour, made accessible by improved transportation systems. Although many of the migrants are from northern Thailand, the largest percentage has always been from the northeast, or Isan. The poorest region of Thailand, Isan also has the least forgiving climate and soil conditions, which means that farmers are usually restricted to one rice harvest a year only. A common pattern has been for rural Isan people to migrate to Bangkok between planting and harvesting, as a way to supplement their income. The number of migrants escalated sharply when the economy entered a 'boom' period in the 1980s (see, eg, Phongpaichit and Baker 1995).

Whereas the initial labour movements to Bangkok from rural areas were dominated by men, in recent years women have accounted for almost half of the migrants, mainly because of companies' preference for young female employees who are considered cheaper to employ and more submissive than men (Jaded 2000: 85). At the time of my research, economic growth had slowed considerably due to the financial crash of 1997, but the number of rural migrants registered as working in Bangkok was nonetheless high. The figures for 1997 collated by the Thai National Statistical Office indicate that there were 193,838 rural migrants in Bangkok, of whom just over half were female, out of a total population of 7,238,953. Such figures are notoriously difficult to compile because they are based on registration of domicile in Bangkok, which most people fail to do since migrants do not settle permanently in Bangkok, but return periodically to their villages for seasonal activities such as harvests. Most of the migrant women I knew planned to return to their villages for good once they had accrued a certain amount of money or could no longer engage in physical labour in the city. Some found that the benefits of earning a wage in the city were outweighed by the relatively high cost of living, and thus decided to move back to the villages (see Brody 2003; Mills 1997, 1999).

THE SHOPPING MALL: DEFINING NEW THAI URBAN LANDSCAPES

My rationale for choosing the domain of the shopping mall as my main fieldwork site was informed by various factors. First, I was fascinated by the phenomenon of urban landscapes and the way in which Bangkok seemed to mushroom upwards in an almost organic way during the five or so years that I lived there. David Harvey has noted the centrality of space in shaping contemporary urban experiences. He makes the point that control over space is the prerogative of the powerful, and its significance lies in the possibilities for communicating and reinforcing social hierarchies and authority through 'spatial organisation and symbolism' (1989: 186). Harvey's comments are useful in finding a perspective on Bangkok, where uses of space, struggles over space and lack of space are implicit features of industrialisation.

The countless newly-erected modern, glittering towers convey messages of affluence and progress. A defining space of the contemporary urban experience in Thailand and much of developing South and Southeast Asia – achieved to its zenith in Bangkok – is the shopping mall. In the shopping mall ideal environments can be carved inside, away from the overpowering heat, crowds and traffic fumes. A cornucopia of consumption possibilities are available for perusal. Importantly, many of the malls are intended for the newly-monied, upper-middle classes, and are places to see and be seen. They constitute an entire leisure experience, complete with cinemas, restaurants and fashionable bars, and are visibly selling an aspirational lifestyle, creating an illusion of luxury that is not matched at the street-level of the city. These public spaces require constant maintenance, and during the five years that I lived in Bangkok, I observed the armies of cleaners in shopping malls and other large buildings. They were usually identifiable as being from Isan by their short, well-built stature, darker skin, prominent cheekbones and flat noses, and were almost always women. These women seemed in many ways to be outsiders to these spaces that were casually occupied by middle-class Thai shoppers.

The women's work blurred the boundaries between 'private' and 'public' by playing a domestic role in a public place. At the same time, the associations of domestic/private with low status, and public/professional with high status, seemed to be reinforced by their work in the malls, which erased the cleaners as participants in their active meanings. It is noteworthy that the Thai phrase for female cleaner or maid – *mae bahn* – also means housewife, literally meaning 'mother of the house.' I wished to gain insights into the ways in which the cleaners were constituted and constituted themselves through the various spaces of the mall, and how they experienced the very physical inscription of their social positioning.

THE CLEANERS

As stated above, my focus in this chapter is on a group of cleaners in a large, central, modern shopping mall. The majority were migrants from northeastern Thailand, a region known as Isan, and their average age was 34. The cleaners were employed by a company that was subcontracted by the shopping mall, and which had an office in its basement. At the same time, the cleaning operations were overseen and monitored by the mall administration. During the period of my research, 150 cleaners were employed at the mall, of whom only 20 were men. The longest period spent working at the mall was five years and the shortest was one month, but this was difficult to gauge because the women would sometimes work for a short time, return to their villages, and then reapply to the company at a later date. The basic wage was 162 *Baht* (approximately £3.00 in 1999–2000), with increases of 20 *Baht* (approximately 45 pence) per day for each year worked. The cleaners were not contracted, but could claim six days' paid holiday and three months' maternity leave after having worked three months for the company.

CLEANLINESS AND CONTROL

Dirt is essentially disorder. There is no such thing as absolute dirt; it exists in the eye of the beholder. If we shun dirt, it is not because of craven fear, still less dread of holy terror ... Dirt offends against order. Eliminating it is not a negative movement, but a positive effort to organise the environment (Douglas 1991: 2)

According to Mary Douglas, dirt marks the boundary between order and disorder and therefore between purity and potential danger, making its elimination imperative to a sense of control over natural forces (*ibid*: 3). The notion of hygiene carries enormous symbolic significance in Thailand and is perceived as marking the difference between civilised and uncivilised places. Most of the Thais I knew who had never travelled told me they imagined England to be a very clean country because it was *'pattana laew'* (already developed). The symbolic power of cleanliness emerged publicly during my research period as part of a scandal involving a Thai pop star. The young woman had referred to Lao women as 'dirty' during a television broadcast which was also shown in Laos. There was an outcry from the Lao women's union, but no apology was given. It was clear that the furore had not simply been caused by the singer's naïve comments, but was triggered by deeper prejudices in her assumptions about the relatively 'undeveloped' status of Laos compared to Thailand.

Sitting across the Mekong river to the north of Thailand, Laos has always occupied a distinctive place in Thai history and popular consciousness. As noted earlier rivalry between the two countries has been stoked over the years, particularly as a result of the Thais' short period as a colonial power over Laos. The sense of Laos as a backward 'little brother' spills over into perceptions of Isan, where the majority of the population is ethnic Lao. The poorest and most infertile region, beset alternatively by drought and floods, Isan is seen as being at the tail-end of Thailand's forward trajectory – the polar opposite to Bangkok's shining example. This lack of evolutionary progress is embodied discursively in constant references to its backward ways, failure to produce conventionally beautiful women, and linguistic peculiarities. The Lao language and accent are often objects of hilarity, connoting country bumpkin ignorance. Discussions with some of the migrant women revealed that it was difficult not to internalise elements of the Bangkok-centric subtext on Isan. The following extract is based on a conversation between myself and some garment factory workers:

> We talked about pride/self-consciousness. They said that a lot of Lao-Isan women don't want to be recognised as Isan in public because they feel ashamed and because people associate Isan with extreme poverty. Those people, they said, won't eat *som tam*[3] or *para*[4] in public, whereas rich people with nice clothes can eat it because everyone knows they are rich. Also those people may not want to speak too much. They feel ashamed that their Thai language is not polite/nice and are therefore silenced.[5] One girl told me a story about a friend of hers who worked in Bangkok and was too embarrassed to speak to her Isan boyfriend in

Lao on the phone in front of her friends. They eventually split up because of her implication that Isan culture wasn't good enough, or was lower than Bangkok culture.

Isan and its people are also considered to be dirty, a trait that apparently worsens the deeper into rural territory one goes. A frequent comment from the urban-based Thai middle-class people I knew – from both Isan and Bangkok – was that I would find Isan villages very dirty (*sokoprok maak*). In fact my own experience was that, although the unpaved roads became mud tracks during the rainy season, house interiors were kept spotless. Given these highly evocative conceptualisations of dirt and cleanliness, it is not surprising that the employment of an army of cleaners is an integral aspect of shopping culture for a recently-created urban middle-class. The maintenance of hygiene helps to create and sustain the illusion of order around which urban 'civilisation' is predicated. That the bodies of poor, rural, largely Isan women and men are responsible for this hygiene completes the image of discipline in which labour, as part of a developed standard of work, is considered a means to survey and correct sloth, ignorance and sloppiness. The theme of dirt as a metaphor for class difference, marking a shift in what constitutes modernity, is echoed by Suellen Hoy in her analysis of the culture of cleanliness in America. She historicises the pursuit of hygiene, linking it not only to medical knowledge and the growth of large cities that were prone to disease, but also to a process of Americanisation. Immigrants from Europe and especially Africa were seen as dirty and in need of education about hygiene; only when they showed themselves able to take on American standards of cleanliness could they begin to be accepted as Americans (Hoy 1995).

As indicated above, the physical removal of dirt is closely bound up with class difference. Demonstrating the capacity to employ others to do this work, usually for low wages, is not only an overt signal of prosperity in the public arena of a shopping mall; it is also an integral aspect of middle-class domesticity in Thailand, where maids are often employed in private houses. As Chin (1998: 12) notes about the Malay middle classes, maids are often employed as part of a lifestyle that revolves around the conspicuous consumption of certain goods and services as a key way to construct identities and lifestyles that distinguish them from the lower or working classes. It is not only dirt removal that marks the class difference, but the very physicality of the work. Certainly, within the middle-class Bangkok-centric conception of moral worth, physical labour is connected with a lack of progress,

coarseness and backwardness, especially if the work is done outdoors. These attitudes are not necessarily restricted to the middle
classes, but also may be employed as a hierarchical distinguishing
device *between* lower-class people in the mall. Supervisors were
employed to oversee the cleaners' work. Dressed in blue uniforms
and not engaged in physical labour, the supervisors ate separately
from the cleaners and referred to them as 'children' (*dek dek*). They
were shocked when, on my first day at the mall, I asked if I could eat
with the cleaners – 'You want to eat with the children?' – and kept a distance from me thereafter. In the mall, the supervisors' self-presentation
and interactions seemed to be partly aimed at marking their distance
from the labourers. They spent a considerable amount of time putting
on make-up and painting their long fingernails, which were clearly
not designed for hard, physical labour. What was interesting was that
these women were from similar backgrounds as the cleaners, often
with similar qualifications; they did not earn much more than the
cleaners and most of them also lived in the slum.

DISCIPLINE, WATCH AND PUNISH

As Foucault makes clear, discipline is not simply an act of external
supervision. Obedience is exacted as much through implicit tech-
nologies of control over bodies and self-supervision, as through direct
observance. He perceives ways of conducting activities and controlling the body's movements as an integral part of extracting labour
efficiently, because consistency and uniformity permit fewer opportunities for corruption (1975: 138).

Every morning the cleaners lined up for registration, with the
supervisors in front. Starting each day with these regulated patterns
appeared to be an embodiment of the cleaners' place *vis à vis* more
senior members of staff. As stated above, the hierarchy was reflected
in the supervisors' description of the cleaners as 'children', perhaps a
term of affection, but one full of significance. In Thailand, power hierarchies may be even more significant than gendered differences.
Older or more powerful people are referred to as '*phi*', while the term
'*nong*' refers to younger, less important people. In calling the cleaners
'children', the supervisors were reinforcing this work hierarchy, even
though they were often younger than the cleaners and lived in the
same slum community. The daily rituals also reinforced the cleaners'
collective uniformity; wearing the regulation uniform was another
physical manifestation of sameness. These mechanisms of uniformity

were further extended through the insistence on specific ways of conducting domestic duties. The cleaners were initially expected to fund a special company training-course. When I asked Daw, the chief supervisor, why this was necessary, she explained that:

> At home [in the village] they [the cleaners] get up early and make breakfast, then go into the fields. Here it's not the same. Maybe they have done cleaning before, but there is more to it here. It's not just a question of sweeping; they have to start doing it very well, otherwise they can't enter the system.

The thrust of Daw's argument was that sophisticated, standardised, taught knowledge provides the necessary transition from an unsystematic rural to a systematic urban approach. Methodological codes were supplemented by more concrete rules of expected behaviour that were enshrined on the wall. The 21 rules forbade talking, joking or eating while working and required cleaners to pay respect to their superiors. Daw explained the reason for the rules:

> We need [rules] because things are so different for people from other provinces (*tang jangwat*). They don't do things in the usual way. They don't have bosses. Here there are supervisors, senior people and teachers. Many things are forbidden, such as drinking alcohol at work. Stealing is forbidden. Some people who come from up-country don't know – they see something nice and they take it.

DIVISIONS IN SPACE AND TIME

In the basement of the mall was the main office of the cleaning company. It was also where the cleaners had their breaks and morning registration. This space was diametrically opposed to the spotless, glamorous space of the mall upstairs. Going there literally felt like a descent into the bowels of the building. There was a pervasive stench of rotting garbage, lack of light or air, and the odd rat scuttling around. This symbolic organisation of space (see Bourdieu 1977, Felt and Basso 1996) was continued in the main body of the mall, in the areas where the cleaners worked. Those in charge of the toilets could not move from their assigned area, except during breaks. The cleaners in the main body of the mall also kept to a specific public area and were chastised if they were not seen to be working constantly. This spatial order evokes Foucault's comment on modern labour practices: 'Each individual has his own place, and each place its individual …

Disciplined space tends to be divided into as many sections as there are bodies or elements to be distributed ... it is a procedure aimed at knowing, mastering and using' (Foucault 1975: 143). In my estimation, the constant presence in the mall of the cleaners was intended as much to be an outward show of hygiene, rather than for any pressing need to endlessly maintain cleanliness. However, the impact of their presence was strategically managed so as to produce the illusion of invisibility. Most notably, in the gregarious, sociable atmosphere of the mall where customers and shop assistants gossiped openly, the cleaners worked alone and silently. The rules stated that they were not to chat to other cleaners, or form groups in order to do so; they were also not permitted to talk to customers unless approached for some reason. The silence of the cleaners in the public spaces was notable in a country where the exchange of banter is a constant backdrop and, I would suggest, an important aspect of social identity.

CLAIMING SMALL FREEDOMS

I have described above some of the ways in which discipline was an implicit manifestation of labour practices in the mall. In this section I will begin to explore ways in which the cleaners reclaimed themselves in the face of this structure and uniformity. The small liberties they sought may seem unremarkable, but I would argue that their culmination was significant. Following Scott (1990), they may be termed 'everyday forms of resistance' or, in my own terminology 'everyday politics'. Controversion took place at the interstices of rural and urban narratives of expectation and behaviour. The 'freedom' (*khwan issara*) of an idyllic rural life was a nostalgic theme for many of the women, who saw constraints on their time, space and movements as irksome. One woman, Gulab, aged 30, from northern Thailand, constantly told me she was tired of working at the mall and that she wanted to go home where she could work and eat when she wanted. She told me that, at home:

> ... whatever you want to do, you can. You have freedom. I was really *sabai* [felt good] at home. I went to the fields [to work] everyday ... When I came home I relaxed. Some days we had a rest or went for *tiaow* (a trip) nearby by motorbike. I was free, but I didn't have any money.

She was thus torn between the need or desire to make money through her links with the cleaning company, and the desire for the quality of life that she experienced at home. This dilemma was heightened when she had a child, whom she desperately wanted to stay and care for, but knew she could not raise without the money that came from her work.

Hirai, in his study on northern Thai factory workers (1998), stresses the qualitative differences between 'village work' and 'city work'. He notes that the concept of '*ngan*' (work, and also festival) when applied to 'village work', is associated with fostering social relationships rather than simply the pursuit of economic reward. Certainly, at particular times such as harvest, work is cooperative; village members help each other to gather the crops. I witnessed this phenomenon when visiting Gulab's village for her wedding; although the work of cutting upland rice by hand under the hot sun was hard work, it was also fun (*sanuk*), a quality much valued by Thais, with lots of talking, laughing and flirting, and time for long breaks. Yet, it should be said that collective memories of such occasions tend to obscure the less *sanuk* work of planting and maintaining rice fields, which some of the women brought to my attention.

CREATING SPACE AND TIME FOR *KHWAM SANUK* (FUN)

One subtle way to subvert the structured, disciplined work regimes was to appropriate spaces within the mall for *khwan sanuk* (fun), enabling the cleaners, to an extent, to impose their own interpretations of work. One woman loved telling amusing anecdotes and would preside outside her allocated toilet, entertaining the other cleaners and employees from the mall. A large store cupboard by the toilets on one floor provided a haven for women's talk, in which certain supervisory staff also participated. Flirtations were also played out in these spaces, mirroring behaviour I had seen in the rural northern fields; Gulab, the northern Thai woman mentioned earlier, conducted a flirtatious romance at work with a security guard, which led to marriage. In these ways, the impersonal work-spaces could to some extent be inscribed with particular personal and nostalgic meanings for the women.

The mall was further domesticated through its relationship with the thriving slum community next door where most of the cleaners lived. The slum was not visible from the main road and was hidden from public view by high metal fences. It was never clear to me whether the people in the community wished to conceal and contain themselves from the outside, or whether the fences were an attempt to preserve the mall's image of modern, sanitary consumption. I suspected the latter. What I found most significant were the ways in which people living in the slum, and working in and around the mall, activated the relationship between the two, and reframed the area linking these two very different places. On hot days women from the slum would often bring their young children to sit on cool marble tiles in the shade outside the mall. Visitors to the mall, particularly the busloads of Taiwanese and Japanese tourists, were targeted by entrepreneurs from the slum selling souvenirs and other items. For the cleaners, going to the slum for breaks and snacks – such as *som tam*, an Isan speciality made of raw papaya and chilli – struck me as a means for them to reclaim themselves and feel re-humanised in a space where they were known as people with lives, relationships and personalities, rather than merely part of a faceless workforce.

By walking next door to their community, they entered a world in whose meanings they actively participated and where they were not surreptitiously monitored for deviance. More than that, the paradox between these two places – symbiotically linked through the women's movements between them but so qualitatively different – highlighted other complexities in the women's lives. At once mothers, wives, providers and community members, the women I knew took pride in their work but saw it as a means to an end, over which they had control. In my conversations with them it was clear that they took pride in their work because of the choices it enabled them to make in other areas of their lives. Unlike in some Asian countries, rural Thai women play a central role in production. Not only do they actively participate in farming activities, but they often also run businesses. It is women who control family finances, and who are expected to contribute financially in the reproduction of their families. As I have noted elsewhere (Brody 2003), being able to provide for parents and children is an important gauge of successful womanhood and personhood. Many of them had family and land back in their home villages, and the money they saved was used for their children's education, and for farming. Thus their work was enabling them to ensure a better future for children who would support them when they were unable to work. It was also a means actively to use and benefit from their land, thus retaining a sense of ownership over the soil of a country that is increasingly being defined from its urban centre. In this complex relationship between the cleaners' work and their vision of self-sufficiency, freedom came from the hope and belief that this was a step to something better.

Finally, I observed what might be termed 'working-class pride and consciousness' in many of the women's references to what they did for a living and their goals. A common theme, particularly among the Isan women, was the ability to withstand hardship/be resilient (*oton lambaak*), and they often drew comparisons between themselves and Bangkokians, whom they accused of being lazy and weak. These perceptions mesh with the popular stereotype of Isan people as honest and hardworking, which was reinforced in my conversations both with northeasterners and with central Thais. These attitudes in the context of low-status cleaning work were succinctly expressed in the life story of Tuk, an Isan cleaner in her late twenties who was a single mother and supported a child and her elderly mother, both of whom were living in rural Isan. She indicated that some of the women she worked with were ashamed to be cleaning toilets for a living. What she saw as these women's fickle attitudes became a foil for Tuk's own attitudes to work, and for the strength of character she saw as integral to her own survival and success. Her commentary reflects her awareness of the value within different types of knowledge, and her unwillingness to accept being labelled as ignorant. The other person in the conversation is myself:

> T: I have a low level of knowledge/education, but those with a high education wouldn't be able to come and do this work. We are low class, but we have knowledge.
>
> A: You've got confidence in yourself?
>
> T: Yes, so I can do this work – I won't let anyone look down on me. I like my work.
>
> A: I feel that Bangkok people look down on rural people, especially when they're from Isan. How do you feel about that?
>
> T: Yes, yes, I agree. It makes me feel disappointed, but the people from Bangkok think we're from upcountry and we don't have any knowledge, and they like to look down on us people who do low-level work. But I don't care. Those who care can't put up with (*oton*) the work, and they leave, but I don't care... I don't like it when other people look down on themselves and say: 'Why do I have to do this kind of work?' If I hear someone talking like that, I ask: 'Do you think you're so high class that you can't do this work?' Some people think it's too hard, but I think if you want to do it, you have to be able to put up with it.

THE LIMITS OF TOLERANCE

There was no formal union for the cleaners, mainly because they were not contracted labourers. Most of them seemed fairly happy with their jobs and felt they were not badly treated. At the same time, most did not appreciate being constantly told what to do and how to do it, and complained to me, particularly when strict work codes were enforced during the cleaning company's bid for International Organization for Standardisation (ISO) status. Life-story narratives from the women indicated that intolerable or exploitative conditions of work would not be passively endured. Even in their younger days as new migrants to Bangkok, many of the women I spoke to had 'run away' (*nii pai*) from work or simply ceased working when faced with injustice or hardship in the workplace.

The women's reasons for working were partly due to a desire for higher wages, but they also illustrated their concern for basic rights. One woman who lived in the slum community told me about her first experiences working in Bangkok. Initially her relatives had found her work in a wood-cutting factory, but she had only stayed seven days because of restrictive practices there. Her second job in Bangkok was on a construction site, building a new bus terminal for a daily wage of 32 *Baht* (less than one pound). She worked on the site for 15 days, telling me: 'and I couldn't stay ... they forced us to do things – we couldn't even sit down for a little rest, so I left again, like before.' These stories often referred to the women's younger days, when work might have been easier to procure due to the combination of a more buoyant economy and their own youth. However, from what I observed, their strong sense of integrity and pragmatism would enable them to overcome the potential risks of quitting their secure work at the mall if they felt it was necessary. Some of the women had grown tired of surviving on the meagre wages, which offered little chance to save because of increasing inflation in Bangkok, while I was there one woman quit work and went back to Isan to start her own business reselling clothes bought directly from factories. Another woman in her late thirties, Bai, had grown increasingly intolerant of the restrictions of her work, coupled with the low wages. She had previously worked in Taiwan for a short while, and decided to return while she was still young enough to work long, tiring shifts in a factory. This decision was offset by the risks involved in taking out a large loan to fund her registration with the employment agency and other expenses, and her guilt and sorrow at leaving her two children for at least a year. However, she felt it was the only way to gain long-term security and a way out of the trap of badly-paid work and long hours, far away from her children.

I would suggest that the managers and supervisors at the shopping mall were aware of the cleaners' limits, and were unwilling to cross those boundaries, preferring to retain a reliable workforce. One way in which this mutual understanding was expressed was their tacit complicity in the small liberties the women took to make their working conditions tolerable, which I have mentioned above. Often I would find the supervisors joining the cleaners in gossip sessions, hidden from view of the 'big' mall bosses, and thus breaking down the structured codes that marked out different work ethics. Such seemingly small yet significant acts indicated that ultimately the boundaries of what was acceptable in the workplace could not be imposed, but rather were a matter of subtle negotiation within the matrices of employer, supervisory staff and cleaners.

CONCLUSION

In this chapter I have shown how a certain urban working ethos is created and maintained in a Bangkok shopping mall, through the imperatives of order and surveillance. I have suggested that cleanliness is a metaphor for a Bangkok-centric vision of a new Thailand, marking a break with the perceived dirt and associated disorder of 'uncivilised' rural existences. Many of the cleaners demonstrated pride or at least conscientiousness in jobs where they were expected to be in direct contact with dirt, in order to prevent others from having to be. Despite the lack of an official union, they retained a strong sense of integrity, humility and justice, which placed limits on their levels of tolerance for certain labour practices. Their strong personal relationships in the mall and in the slum community enabled them to claim and reframe spaces as their own. Above all, the women's work within the urban-based economy provided a means to maintain local values, such as pride in farming one's own land, while opening up possibilities to participate in Thailand's modern vision through their educated children. The cleaners' linkages with and support of their rural home territories were an implicit, yet effective refusal to accept uncritically the dominant narrative of Thailand's future. In this way, the 'everyday politics' of life and work in a shopping mall were part of a subtle challenge to the hegemony of the urban centre.

Notes

[1] See, for example, Fuller and Lightfoot 1984; Goldstein and Pitaktepsombati 1974; Goldstein and Goldstein 1980; Phongpaichit 1982; Mills 1992, 1993, 1997, 1999.
[2] Mongkut was King of Siam from 1851 to 1868. He was responsible for introducing Western-style education, in addition to supporting infrastructural projects such as road-building.

[3] A typical Isan dish, made from raw papaya and chillis, which is becoming increasingly popular as a snack among trendy young Bangkokians.

[4] Another typical Isan dish of fermented fish, with a characteristic taste and smell, used as a condiment with rice.

[5] Lao is the first language for rural Isan people, which they speak amongst themselves; they usually only learn central Thai, the national language, when they start school at the age of five or six.

References

Bourdieu, P (1977) *Outline of a Theory of Practice*, Cambridge: Cambridge University Press.

Brody, A (2003) 'Agents of change: struggles and successes of Thai women migrants in Bangkok', unpublished PhD thesis, SOAS, University of London.

Chin, C (1998) *In Service and Servitude*, USA: Columbia.

Douglas, M (1991) *Purity and Danger: An Analysis of the Concepts of Pollution and Taboo*, Routledge: London.

Escobar, A (1995) *Encountering Development: The Making and Unmaking of the Third World*, Princeton: Princeton University Press.

Evans, G (1999) *Laos: Culture and Society*, Thailand: Silkworm Books.

Felt, S and Basso, K (eds) (1996) *Senses of Place*, Sante Fe, New Mexico: School of American Research Press.

Foucault, M (1975) *Discipline and Punish: The Birth of the Prison*, Harmondsworth: Penguin.

Fuller, T and Lightfoot, P (1984) 'Circular migration in Northeastern Thailand', in Brummelhuis, H and Kemp, J (eds), *Strategies and Structures in Thai Society*, Amsterdam: University of Amsterdam, 85–94.

Goldstein, S and Goldstein, A (1980) *Differentials in Repeated Return Migration in Thailand*, Bangkok: Institute of Population Studies.

Goldstein, S and Pitaktepsombati, P (1974) *Migration and Urban Growth in Thailand: An Exploration of Interrelationships Among Origin, Recency and Frequency of Moves*, Bangkok: Chulalongkorn University.

Harvey, D (1989) *The Urban Experience*, Oxford: Blackwell.

Hirai, K (1998) 'Women, family and factory work in Northern Thailand: an anthropological study of a Japanese factory and its workers' lives', unpublished PhD thesis, London School of Economics, University of London.

Hoy, S (1995) *Chasing Dirt: The American Pursuit of Cleanliness*, New York: Oxford University Press.

Jaded, C (2000) 'Life after redundancy: the effects of the termination of employment of Thai workers', in Brody, A (ed), *Uniting Voices: Asian Women Workers' Search for Recognition in the Global Marketplace*, Bangkok: Committee for Asian Women.

Mills, M B (1992) 'Rural women working in Bangkok: modernity and gender vulnerability', in Van Esterick, J and Van Esterick, P (eds), *Gender and Development in Southeast Asia*, UK: CASA.

Mills, M B (1993) 'We are not like our mothers': migrants, modernity and identity in Northeastern Thailand', unpublished PhD thesis, Berkeley.

Mills, M B (1997) 'Contesting the margins of Thai modernity', *American Ethnologist*, 24(1) 37–61.

Mills, M B (1999) *Thai Women in the Global Labour Force: Consuming Desires, Contested Selves*, New Jersey: Rutgers University Press.

Ngaosyvathn, M and Ngaosyvathn, P (1994) *Kith and Kin Politics: The Relationship Between Laos and Thailand*, Manila: Contemporary Asian Publishers.

Phongpaichit, P (1982) *From Peasant Girls to Bangkok Masseuses*, Geneva: ILO.

Phongpaichit, P and Baker, C (1995), *Thailand: Economy and Politics*, New York: Oxford University Press.

Rajadhon, P A (1972) *Watthanatham* (Culture), Bangkok: Samnakpim Banakarn.

Scott, J (1990) *Weapons of the Weak: Everyday Forms of Peasant Resistance*, Delhi: Oxford University Press.

Turton, A (1984) 'Limits of ideological domination and the formation of social consciousness', in Turton, A and Tanabe, S (eds), *Historical and Peasant Consciousness in South East Asia*, Osaka: National Museum of Ethnology, 19–74.

7 Fast Money in the Margins: Migrants in the Sex Industry

Laura María Agustín

In the tense debates about immigration in Europe, laws affecting how people gain entry and whether they may work are understood to be changeable. In contrast, regulations affecting whether jobs 'count' as the basis for residence seem to be written in stone. Typical discourse describes those who should be excluded from Europe as 'economic migrants', as though wanting to work were bad, even when there are plentiful jobs on offer. However, economic motives *are* acceptable if migrants find jobs in the so-called 'formal' sector of the economy; only when the jobs are said to be in the 'informal' economy are they unacceptable. Migrants from outside Europe have a better chance of being allowed to stay if they can be categorised as victims (refugees, asylum-seekers, 'trafficked women') than if they are simply healthy people willing to do non-prestigious work for low pay. In fact, migrants *are* employed in great numbers in a variety of informal businesses, which means there is a demand for their labour. But since work permits are rarely issued for informal jobs, these workers are cut off from regularising their status. This schizophrenic situation results in the labelling of vast numbers of migrants as 'undocumented', 'illegal', opportunistic and even criminal.

Women and women migrants predominate in informal-economy jobs, the great majority working in services still considered traditional to women: domestic, 'caring' and sexual. Most domestic and caring work is carried out in informal – often feudal – conditions. Although these jobs are broadly considered to constitute morally dignified labour, they pay so badly for so much work under such trying conditions that many migrants prefer to sell sex as a primary or second job, despite the stigma attached. Many proponents of recognition and good governance for domestic and caring work refuse to recognise sexual labour of any kind, which is only considered in formal debates on whether 'prostitution' should be accepted as work or be 'abolished' as inherently violent (Pateman 1988; Sullivan 1995). While interesting to some as an ethical question, these debates do not begin to address the current European situation, in which sexual markets grow and jobs abound, in a proliferation of products and services typical of contemporary capitalism (Sanchez 2003). Two social changes may help to account for this growth. First, with sexual identity increasingly seen as central to the understanding of the self, the individual is seen as having a duty to discover him or herself and experimentation is encouraged. Secondly, changes in ideas about commercial consumption mean that people find it acceptable to buy more products and services, including erotic activities (Agustín 2004a). The sex industry thus provides a paid occupation for many millions of people worldwide, providing much higher wages and often more freedom and flexibility than other jobs available, as the following testimonies attest:

> The alternative would have been working for one of your Italian firms that have come to Albania to exploit our work. Two years ago, when I left home, a worker in one of your shoe factories made 150,000 *lire* a month (€77). A woman, half that amount. I don't understand why Italy is amazed if young Albanians come here to try to make money the fastest way possible. Girls like me in one evening earn 800,000 *lire* (€413) and sometimes more than a million. Should we be making shoes for 150,000 *lire* a month? (Albanian woman in Italy, from *Corriere della Sera*, quoted in Danna 2004: 85)

> Sometimes I enjoy working, I can travel and see beautiful places. I can go to nice restaurants. I enjoy that the Turkish men view us as desirable. (Ukrainian woman in Turkey, Gülçür and İlkkaracan 2002: 419)

> One day I met a friend of mine while I was walking in the town centre … I learned that she was a prostitute so her children could live in a decent way. This work has the advantage of financial ease and freedom to work schedules that allow spending more time with the children. (French woman of Algerian parents in France, Cabiria 2002: 286)

These accounts indicate that motivations vary for selling sex and should not be reduced either to the usual moralistic debate about 'prostitution' or to an economic argument (Agustín 2005a). Nor should the gaze be limited to one relatively less lucrative and commonplace segment, sex sold outdoors (Høigård and Finstad 1986; McKeganey and Barnard 1994).

Mention is often made, in an accusatory tone, of the enormous profits generated by the sex industry; but the fact that most of this money comes from an unregulated economic sector, much of which cannot easily be constructed as 'prostitution', is not widely understood. In this chapter, the informal status of sex businesses is linked to job markets for migrants, and brief ethnographic descriptions of selected sites illustrate how the usual stigmatisation of these jobs as abject fails to examine the complex and diverse social realities involved, including the possibility of making a lot of money quickly.

THE CONSTRUCTION OF MARGINALITY

When governments recognise businesses and business sectors, information and statistics on them are entered into government accounting, and they must submit to government regulation and law; obtaining permits, undergoing inspections, providing basic conditions and rights to workers, paying taxes and so on. Recognised businesses are said to belong to the 'formal' economy, a concept derived from partial statistics such as tax returns, payroll data and company records. All other economic activity not recognised in government accounts is characterised as 'informal'. For the last 30 years, informal economies have been allowed to grow uninhibited on the theory that this policy would assure basic livelihoods for many people (ILO 2002).

The formal economy, simply by virtue of being officially recognised, is inevitably thought of as 'real', with an assumption that these businesses are good, productive, and normal. Informal economies are called grey, black, submerged, underground and are often (perhaps unconsciously) thought of as bad, undesirable, temporary, not serious or not productive. Informal businesses are often imagined to be small, composed of street traders and freelancers, a notion contradicted by the sex industry, the majority of whose businesses are also informal. The sex industry is not recognised *per se*, although many of its venues, such as bars, saunas and hotels, are recognised as other kinds of business. Yet although most commercial sex is prohibited, unregulated, ignored and deplored, it generates billions of dollars worldwide, millions of euros within Europe and provides an income for vast numbers of people. Some informal activities, conducted in cash or otherwise outside tax-collecting authorities, have been valued in the UK at £700 million for stolen goods, £800 million for gambling,

£9.9 billion for drug-dealing and £1.2 billion for 'prostitution' (Kellner 1999: 21). This last category, however, will not have included most of the myriad forms of trade found in the sex industry, which means that figures for commercial sex must be much higher.

In Europe, sex industry sites include bars, restaurants, cabarets, clubs, brothels, discotheques, saunas, massage parlours, sex shops with private booths for watching videos or live shows, hotels, flats, dungeons for bondage and domination, internet webpages and chat-rooms, cinemas, parks, and streets. Other locations where sex is offered for sale on an occasional basis include stag and hen parties, on board ships (both merchant and tourist) and in mainstream pubs. Products and services include erotic phonelines, escort and matrimonial services, newspaper and classified advertisements, films and videos, souvenirs, toys, clothes, equipment, lap and other erotic dances, live and virtual spectacles via web cameras and the sexual 'acts', both penetrative and oral, conventionally associated with the industry. Sometimes, art exhibitions and theatre productions appear temporarily to form part of the industry, and many of the sites and forms mentioned also promote and sell non-sexual products and services, thus mixing confusingly with unstigmatised daily life. Commercial sex sites and the names given to them vary from country to country both within Europe and throughout the world, but no country is without a variety of venues and forms.

According to the International Labour Organisation (ILO), fully a third of those employed in sexual businesses in five countries within south-east Asia do not directly sell sexual services, but without their labour sales could not take place (Lim 1998). These include business owners and investors, independent contractors and support employees (cooks, managers, waiters, cashiers, guards, drivers, accountants, cleaners, lawyers, doctors) and middlemen who facilitate business processes (travel agents, guides, estate agents, taxi drivers, matrimonial agents, newspaper and magazine editors, internet entrepreneurs). Society does not treat all participants equally, valuing some highly (the capitalist entrepreneurs), criminalising others (the middlemen, often called pimps and traffickers), victimising some (women who sell sexual services) and ignoring many (men who sell sexual services). Some participants are Europeans who enjoy standard citizens' rights, while others are non-Europeans with limited rights living in vulnerable conditions. But earnings are not correlated with social valuations or civil status, and what for many is conceived of as socially or morally marginal can produce economic gains that can lead to significant social empowerment.

MIGRANCY AND THE SEX INDUSTRY

A number of structural changes in the world economy have spurred migration, including industrialised countries' shift to a service economy, manufacturing's move to developing countries, multinational corporations' increasing dependence on subcontracting, and 'structural adjustment policies' of the International Monetary Fund (IMF) that cut social programming. Most newly independent States in Europe have also found themselves facing severe economic problems as part of their conversion to free markets. All these factors contribute to a demand for women workers in new sites and to the (perhaps temporary) disintegration of families under stress from lack of income. The result is that more people look for alternatives away from home and migration becomes a conventional solution. The economic impulse is clear, but migrations are not only motivated economically. It is clear that choice is involved, even with the poorest migrants, simply because not everyone migrates from places of poverty and violence.[1] Exposed to media images that depict travel as essential to education, pleasure and worldliness, people in poor as well as rich countries may want to see famous places, experience glamour, be admired, meet new people, marry, and become independent (Agustín 2004b and 2006).

For migrant women, the two job sectors widely available in Europe are in domestic and caring services, where conditions are often referred to as servile, feudal or even semi-slavery. In many European families, live-in maids are increasingly required to be present from morning in order to night to perform a wide and often undefined range of tasks. Although the literature on an 'ethics of care' and a sociology of emotions does not yet agree on whether women are inherently better at caring (Abel and Nelson 1990), these jobs are still widely viewed as 'natural' to women. Some tasks are intimate or involve taboos (such as preparing and serving food, cleaning bathrooms, washing underwear), and some employees have charge of the most personal and delicate of bodily tasks. Even the maid or babysitter who comes in for a few hours and then leaves is privy to intimate family details.

But domestic and caring work is physically trying, badly paid and largely invisible to the outside world. Jobs that involve living inside another family's home often mean endless work shifts and total lack of private space and personal time. Many employers demand acts of pointless servitude from domestic workers or unreasonable educational skills from ill-paid nannies (Anderson 2000). Migrants who have left their own children behind to make money abroad caring for others' children face tremendous emotional dangers, feelings of guilt, inadequacy and rage (Parreñas 2001). Thus, for many migrants, the sex industry is preferable to domestic work.

JOBS IN THE SEX INDUSTRY

Given the diversity of commercial-sex venues and businesses, it follows that the jobs available are also enormously varied. When the term 'sex worker' is used instead of 'prostitute', the intent is not necessarily to avoid stigmatising language, but because 'sex worker' refers to *all* the many forms of sexual labour, only some of which can be considered 'prostitution'. For example, there are workers who only talk on the telephone and never see their clients; there are dancers who are never touched; there are those who perform sex acts for a camera or behind a glass panel. The principal task of many sex workers is conversation aimed at encouraging customers to buy highly-priced alcoholic drinks.

Moreover, these jobs differ according to local norms. Workers who have more control in some venues can determine their own schedule, who they accept as a client and how much they charge. Many people work part-time or occasionally, which are significant advantages for mothers and students. Many sex jobs do not require formal training or education, and some people find it easy to perform certain jobs, while others find them difficult. As in every job, the worker has more opportunities to choose, control and move up after being in the business for a certain amount of time. This is an industry of highly personalised services.

It is often imagined that migrants have few options but to work in the street, and some do prefer that venue. But again, given the lack of regulation in the sex industry, there is no reason why migrants *cannot* work in any and all jobs. That is, when irregular civil status is the norm and work permits are non-existent, migrants with the right contacts can arrive at a deluxe site and, depending on their individual abilities and talents, be successful there. All migrants depend on knowledge they themselves do not initially have – such as which flights to take, which entry-points and airports to use, the latest visa conditions, and the names of potential employers.

> Once I was talking with a friend and she asked if I wanted to go to Spain. I knew why, so I said: 'Ah, do you want to?' … and I don't know where she met this guy, he got the papers for us … the money and we left … This guy went to look for work, where are the best places to

work, where there are men...Because one place has a lot of men, another doesn't ... I worked in Logroño a month or so ... then back to Málaga ... a month or two, then I came here ... He talked first with the boss of this place ... said he was looking for work for us. (Ukrainian woman in Spain, Agustín 2004c)

Clearly, personal relations and luck play an overarching role in finding work, getting along in it and making money. Given the illegality of much of the activity, an ability to tolerate and manipulate both criminal and police interference may be vital. Finally, the capacity to maintain a healthy emotional state may be most important ability of all in work that society deplores and workers themselves may stigmatise. Many who work in the trade feel they are guilty of having sinful relations; others describe a great weight on their hearts. As to the sex itself, many say they don't feel anything when they are with clients, while others feel disgust, fear, loneliness or sadness. But then, migrant domestic and caring workers say the same kinds of things.

RESEARCH IN A MARGINAL PLACE: GEOGRAPHIES OF EXCLUSION

For a long time I worked in *educación popular* in various countries within Latin America and the Caribbean, and with Latino migrants in North America and Europe, in programmes dedicated to literacy, AIDS prevention, health promotion, preparation for migration and *concientización* (a term that cannot be translated precisely into English but which combines the concepts of 'consciousness-raising' and 'empowerment'). My concern about the vast difference between what first-world social agents (governmental, NGO workers, activists) say about migrants, and what migrants say about themselves, led me to study and bear witness on these issues. In Europe, I deliberately located myself on the border of both groups, the migrants and the social sector – including all those claiming to research them and work on their behalf – spending time in brothels, bars, houses, offices, outreach vehicles, conferences and 'the street', in its many incarnations.

Although researchers and NGOs have been working with migrants who sell sex for nearly 20 years in Europe, publication of their findings remains outside mainstream press and journals. Most of the people who meet and talk with migrants are neither academics nor writers. They do 'outreach', which is conceptualised as distinct from 'research' and is often funded as HIV/AIDS prevention, with the result that the published products of outreach research are generally limited to information on sexual health and practices, and many other kinds of information collected remain unpublished. Some who work in these projects have the chance to exchange such information, but most do not. Recently, a new kind of researcher has entered the field: sociology and anthropology students, mostly women, who are interested in migrations. These researchers want to do justice to the reality around them, which they recognise as consisting of at least as many migrants selling sex as doing domestic or caring work. This research often consists of small-scale interviewing. Hegemonic discourses often marginalise or disqualify this kind of knowledge, claiming that the data is not systematised. In my research, I seek out this kind of information (and have a list of more than 30 such projects in Europe, 60 worldwide). I have also undertaken qualitative interviews myself, in both Latin American countries and Europe (Agustín 2007).

LOCAL PARTICULARS: EXAMPLES FROM SPAIN

The following ethnographic descriptions illustrate the widely differing commercial and social settings in several regions of Spain. Many kinds of venues are not mentioned, and no conclusions should be drawn relating any one kind of setting with a particular region. This material represents a small sample of the available diversity, and benefits from a number of relatively recent research projects from Spain (Agustín 2004c; APDHA 2003; Bonelli 2001; Casal 2000; Cuanter 1998; de Paula 2000; Hart 1999; Oso 2003; Ribeiro and Sacramento 2005; Riopedre 2004; Rodríguez and Lahbabi 2004; Roldán et al 2003). The four industry segments described are: large clubs, private flats, small houses associated with industrialised agriculture and a cosmopolitan coastal zone. For each description, I highlight some elements significant to those who work there.

Highway and road clubs

Commercial sex forms part of the road culture that exists along routes connecting Spain with France, Germany and other States to the east, and Portugal to the west. Long-distance truck drivers break up extended stints of solitary driving with stops for rest and recreation at clubs, which also offer local businessmen and youth sex-sites away from prying eyes. Known informally as *puticlubes* (whoring clubs), they may house 50 workers or more, and in some areas there are so many clubs close together that they form a genuine erotic shopping area.

Multi-floored, luxuriously decorated and offering a range of activities, including videos, live shows, jacuzzis and 'exotic' music (for example, the latest rock from Moscow), many of these clubs are sites of conspicuous consumption where customers pay as much as 10 times the ordinary price for drinks. Since this is the major source of income for club owners, employees are expected to get clients to buy as much as possible, including expensive champagne drinks for themselves. The array of women, transsexuals and men living in a club at any given time is a phenomenon surely unique to the sexual milieu, where European truck drivers and businessmen find themselves amidst a kaleidoscope of nationalities including Romanians, Nigerians, Colombians, Ukrainians, Brazilians, Moroccans – the list never ends. In these settings where people from very different cultural backgrounds mix and use creole and pidgin forms of communication, it's possible to experience a kind of extravagant cosmopolitanism. Some customers use the more lavish venues to entertain and impress business clients; groups of young men spend a night out (with perhaps a sexual initiation for one of them); and lovelorn bachelors and widowers seek companionship. Many spend hours drinking, talking and watching without purchasing any 'sex' at all. If they do, it typically occupies no more than 15–20 minutes, since the house rules usually ensure that workers are back promoting drink as soon as possible. A large number of support personnel is needed to keep these high-overhead businesses going, and since owners employ undocumented migrants, they must keep good public relations with local police. Workers move on after their three-week stints, assuring that novelty will always be available.

To consider this venue as only 'prostitution' requires focusing exclusively on the short period when workers retire to private rooms with clients, but research shows that for those who have learned the ropes and adapted to the job, other aspects are more important than the sex. Workers call these venues *hoteles de plaza*, referring to the 'places' they pay to live and work in, for three-week stints. Food and a room are always provided, but conditions vary enormously, with owners free to impose capricious rules and fines on employees who are unable to protest or denounce abuse to local authorities. Workers must also adjust to making large amounts of money; €5000 a month is a conventional sum earned by people with sufficient talent, ability and dedication.

> What I try to do is get the client to invite me to his table, get into conversation in order to make friends and so he doesn't feel he is paying and I don't feel he is paying me. I have regular clients who are rich who buy me champagne that costs €250 or €300 a bottle. You try to make it

last ... and then you don't have to be with so many people. (Dominican woman working in a club, Casal 2000)

Such earnings for those unaccustomed to it can provoke both huge shopping sprees and expensive habits, including drug consumption. Workers must learn to budget and pace themselves, as well as resist drinking too much or accepting drugs on the job, using strategies such as arranging to be served soft drinks disguised as cocktails.

Those workers who have paid to be 'smuggled' into the country arrive with debts, over which, in many cases, they have control and can pay off on their own account. Others have less control over debt repayment:

> In some places they ... have to work 15 hours a day ... and if one day they don't want to work or get sick they are fined €240, so the debt goes up. The majority that come to us owe money to a friend, to a club owner or to whoever brought them and they usually take between one and three months to pay. Afterwards they are free to go on working where they want or leave it. (Spanish social worker in Caritas, Casal 2000)

Some debts are much greater and take longer to pay off, and the control exerted by an owner or intermediary can be extremely oppressive, but this is not the most common situation. It is important to recognise the diversity of experiences that are produced by so much clandestinity and informality, and to attend to the details of individual stories.

One view of this kind of locale sees workers as enslaved, but this is not true much of the time:

> When you live in the club it's cheaper, because it's a daily rate that you pay for food and lodging, while if you live outside you have to pay the expenses of flat, food, transport... Most of the time you're in the bar, you save more. My sister and I finished working, went to bed and slept as much of the day as we could to avoid expenses and to feel that the time was passing faster. (Colombian woman in Spain, Bonelli et al 2001: 81)

> When you work a lot in one place then you ... you get tired of the clients ... Even though it will be the same, you imagine another place with other people, and then you come to life inside ... I go to another country, another city. Lately I live between Mallorca and Barcelona ... In summer I always go to Mallorca to spend a little time with my son. (Latin American woman in Spain, Cuanter 1998: 93)

The club culture of three-week verbal contracts means constantly having to worry about and arrange for the next job but also allows for flexibility and the ability to take time off.

Private flats

Whereas many clubs specialise in ostentation and publicity, private flats offer discretion. All towns have them, in the kind of buildings and neighbourhoods that suggest tenants belong to the respectable middle-class. Clients first ring up to make an appointment, and managers arrange for clients not to run into each other. The flats themselves appear ordinary inside, displaying few or no sexual signs. On the contrary, they may have floral-patterned spreads and stuffed animals on the beds, crucifixes and images of saints on the walls and the smell of home cooking wafting from the kitchen (although a chain and cuffs hanging from a hook on one wall may indicate special services offered). If the customer has not requested a worker he already knows, he makes his selection and goes to a bedroom. Again, the mix of nationalities and ethnic groups is notable. These businesses rely on classified advertisements and mobile telephones, the two elements that also make possible the boom in independent workers who run businesses from home.

Workers have two options here: living in the flat itself, or living outside and arriving for work shifts. In the first case, the atmosphere is that of a shared flat. In the second, workers spend more money on living expenses but feel more independent and are able to come and go as with a conventional job. Again, individuals can earn very large amounts, depending on their abilities and perseverance. It is common to hear that heterosexual clients want 'exotic' women to have sex with, but it must be remembered that exoticism is relative and changeable according to local and temporal conditions. In flats as in clubs, national and ethnic origin may be an advantage with some clients, and a disadvantage with others. From the point of view of the person choosing workers, it is important to have a variety of phenotypes and nationalities to offer:

> The difference is with the clients, if they tell me 'a Spanish woman' then I send a Spanish woman; it's not racism because I have some girls as blonde and white as the Spanish and they don't work ... 'I won't give my money to a foreigner', and a foreigner can be white, from India or from wherever you like, but she's foreign ... There's something for everyone here, this is a boutique. (Dominican woman running a flat in Spain, Agustín 2004c)

This atmosphere of variety applies to gender and sexuality, as well, so that flat managers keep men (gay, straight, bisexual) and transsexuals on their lists, too.

> Gentlemen come here who have their lives set up, but they have this deviation and the only place where they can express it is here. (Dominican woman running a flat in Spain, Agustín 2004c)

Transgendered people (who may have bodies equipped with organs of both sexes), many of whom are fleeing violence and intolerance in other countries, find they have come to occupy a special place in the European sex market. Some women believe that trans workers enjoy an advantage over themselves, since not only can they be penetrated, but they can penetrate clients as well.

The agricultural world

In the southern province of Almería, a large proportion of the tomatoes and other vegetables Europeans eat are grown under plastic in vast plantations operated under semi-feudal conditions. Nearby, several kinds of sex businesses coexist, ranging from luxurious bars with private cubicles to rustic, poor housing where tenants open their doors to clients. The luxurious sites are located close to the plantations, even directly across from them, and those who enter and pay the high prices are Spanish owners and other 'whites' from the managerial class, many of whom have moved up fast from being agricultural labourers themselves. Women who work in the central clubs tend to come from Eastern Europe and the former Soviet Union. The rustic sites are located much further away, sometimes up inconvenient roads with few public services where Nigerian women offer sex and a domestic atmosphere inside their own houses (meals, drinks, music, a place to stay the night). Here, customers are usually undocumented migrants from northern and western Africa, and the scene resembles a traditional form of commercial sex associated with migration in Africa (Nelson 1987; White 1990). In the case of Almería, two kinds of informal labour, agricultural and sexual, are linked with each other and with migration, and we see how the most subaltern migrants create niches and support each other.

Ethnic and cultural reasons are often given by workers as 'explanations' for why certain groups are found in certain places.

> Normally in a club they don't accept more than three or four Africans, because they have a very bad way of working. They approach a client and if the client doesn't want anything they just stay and stay until the client leaves … The Russians have messed up the job. They do whatever they are asked, anywhere and in front of anyone. (Colombian woman in a club, Bonelli 2001: 83)

Where there are Nigerians there are no Russians. The Russians don't accept the Nigerians who are very difficult and fight a lot, the managers say because they drink a lot … The Casa de Campo [a large park in Madrid] is full of Nigerians, so there's a lot of discrimination in clubs between white and dark people. (Colombian woman in a club, Casal 2000)

Similar stereotyping comments are made by members of every group towards every other one, and need always to be taken sceptically. In the case of the plastic-roofed plantations, the segmentation by ethnicity is undoubtedly related to an agricultural industry where many undocumented men are employed.

The cosmopolitan frontier

This is a region where Spanishness fades and tourism, expatriate culture and hybridity reign. Businesses in Torremolinos, Marbella and smaller towns along the coast highway of Málaga advertise in a brochure called *Encuentros* (meetings), which categorises its offerings under the terms Gay Bars, Swapping, Private Establishments, Contacts and Sex Shops. A plethora of clubs, bars, party rooms and flats advertise, highlighting specialities such as piano-bars, saunas, jacuzzis, Turkish baths, dark rooms, go-go shows, striptease, escort services, private bars, dance floors, a variety of massages, private booths with 96 video channels, gifts for stag and hen parties, latex wear and aphrodisiacs. Apart from the sexual products and services available, other services advertised include air conditioning, valet or private parking, swimming pools, credit card acceptance, select clientele, television and accessibility for the handicapped. Many adverts play down the commercial aspect by emphasising the 'non-professionals' present. Fitting the international environment, businesses are called Milady Palace, Play Boy, Melody d'Amour, Dolly's, New Crazy, Glam Ur Palace Club and Titanic. Many are located in ordinary shopping-strip zones.

With so much variety, it is impossible to generalise about workers' experiences. Go-go shows, striptease and dance floors require dancing and performance talents; Turkish baths, saunas and jacuzzis may demand the ability to do erotic massage. Working with disabled clients certainly involves particular skills, such as the ability to listen and accept differences. Knowing languages may be important, as well as the capacity to act like an amateur – fulfilling the fantasy of some clients to believe that they are paying, yes, but not for a 'professional'.

Opportunities for workers with flexible gender and sexual orientations are indicated by the presence of dark rooms, saunas and baths. I include information about commercial sex in this region, where little research has been carried out, to give some idea of the considerable variety available in a single small geographic area.

THE SEX IN SEX WORK

At the heart of many jobs are social relationships with a physical and/or sexual aspect. 'Sex acts' are sometimes assumed to be an obvious activity that everyone does in more or less the same way. They are also imagined to consist of 'natural' and 'unnatural' acts. But those who sell sex are aware of the variety in human capacities, desires and tastes, and those who have migrated between cultures know that they differ in their assessment of acts as 'good' and 'bad'. Workers learn to *perform* sexual and emotional acts aimed at satisfying the person paying, as well as to manoeuvre situations so that they receive the maximum amount of money for the minimum of work. Since workers are also individuals with tastes and values, they tend to find work sites where they can tolerate the acts required of them:

> The flats are where the sadists go, the masochists, all those people that ask you to do water sports and that. Some people go to work in the clubs because they can't stand it. I have a friend who works with me now who used to work the telephone in a flat. She took the calls and says that the most depraved people go there. (Colombian woman working in Spanish clubs, Bonelli 2001: 85)

For migrants, learning about unfamiliar sexual norms can provoke either puritanical condemnation or adaptation, depending on the individual. Even the acts conventionally associated with 'prostitution', penetrative and oral sex, do not amount to the same thing when carried out in a sex therapist's office, in a film studio, in a brothel or in a car. Some people prefer to get these acts over with as quickly as possible, while others associate them with social pleasantness. Street work, often deplored by outsiders as the most miserable, offers one of the few jobs which workers can decide upon and do immediately, and receive instant cash, thus enabling the buying of food and the survival of self and family in a matter of hours. It can also be the most autonomous and flexible form of sex work, and is preferred by many who could operate in other ways.

FLEXIBILITY, INFORMALITY AND THE MARGINS

This chapter has considered only a few of the common sex-work scenarios in which migrants are found working: big clubs, small flats, rural areas, hybrid tourist zones and the street. All of these involve a wide range of activities operating in complex cultural contexts in which the meaning of 'buying' and 'selling' sex is not always the same. I have elsewhere proposed the *cultural* study of commercial sex, an interdisciplinary approach that relates commercial sex to other social and cultural concepts, and breaks with a research tradition that focuses on transactions called 'prostitution', particularly on individuals' personal motivations (Agustín 2004b and 2005b). With the academic, media and 'helping' gaze fixed almost exclusively on women who sell sex, the great majority of people and phenomena that make up the sex industry are ignored, and this in itself contributes to the intransigent stigmatisation of these women. While the sexual cultures of lesbian/gay/bisexual/transgender people are being slowly integrated into general conceptions of culture, commercial sex is usually disqualified and treated only as a moral issue, meaning that a wide range of ways of study are excluded (Agustín 2005b).

The reduction of this wide field to a narrow, moralistic zone also creates opportunities for businesspeople to operate outside government rules and regulations and make large profits; and, for migrants (including those considered 'illegal'), to make money faster than in any other jobs available. They provide openings for 'flexible' workers, those willing to adapt to changing markets. In these sites of very different moralities from those manifested by hegemonic social discourses, workers use sex as an instrument to accumulate not only financial but also social and cultural capital. The sale of sex can generate positive changes in workers' countries of origin via the substantial remittances that are sent home. This means that these jobs are in the margins, but with an economic difference. The generation of money is not an unquestionable good, but the traditional feminist 'prostitution' debate does not adequately consider the extent to which money *is* important for both migrant and non-migrant workers and their families. Nor does it consider the diversity of activity demonstrated here or the social functions (apart from sex) that may be implicated.

Informality, however, produces highly unjust working conditions and rampant opportunities for abuse, in which migrants enjoy no labour rights, protections or benefits. Their safe standing in any given business depends on the personal relationships they are able to develop with owners, managers and other employees. If something goes wrong, or they fail to measure up to someone's particular desires for how they should act, sex workers are completely vulnerable, unable to appeal to government authorities and afraid to ask for redress in the criminal-justice system.

Societies that allow sex businesses to flourish and proliferate should include them in government accounting. This decision would subject businesses to conventional government controls: a) norms for permits to operate (eg, safe construction, proper compliance with zoning); b) requirements for health and safety standards in the work-place; and c) normal labour protections for employees, including inclusion in State social-security systems whether they are migrants or not.

Recognition of this economic sector would be only the first step and is not identical to traditional notions of 'regulation' associated with commercial sex, which consider only 'prostitution' and which arrange workplaces for the convenience of business owners, manage-ment and clientele – never workers. Many regulatory proposals auto-matically require workers to submit to medical examinations, while clients are always imagined to be 'clean'. This antiquated model of regulation is opposed by those who sell sex everywhere. In contrast, my proposal agrees with the ILO that the only way to protect those employed in sex businesses is for governments to recognise their exis-tence (Lim 1998).

For migrants, being employed by a European business should mean being treated as an employee. Individual judges have drawn this conclusion in a number of cases in Spain, informing the owner of a business that his employees are, indeed, just that, and as such must be covered by the social-security system, regardless of the current lack of legislation for this situation. Logically, then, work-permits should be granted to those who are employed, if the employers are allowed to operate: any other conclusion is incoherent.

Official recognition of so few economic activities constructs an inflexible, unchanging centre and large, ever-expanding margins. It is certainly not chance that women outnumber men in the informal economy and, at the same time, that so much of traditional women's work remains unrecognised. A high proportion of migrant women are thus employed in informal-sector jobs and forced into illegality.

Would the sex sector resist such proposals? Some business owners would, since operating clandestinely is beneficial in so many ways. But some would not, because they prefer to see themselves as 'nor-mal' or do not like operating in the margins and being associated with criminal underworlds and social perversions. Given the vast number of businesses involved and their growing variety, clichés about who business owners are should also be resisted.

THE LAST WORD

It makes me laugh when they think that I am not an honest woman because I do this job. Of course, as a job it's ugly, and I don't understand why in Italy they don't let us do it in organised places; I don't understand what is bad about selling love for money ... With this job I have made it possible for all my brothers to study and I have supported my mother, so I am proud of being a prostitute. (Nigerian woman in Italy, Kennedy and Nicotri 1999: 32)

Note

[1] The number of migrants worldwide (people living outside their home country) now totals more than 175 million, a bit less than 3% of the world's population (UN 2004). Numbers are higher in specific countries at particular times.

References

Abel, E K and Nelson, M K (1990) *Circles of Care: Work and Identity in Women's Lives*, Albany: State University of New York Press.

Agustín, L (2004a) 'A migrant world of services', *Social Politics*, 10(3) 377–396.

Agustín, L (2004b) 'Daring border-crossers: a different vision of migrant women,' in Day, S and Ward, H (eds), *Sex Work in a Changing Europe*, London: Kegan Paul, 85–94.

Agustín, L (2004c) 'Mujeres inmigrantes ocupadas en la industria del sexo,' in *Trabajar en la industria del sexo, y otros tópicos migratorios*, San Sebastían: Gakoa, 109–186.

Agustín, L (2005a) 'Migrants in the mistress's house: other voices in the "trafficking" debate', *Social Politics*, 12(1) 96–117.

Agustín, L (2005b) 'The cultural study of commercial sex', *Sexualities*, 8(5).

Agustín, L (2006) 'The disappearing of a migration category: migrants who sell sex', *Journal of Ethnic and Migration Studies*, 32(1) 29–47.

Agustín, L (2007) *Sex at the Margins: Migration, Labour Markets and the Rescue Industry*, London: Zed Books.

Anderson, B (2000) *Doing the Dirty Work: The Global Politics of Domestic Labour*, London: Zed Books.

APDHA–Asociación Pro Derechos Humanos de Andalucía (2003) 'De la exclusión al estigma', Almería.

Bonelli, E, et al (2001) *Tráfico e inmigración de mujeres en España: Colombianas y ecuatorianas en los servicios domésticos y sexuales*, Madrid: ACSUR–Las Segovias.

Cabiria (2002) *Rapport de synthèse*, Lyon: Le Dragon Lune.

Casal, M (2000) 'Inmigración femenina y trabajo sexual: Estudios de casos en Madrid, Pamplona y Bilbao', in Izquierdo, A (ed), *Mujeres inmigrantes en la irregularidad*, unpublished report, Madrid: Instituto de la Mujer.

Cuanter (1998) *Las notas características de la prostitución y su acceso a los servicios sociales,* Madrid: Instituto de la Mujer.

Danna, D (2004) *Donne di mondo: Commercio del sesso e controllo statale,* Milan: Eleuthera.

de Paula Medeiros, R (2000) *Hablan las putas,* Barcelona: Virus.

Gülçür, L and İlkkaracan, P (2002) 'The "Natasha" experience: migrant sex workers from the former Soviet Union and Eastern Europe in Turkey', *Women's Studies International Forum,* 25(4) 411–421.

Hart, A (1999) *Buying and Selling Power: Anthropological Reflections on Prostitution in Spain,* Boulder: Westview Press.

Høigård, C and Finstad, L (1986) *Backstreets: Prostitution, Money, and Love,* University Park: Pennsylvania State University Press.

ILO (2002) 'Unprotected labour: What role for unions in the informal economy?', *Labour Education,* 2002/2, No. 127, Geneva.

Kellner, P (1999) 'We are richer than you think', *New Statesman,* 19 February, 21–22.

Kennedy, I and Nicotri, P (1999) *Lucciole nere. Le prostitute nigeriane si raccontano,* Milan: Kaos.

Lim, L (1998) (ed) *The Sex Sector: The Economic and Social Bases of Prostitution in Southeast Asia,* Geneva: International Labour Organization.

McKeganey, N and Barnard, M (1994) *Sex Work on the Streets: Prostitutes and Their Clients,* Philadelphia: Open University Press.

Nelson, N (1987) '"Selling her kiosk": Kikuyu notions of sexuality and sex for sale in Mathare Valley, Kenya,' in Caplan, P (ed), *The Cultural Construction of Sexuality,* London: Tavistock, 217–239.

Oso, L (2003) 'Estrategias migratorias de las mujeres ecuatorianas y colombianas en situación irregular', *Mugak,* 23, 25–37.

Parreñas, R (2001) *Servants of Globalization: Women, Migration and Domestic Work,* Stanford: Stanford University Press.

Pateman, C (1988) *The Sexual Contract,* Stanford: Stanford University Press.

Ribeiro, M and Sacramento, O (2005) 'Violence against prostitutes: findings of research in the Spanish-Portuguese frontier region' *European Journal of Women's Studies,* 12(1) 61–81.

Riopedre, P (2004) *Mara y sus amigas: Investigación sobre la prostitución en Galicia,* Lugo: Manuscritos Ed.

Rodríguez, P and Lahbabi, F (2004) *Migrantes y Trabajadoras del sexo,* León: Del Blanco Editores.

Roldán, A, et al (2003) 'El oficio de la prostitución en Navarra: estigmas y modo de vida,' Asociación ABIATZE, Pamplona.

Sanchez, L (2003) 'Sex and space in the global city,' in Perry R W and Maurer, B (eds), *Globalization Under Construction: Governmentality, Law, and Identity,* Minneapolis: University of Minnesota Press, 239–271.

Sullivan, B (1995) 'Rethinking prostitution,' in Caine, B and Pringle, C (eds), *Transitions: New Australian Feminisms,* New York: St. Martin's Press, 184–197.

United Nations, (2004) *World Economic and Social Survey,* New York: Department of Economic and Social Affairs.

White, L (1990) *The Comforts of Home: Prostitution in Colonial Nairobi,* Chicago: University of Chicago Press.

8 Begging Questions: Leprosy and Alms Collection in Mumbai[1]

James Staples

INTRODUCTION

This chapter sets out to explore the practice of begging from the perspectives of those engaged in it. In the process of doing so it aims to unravel how begging – a marginalised occupation *and* an identity category – is practically and symbolically constructed by its practitioners. The particular research on which the chapter draws was carried out during 1999 and 2000 with leprosy-affected people from a self-run leprosy colony called Bethany in coastal Andhra Pradesh, south India. Groups of people from this settlement regularly migrated to Mumbai (formerly Bombay) on the opposite side of the country where they stayed in smaller, temporary, settlements and successfully begged for alms to take or send back home.

As a form of interaction, begging necessarily involves relationships with others, so I also want to use this chapter to examine the ways in which these 'others' help constitute the categories of 'beggar' and 'begging'. In particular, the chapter looks at institutional perspectives – those of State institutions and of donor agencies – alongside those of a lay public, and examines the interrelationships of these groups.

Currently, there is very little published research on begging from the perspectives of those who beg. From the classical Hindu texts, such as the *Rigveda*, which cites the giving of alms as 'a necessary tool to seek salvation' (Makhan 1979: 23), to more recent ethnographic studies (Chaudhuri 1987; Gore 1963), much greater emphasis has been given to those who give than to those on the receiving end of such charity. Alms giving, in these accounts, is described as a way for Hindus to earn merit (*punya*) and offset sin (*pap*) (Bayly 1983: 126; Chaudhuri 1987: 5); similar benefits to those accrued by Muslims (Islam 1996: 7) and, in medieval Europe, to Christians (Munzer 1999). The notion of 'gifting', then, has received a great deal of attention in anthropology, from Malinowski's exploration of *kula* exchange in Melanesia (1922) through Mauss (1954), Lévi-Strauss (1969) and Firth (1973) to Parry (1986) and beyond. While Mauss had a point when he argued that the 'economy of gift-exchange fails to conform to the principles of so-called natural economy or utilitarianism' (1954: 69), a crude dichotomy between economic and gift exchange implies a separation between the two that is not always apparent from the ground.

Begging, in contrast, is 'an interaction … which seems to operate in that grey area between routine market exchanges and the obligations of gift giving' (McIntosh and Erskine 2000: 1.4). Moreover, begging focuses attention on the less examined perspective of the receiver, in this case the beggar. While the most common Telugu term for begging – *bikshatana* – emphasises the gifting of alms (from the Sanskrit, *bhiksha*) rather than soliciting of goods, the English word begging is regularly employed in Bethany. This suggests that the practice is now understood more in terms of missionary and development discourses than as a quasi-religious activity. I thus use the English term 'begging' in this chapter.

Before tackling key questions surrounding the production of identities through begging, some ethnographic material on which to base my analysis is called for. I begin, then, with some background material on leprosy in India, before looking in some detail at the practices defined as begging by people in Bethany. [2]

BETHANY, LEPROSY AND BEGGING PRACTICES

Bethany's particular history of begging began with the formation of the community – named after the village of Bethany, near Jerusalem, which the New Testament identifies as home to Simon the Leper – in the late 1950s. The discovery of a cure for leprosy meant it was possible for those treated for the disease to be discharged from the mission hospital where they had converted to Christianity and, in many cases, had been resident for several years. Long estranged from their mainly

Hindu natal homes, they settled on wasteland close by the hospital, and sought out ways of making a living.

Although casual seasonal labour on neighbouring farmland was occasionally an option for those who were physically able, other mainstream occupations were not. Leprosy was, and to a significant extent remains, negatively constructed as a highly stigmatised state of being. Defining someone as a 'leper' can legitimate their rejection because leprosy has long been perceived, literally in the case of classical Hindu law (Strange 1859: 155), as the manifestation of wrongdoing on the corporeal body. Wise, a nineteenth century scholar of classical Ayurveda, noted that 'when a person dies with it Hindus believe that the person will be affected with it in the next life, unless he performs *praschitta*, penance' (1845: 258). Missionary discourses of the mid- to late nineteenth century reinforced these perspectives by appropriating the leprosy-deformed body as a metaphor for the diseased soul (cf Skinsnes and Elvove 1970; Brody 1974; and Stephen 1986; Buckingham 2002; Staples 2005).

Fragments of this multiply-constructed 'leper' as 'a public nuisance' (Selections 1896: 23) and a potential source of disgrace to his or her relatives remains, in various guises, in contemporary India. De Bruin notes that for her south Indian informants leprosy is seen as 'the result of the transgression of a sexual or social norm' (1996: 34), while Tandon reports similar findings from Uttar Pradesh, north India (Tandon 1999). Leprosy is also seen as highly contagious. Some outside visitors to Bethany still tie handkerchiefs across their mouths and noses to avoid the perceived risk of contagion, while the incidence of leprosy in a family continues to disrupt marriage and employment opportunities.

As a biomedical disease, however, leprosy is curable and, in any case, is only very mildly contagious, with most people having a natural immunity to the disease. In addition, it becomes non-contagious within days of drug treatment commencing. Multi-drug therapy, currently seen as the most efficacious treatment, has been widely available since the 1980s. Other forms of drug treatment were available from the 1950s onwards.

Left to its own devices, the disease attacks the nerve endings, causing loss of sensation in the extremities and rendering them prone to injury and infection. Amputations of toes, fingers (and sometimes whole limbs) are thus common, as is muscle wastage and the 'clawing' of hands and feet, which – coupled with the loss of eyebrow hair and the collapse of the nose – create the archetypal leonine face and deformed body of 'the leper.' Despite the havoc it wreaks on culturally acceptable bodily norms, however, leprosy is not literally deadly. Untreated, having inscribed itself on the body, the disease eventually burns itself out, leaving a lasting and public reminder of where it once was.

Bethany's earlier settlers, treated prior to the onset of multi-drug therapy in the 1980s, for the most part no longer had the disease in a medical sense, but they bore its marks. In some cases the extent of their deformities would have anyway rendered conventional employment physically problematic. More often, however, it was fear of their disease, and a parallel fear on the part of those affected by leprosy of the responses they would evoke, that ruled out a good many of the livelihood options otherwise available to the rural poor. An alternative was called for – one that would allow their disfigured bodies to work in their favour.

The idea for what were called *zanda* (flag or banner) groups was said to have came from Pastor Prasad, Bethany's founder. There were, of course, earlier examples of alms collection in India as an ascetic practice on which his brainwave undoubtedly drew (see, for examples, Sikhare 1920: 22; Gore 1963; Makhan 1979; and Chauduri 1987). As an *alternative* to begging, Prasad told earlier settlers to go out in a group of up to 20 people with cloth-topped collection tins and a banner explaining where they had come from. 'He told us not to ask for money,' remembered Esther, an early settler, 'but to go on the road, sing Christian songs and make music with tambourines and rattles … passers-by would [*then*] give us something.'

What evolved from this innovative format was a network of similar but smaller groups of seven or eight members, each organised by a *zanda maistry*. The *maistries,* who often doubled as village money-lenders, would offer cash advances to those recruited to their groups and – in exchange for a larger share of the takings – would also provide hats, begging tins, cooking vessels and other essential equipment for the trip. If there were eight people in a group, for example, income would be split nine ways, with the *maistry* taking two portions.

Hats, always red, had the word 'Help!' – often in two languages – stitched on to them, and the banner explained, in four languages, where they were from and why they were deserving of alms. Instruments provided included drums, tambourines and *kaiah* (rattles).

Whereas Prasad's initial groups had begged locally – sometimes returning mid-morning to bring rice for their families – *zanda* groups went much further afield, to major cities and tourist centres, and stayed away for up to 40 days at a time. Most stories about *zanda* groups – even when recounted by those who have never been begging – emphasise the physical hardship they entailed and the abuse suffered at the hands of the general public and officials. A former *maistry* recalled, during a life history interview, the difficulties of finding somewhere to rest after a full day of marching through the streets:

> We went somewhere and tried to cook something. Someone came out from their house and upset our pans from the fire and told us to get out, that we couldn't stop there. So we gathered up our things and went to another place where we finished our cooking. We were very anxious – there was no place where we could eat and sleep safely. We actually cooked in the place where other people go out to the toilet, but even then some people complained. Anyway, usually I kept my begging money in my top shirt pocket, and at night I'd take the shirt off and use it as a pillow. On that day I was so worried about where we could cook I forgot to take it off and in the night someone came and stole all the money.

Thefts like this one, and incidences of violence or sexual harassment, are common features in accounts of begging trips. Although they occurred, they were less common than the more mundane, and therefore less remarkable, hardships. These included the lack of a water supply or space for bathing; few proper meals; no changes of clothes over a long period; and the physical difficulties – especially for those most impaired by leprosy – of walking around all day without access to medical attention.

By the time I began fieldwork in November 1999, this form of begging had reduced drastically. Of the 166 people in the village who, during a house-to-house survey, described their main occupation as begging, fewer than 10 relied exclusively on *zanda* groups. The total number of people begging was rather more than the figure quoted by Bethany's office in official reports to donors of 'less than 100'. From a total population of 913, of the 166 (98 men and 68 women) people engaged in begging, seven of the women were also engaged in part-time work within the Colony. An earlier survey, in 1989, found that 199.5 of a population of 843 went begging (Staples 1990: 31). The reduction in numbers of people begging is attributable, in large part, to the fact that since the early 1980s, several NGOs had been involved in supporting social welfare and income generation projects established specifically to help provide alternatives to begging. These projects were overseen by elected village Elders and by an external committee of donor and beneficiary representatives, and managed on a day-to-day basis by an office – staffed by villagers – within Bethany (Staples 2003 and 2007). These projects, which included, for example, a weaving and tailoring workshop that employed around 200 women part-time and several full-time male and female weavers, had certainly had an impact on the numbers of people now begging. What is noteworthy, however, is that, after more than two decades of such projects, nearly 20% of the total population still relied directly on begging. The reasons for its persistence will be further explored later in the chapter.

The 156 people who did not rely exclusively on *zanda* groups begged singly or in couples, either in Mumbai (although known in Bethany by its former name, Bombay), the most popular location; in Delhi, Kolkata (Calcutta) or Chennai (Madras); or more locally in the nearby cities of Vijayawada and Guntur. Although begging was carried out alone, during their time away from the Colony they continued to live as part of a much wider group of others involved in begging in their respective locations.

In terms of distinguishing who went begging, there was no single defining factor. Children and most young adults (18–25 year olds) were excluded, with the youth discouraged from begging by their parents and children left behind with relatives and neighbours. So were many of the oldest, most deformed leprosy-affected people, for whom welfare benefits were available in Bethany. Otherwise the settlement was very heterogeneous: there were few Bethany families that were not represented there. Participants in begging varied from the very poorest in the community to moneylenders for whom begging provided capital. A common reason given by some who had given up paid employment to return to begging was that their debts to moneylenders – typically borrowed to fund a daughter's wedding – were higher than their salaries could ever repay. Many people also moved in and out of begging over time, combining it with casual labouring work or odd jobs in Bethany, for example, or with membership in NGO welfare programmes. Others begged for limited periods to finance a particular expenditure, attempting to return to lower-paid work within Bethany once the expenditure had been met. One man I knew, employed full-time in an NGO-sponsored income generation programme, used his annual leave to travel to Mumbai to beg as a supplement to his income.

A common explanation for the shift in form of begging was that, as they became more experienced, beggars were less reliant on the expertise of a *maistry* and could make more money singly than they could in a group. 'Single' begging – as it was referred to – also offered a greater degree of personal autonomy ('we don't have to commit ourselves to 40-days at a time') and, according to some, reduced the risk of arrest. 'A single person can avoid the police,' I was told. 'When you're in a group of eight people with a banner and instruments, it's easier for them to catch us all.' While I am not denying the validity of these explanations, other accounts – such as the counter-claim that there was 'safety in numbers' – suggest that they have been applied after the event to explain a more gradual shift. This seemed to have been prompted at least in part by a series of conflicts between *maistries* and their group members over money. Whatever lies behind the shift, however, the change drives home the point that begging is not a fixed activity, its practitioners adapting it according to a whole range of external factors.

In Mumbai, the only begging location where I spent any prolonged period, there was a single place where all Bethany people, and a few others, stayed. At the end of my stay – when many had already left the site to return to Bethany for prayer meetings held over Easter – the watchman had counted 51 people from Bethany, nine from a colony in Rajahmundry, and three from a colony in Vizakhapatnam. At peak times, I was told, there were as many as 150 begging people staying there. Until recently, their resting place had been a small patch of railway-owned land within the boundaries of a suburban-line station, discovered back in 1982. Assisted by someone who worked for the railway, they had even constructed makeshift shelters from black plastic sheeting to sleep under during the monsoon.

In December 1999, however, the station was cleaned up – and the beggars were cleared out – in preparation for a Government minister's visit. 'Once he's gone,' it was predicted at the time, 'our people can pay some money to the local police – Rs 50 each – and then they can go back.' I was persuaded to postpone my own trip for this reason but, by March the following year, it seemed unlikely that the railway authorities would ever let them return. 'Encroachment' – the squatting of publicly-owned land, residentially or by street traders – was a major issue in Mumbai at this time. Government action against it, for example, was cited as one of the reasons for the *bandh* (strike) in the city on 25 April 2001 (*The Indian Express* 2001). When I visited in April 2000 – spending my nights in the relative comfort of a nearby hostel, along with Yobu, a friend and Bethany villager who accompanied me – they were eating and sleeping on a narrow stretch of land that ran alongside a busy main road leading away from the station. The camp was separated from the main road by low-level, fancy white iron fencing, and had been planted at 10-foot intervals with saplings, encircled by more white fencing and supported with lollipop-like signs displaying the logo of the plantation's sponsor: Proctor and Gamble. The garden was not big enough for everyone; a large number also slept on the pavement on the other side of the road, shielded at night by a line of city taxis that parked there.

One Bethany man, Ishmael, remained on-site all day as a watchman. Everyone kept their own things – which included bedding (made from stitched-together sacks), cooking utensils and sometimes a kerosene stove – in sacks that they handed to Ishmael before setting off each morning. When they returned at night, he either handed them back their sack or gave them the items from it they required. For this service he charged Rs 2 per sack per day.

Cooking the evening meal was generally conducted in small groups of family members and/or neighbours from the village, with a larger proportion of men than is usually involved in food preparation. 'The women are more tired after being out all day' suggested one man when I asked him why he thought this was. As everyone cooked and ate in the open, within a fairly confined space, groups tended to cook the same dishes 'so there's no jealousy.' Meat – chicken or goat mutton – was served on Sundays and Thursdays; egg or goat's head on Fridays; *dhal* (pulses) on Mondays, Wednesdays and Saturdays; and vegetables on Tuesdays. A portion of rice was usually saved for breakfast the next morning, before setting out, and most people went without a rice-based meal at lunchtime.

There were no water facilities on-site. Drinking water was sourced (at a price) from local cafés every morning and evening and stored in begging tins and plastic jerry cans. Most people bathed only once a week – on Sunday afternoons – using two wells in a derelict and overgrown mill five minutes' walk away, where they also washed their clothes. They shared this facility with the motor mechanics whose shops lined the same street. 'They objected to sharing this place with leprosy patients to start with,' someone told me, 'but the watchman from the next building [*who received Rs 5.00 per bathing person*] told them to leave us alone, and they did.' It could have been the prospect of sharing facilities with beggars rather than with leprosy-affected people *per se* that led to the objections, although my informants were mostly loath to concede this. Leprosy, like other stigmatised diseases, might have also become a hook on which all failings could be hung (Goffman 1963: 21).

In general, however, relations with local traders appeared to be good. Several swapped collected loose change for paper money; one shop provided a postal address; and others provided a safe place to keep begging money until it could be taken back to Bethany. Sugar cane and fruit juice vendors, whose stalls Bethany people kept watch over at night, lined the pavement leading from the settlement to the station. A coffee seller – steel urn in one hand and tray of glasses in the other – arrived early each morning and again in the evenings to sell coffee to Bethany people as they left or arrived back. Consequently, although this was not a predominantly residential area, there was little sense of ostracism from the people living and working in their immediate vicinity. This suggested a disparity between the representation in narratives about the begging of outsiders as hostile and separate, and the supportive, often mutually beneficial, relationships that existed with many of them.

Communication with family back home was conducted by telephone. They called Bethany's office from a kiosk and asked the watchman to call people from their homes. Sometimes people even visited them in person. 'It used to be a big thing to go to Bombay,' one (non-begging) man told me. 'Now they behave as if they are just going to market.' Moneylenders and chit-fund managers, for example, occasionally made the round-trip to Mumbai to collect overdue debts, and non-begging family members sometimes went to spend a few days 'for tourism purposes'. The spatial boundaries within which Bethany people lived were becoming wider.

There were difficulties, however. On at least two occasions officials had arrived with water jets and hosed them out, and when monsoon rains came a month or so after my visit there was nowhere to take shelter. Only a very few people braved the worst of the weather, either returning to Bethany to make daily outings to begging spots in local towns, or joining new *zanda* groups that were heading south to Chennai. In addition, there was always the risk of incarceration.

Back in Mumbai, most days started at around 4:00 am, when residents of the camp got up to attend to their ablutions before the rest of the neighbourhood did. Women were able to use the undergrowth in a disused railway siding to one side of the nearby station. Men had to cross the tracks and use the rails on the far side, avoiding the suburban trains that ran every three minutes (two people had been injured on the tracks already that year, one of them fatally).

Unless they had obviously deformed feet, most people wore old trainers – allowing a suggestion of deformity even when there was none – and some people bound up their hands to accentuate or emulate impairments. Women generally wore baggy, torn men's shirts over their saris and scarves on their heads. Some men dressed as if for a *zanda* group, with red hats and matching sashes. Everyone carried a shoulder bag, stitched in Bethany from plastic sacks; a begging tin, usually an old powdered milk can with a wire handle looped through holes near the rim; a rattle; and, inside the bag, a steel glass for water.

Groups set off to their respective spots in different parts of the city between 5:00–6:00 am, usually congregating in smaller groups for a prayer before going to their individual locations, and arranged to cross each others' paths during the day as an added safety check. Once they were on their own, different people favoured different techniques, although the use of a *kaiah* seemed to be a distinct Bethany tradition, enabling me to distinguish between Bethany and other begging people from a distance. Some people focused on traffic, going up to car windows and asking for money; some went from shop to shop; while others – especially the most infirm – stood or sat in a particular place and called out to passers-by.

Different places were popular on different days of the week. On Wednesdays, for example, there were services all day at St Michael's, a Catholic church in Mahim, which large numbers of Bethany people visited throughout the day. Tuesday was alms-giving day at a Hindu temple in Dadar, while Muslims tended to give outside a mosque in Mumbai Central on Thursdays. In addition, different individual benefactors gave at set times. There was a Jain businessman, for example, who distributed packets of cooked rice and *dhal* and ten rupee notes to the destitute from a centrally-located teashop every Monday. One evening during my stay, a wealthy Christian – looking for a way to mark his birthday – arrived with vats of chicken *pulao* (with not enough salt or chillies, the beneficiaries complained afterwards) and accompaniments to share with everyone there. Others sometimes brought bundles of clothes and took photographs of those they gave to. 'They give us second-hand old rags,' one man suggested, 'and probably use the pictures they take to impress their friends or to raise money for themselves.' I will return later to the workings of these relationships with benefactors.

Working hours varied from person to person, but most were back before nightfall. In addition to money – usually between Rs 50–Rs 100 per day – they brought back with them vegetables and foodstuffs donated from shopkeepers, pieces of firewood collected from the streets, and any garments or footwear they had been given.

INSIDER PERSPECTIVES: BODIES AND SYMBOLS

While the above account provides some detail on the everyday lives of those engaged in begging, it says very little about the actual practice and experience of begging or how, through its practice, begging is relationally and dynamically constituted and embodied. I address this in the following sections of this chapter, starting here with an exploration of how begging is constructed and/or interpreted subjectively both by those who beg and by the non-begging people they live alongside. There are also important differences, I shall argue, between begging as it is practically constituted in 'the field' and begging as it is invoked and talked about in other contexts.

One of the most striking things about begging – as Navan (1998: 98) has pointed out – is that, for its participants, it requires the cultivation of negative images, upturning identities cultivated in other contexts. Whereas leprosy deformities are disguised in most other interactions, in order to beg they are accentuated or, in some cases, even invented. One man I knew, for example, improved his credibility as a beggar by wrapping his healthy hand – the one he held outstretched to passers-by for alms – in a length of bandage before setting out each morning. Another woman, who followed the same approach, also inserted padding into one of her training shoes to give the impression of a limp.

If they did not present themselves in this way, I was told, they faced moral disapprobation, and many people recalled being told things like: 'Your hands are good, you could get a job!' This certainly fits with the view expressed by many of the non-leprosy-affected people I met away from the Colony, who applied the Victorian distinctions between 'deserving' and 'undeserving' poor. The latter category, in Caplan's (1999: 291–292) analysis, includes those with 'bad habits' (those who drink alcohol, take drugs, or go into prostitution) and those of working age. The deserving poor, on the other hand, are made up of the elderly and young children, widows and those with impairments or chronic illnesses. Leprosy would certainly come into this category, but increasingly effective drugs have meant that in many cases people no longer have the evidence of their disease physically inscribed on their bodies. I shall come back to look at donors' ideas about and engagement with begging in the final section of this chapter.

In the upturned world of begging, then, the deformities that prevent those affected by leprosy from getting employment elsewhere allow them to construct 'marketable selves' (Featherstone 1991: 171). Those engaged in the practice are all too aware of the obvious differences in income between those with few physical deformities and those with many. While most beggars reckoned to make around Rs 2,000–Rs 3,000 after living expenses per month, for example, those without use of their legs, deformed faces and no fingers could use their bodies to raise up to Rs 4,000 and above. As my field notes also illustrated, 'bodily techniques' (Mauss 1979) – the ways in which deformities were intentionally exposed to create a momentary moral relationship between the donor and the recipient – also correlated directly with begging success. I jotted down the following as I observed one man I knew beg on a busy shopping street in Mumbai Central:

> [*He's*] sitting on the ground with a 'Help!' hat on his head, and he puts out his right hand to every person who goes by after first touching his forehead. This shows off his hand deformity – he has no fingers – to the full, and his mutilated leg is stretched out in front of him. His begging tin is to the side, and passers-by are encouraged to throw money into it. He speaks in short sentences – just enough to get heard – things like 'please help' or, simply, 'Amma!'

Begging, as Appadurai explains it, is 'an exaggerated and intensified enactment of forms of dependence and types of interaction that are widely institutionalised in Indian society' (1990: 101). Beggars use what he aptly describes as 'coercive subordination' to trap benefactors 'in the cultural implications of their roles of superiors, that is, the obligation to be generous' (*ibid*). Deference; violation of norms concerning physical exposure and contact (touching feet, for example); and the play upon the rituals of worship (the touching of the forehead and other gestures) were all embodied strategies employed by those I observed to achieve this. Few of them verbally categorised their actions in this way if I questioned them directly about 'how to beg' – suggesting that begging practices formed part of a 'habitus' (Bourdieu 1990: 52ff) – but among the less inhibited, many were willing to demonstrate their answer by acting out the practices I describe above. Disguise – reconstituting oneself as a 'beggar' *and* a 'leper' – was as important as revelation in non-begging situations.

Raju, for example, was a cured leprosy-affected man – whose body bore no obvious signs of his disease – whom I spent a lot of time with while I was in Mumbai. He made an explicit distinction between his begging-self and the self he presented in other contexts. I met him one day at the end of a morning's begging in the vicinity of a church, when he was due to accompany me to another part of the city for lunch. After taking off the obvious markers of his beggar identity – his hat, the bandage he wore around one hand, his shoulder bag and his begging tin – Raju also took off his shirt and baggy, grimy white trousers, to reveal well-pressed jeans and a clean polo shirt beneath. He combed his hair, splashed water in his face, and, after dropping off his things with the watchman, walked with me to the station and, unusually, bought tickets for both of us. 'I don't have my passport with me this time,' he laughed, referring to the begging uniform that not only allowed him to travel free, but which justified it to himself in a way that it did not when he was 'off duty.' Not only was Raju dressed and groomed differently: his bodily demeanour had also radically changed. He walked faster and carried himself in a more upright posture than when he was begging; he held his head high and retained eye contact during conversation, rather than deferentially lowering his gaze to the floor; and his arms swung loose at his sides. Just as he embodied the beggar identity, now he appeared to occupy an alternative body, one suitable for moving around urban space in relative anonymity.

All this is literally the stuff of Blacking's definition of an anthropology of the body, which 'is concerned with the interface between body and society, the ways in which the physical organism constrains and inspires patterns of social interaction and the invention of culture' (1977: v–vi). In begging interactions – which by their nature tend to be brief – the disfigured body, complemented by speech, is the primary means of communication. Bethany's beggars are all too aware of the meanings society attributes to their bodily deformities and have successfully manipulated those meanings accordingly.

Despite the obvious imbalance in the relationship between the beggar and his donor, the interaction between the two is not always as straightforward as it may appear. In interpreting the donor's motivations, for example – as my friend did in suggesting that a donor who took photographs did so 'to impress her friends' or to make financial gain – he inverted the balance of the relationship. In telling the story he represented himself as the patron and the philanthropist as the client. The group's muffled complaints about the Christian donor's chicken *pulao* suggests a similar recognition of the donor's need; in this case, perhaps, they see him as averting divinely imposed ill-fortune. This allowed them to negotiate, within tight parameters, over the quality of the food provided. When a benefactor does not fulfil the expected criteria, the beggar also reserves the right to go elsewhere. For example, few of Bethany's beggars now visited the Jain businessman who gave away food packets and cash incentives because, as one informant put it, 'he expects us to eat the food there and wait around a while.' In the time that it takes to consume what he has to offer, an individual could have secured greater gains through conventional begging.

While this extends the viable options available to the beggar, it would be wrong to overstate the power he wields in any particular encounter. Donors generally want to give on their own terms, maximising the more elusive benefits they gain for themselves in the giving (such as the reduction of guilt; fulfilment of religious obligations; the satisfaction of having helped; or the enhancement of their own social status). Those begging, in this context, need to *appear* to subordinate themselves to the needs of the donor – for example, by making a public show of accepting what is offered, and by embodying their subordination – rather than trying to negotiate. The beggar/donor relationship is fleeting yet complex and ambiguous, because 'begging' occupies opposing extremes of a moral scale simultaneously (also mirroring the kinds of negotiations that go on between fundraising agencies and the larger donors on whom they rely).

Trying to explore what people involved in begging felt and thought about the way they made their living was problematic. As I shall show, dominant institutional discourses about the issue were such that there was little or no forum – other, perhaps, than the explicitly religious – in which to discuss the possible merits of begging. This difficulty was aggravated by Bethany people's prolonged relationships with donor agencies. Not only is it the donor's purpose to provide alternatives to begging – and a positive presentation of the practice would thus undermine that purpose – the donor is also seen as being *morally* opposed to begging. Even those people who, as I saw it, had accepted the economic and other benefits of begging over the alternative of poorer paid work within the community, still maintained the line that begging was a negative practice that they would prefer not to be involved with.

Almost everyone in the community who spoke to me about begging, whether they had ever begged or not, emphasised certain of its negative aspects. During a lighthearted, jokey discussion about begging in one of Bethany's tea shops one day, for example, the speakers were keen to close on a solemn note, impressing on me the serious downsides of the practice. After the laughter had died down, one of the speakers turned specifically to me and said:

> It's not as easy as you may think. Begging people have to walk maybe 20 or 30 kilometres a day in all weathers. They have to bend down and grovel for alms, and their limbs get stiff and ulcerated. People who go for begging have no regular place to sleep, to cook and eat, and nowhere to bath regularly or wash their clothes. They face all these problems, so we shouldn't just think it's an easy option.

After I returned from Mumbai, a leprosy-affected man who used to beg took Yobu, the friend who had accompanied me, to one side and said to him: 'I hope you didn't let James think begging was an easy way to make a living, did you?' People in the village were very clear about how they wanted me to understand begging. Morally negative aspects were played down (except in contexts where they might offer greater leverage with donors who they wanted to provide alternative options), and hardship – particularly for bodies that were already suffering – was emphasised.

In addition, at an organisational strengthening workshop held in the community, participants firmly identified begging as a negative aspect of the village's development. The workshop was one of a series of training programmes – facilitated by outside trainers from Chennai – that took place during my fieldwork. Funded by an overseas donor, the courses were attended by representatives of different parts of the community – such as employees, Elders, women and youth – and were, in the words of the trainer, intended 'to improve the efficacy of the various units of the Colony' (Senthilathiban and Duraiswamy 1999: 10). A male representative of the community's youth – who had never been begging, but whose parents had and still did – used the forum to describe begging as a negative practice for four main reasons. First, it caused a deterioration in health; secondly, it led to harassment and possible beatings by the police; thirdly, living conditions while away begging were poor; and, finally, it took place too far away from home, making it difficult to seek medical help if they fell ill. In short, criticisms of begging related to the direct effects of the practice on its practitioners' bodies rather than the morally negative aspects of begging.

Although no positive aspects of begging were identified during the training course – pertinently, participants were never asked if there were any – it became clear to me that begging was considered more than just the last resort. For one thing, and particularly for women, whose voices were also the least heard, it offered a kind of freedom and lifestyle not available within the constraints of village life (alongside the more often reported disadvantages of sexual harassment from passers-by). 'They like being there, being free, being able to drink beer and do what they like,' claimed one (male) non-begging informant (whose opinion would no doubt have been contested by many women had he made it publicly). 'Then they come back to the village and dress in silk saris and walk around like they are big people.' Economic advantages aside, since many people went begging without their spouses – and nearly always without their children – they were able to live in ways that might not have been acceptable at home. Men did much of the cooking, for example, which suggested a bending of gender rules in the camp, perhaps reflecting women's more equal status as beggars, and which would be impossible within a conventional environment. A male beggar told me, for example, that women evoke more compassion than men and, therefore, raise more money. Caplan, while noting the ambiguity of women as receivers of alms, offers a similar explanation (1999: 292). While this changes the balance of power between men and women who beg, it also emphasises the importance attached to the kind of body one has – and how it might be read – to the successful begging encounter.

Financially, the rewards of begging were higher than the alternative of working in one of Bethany's income generation programmes. While conventional employment could be expected to pay out Rs 1,000 per month, begging could generate two or three times that income over the same period. In some cases, such as when people had large debts to repay to moneylenders, these factors made begging a perceived necessity.

For others, it enabled them to reclaim some of the status their leprosy had cost them. One very deformed person affected by leprosy explained to me that through begging he had been able to save enough money to provide a communal meal for everyone back in his native place, to mark the death of his mother. Before, he had been stigmatised because of his disease. Now that he had money, he claimed, the people in his village cared less about his deformities and saw him as a 'big man' to whom 'the Gods have shown favour,' all as a direct result of his economic prowess.

Nevertheless, begging was not a proper form of 'income generation,' claimed the Community Development Officer (CDO), himself a person affected by leprosy. Although he was reliant on begging income from his own family members, he argued that begging could not be classified under the rubric of income generation because the two categories were directly opposed. The whole purpose of the latter, he explained to me, was to prevent the former. This was an illustration of the ways in which categories are externally classified in such a way as to constrain our discussion – if not our thinking – of those same categories.

Even though the man who gained prestige by feeding his former community did so with income from begging, it was likely that he also concealed the source of that income from most if not all of the diners. In the same way that people concealed their leprosy deformities in non-begging situations, they also concealed the fact of their begging from other outsiders. While many people's families knew about their disease, for example, those who begged often kept this aspect of their lives from family members outside the community, suggesting that begging – perhaps because it involved issues of choice – was a more stigmatised category than the disease itself. This appears to be the case elsewhere: according to Navan (1998: 89–105), begging is a key source of the contemporary leprosy stigma in Thailand, where sufferers were visible *only* in the context of begging. Here, she argues, the negative image of leprosy is thus constructed through their designation as beggars. The same might well be argued for India.

The concealment of begging in Bethany, which no doubt reinforced the negative self-image of begging described above, is also revealed in the language used to talk about the practice. 'If we accidentally mention a *zanda* group when we're with relatives', as one man put it, 'they won't know we mean a begging group.' (His sister's husband, for example, only found out that her parents went begging more than 10 years after he married her.) In addition, when I asked people what they did for a living, it was rare for them to use one of the Telugu derivations of the verb 'to beg' (*bikshatana* or *adukuntum*) in their replies. They would tell me, euphemistically, that they would *'Bombai velatharu'* (go to Mumbai) or *'Dilli velatharu'* (go to Delhi).

This language of concealment extended to children. As part of a children's workshop I organised, the participants – aged between seven and 10 – were asked to write down what their parents did for a living and the jobs they would like for themselves. Ten of the 29 children had parents who went begging: eight of them expressed that using the same linguistic device as their parents (ie, *'Bombai velatharu'* or *'Dilli velatharu'*), and only two of them referred explicitly to begging. One wrote the phrase *bikshaniki vastadu* (going begging), the other used the form *adakutanaru* (begging). In both cases, when they read out their answers the other children laughed – reinforcing that this was not a usual or acceptable form of expression – and both were scolded by Lakshmi, a member of crèche staff who had come to help with the session. She told them they were using 'wrong words' (*tappudu matalu*). Even though the CDO – also there to assist – supported the ways in which the two boys had replied, it became clear that the ways in which begging could be articulated within the community, and to outsiders in non-begging contexts, were instilled during early socialisation.

INSTITUTIONAL PERSPECTIVES ON BEGGING

Turning now to 'outsider' perspectives, there are disparities between popular ideas about begging among the donor-public and those who receive official sanction from the government and other agencies, such as overseas donors and local NGOs. Somewhere between these categories are local philanthropists: the individuals who engage with Bethany's beggars collectively in 'the field', visiting them to make their gifts rather than sending a cheque through official channels or dropping coins into a begging tin. The latter relationship, at least from the beggar's perspective, has already received some attention earlier in this chapter. What I want to look at in this final section is how officially sanctioned, institutional perspectives on begging have been constituted, and the ways in which they are perpetuated by, and passed on into, popular perspectives.

At the State level, vagrancy remains technically outlawed in much the same way as it was under the British (Sikhare 1920). Under the Bombay Prevention of Begging Act 1959, which has subsequently been extended to cover Delhi, there are clear provisions for the segregation of leprosy-affected people arrested for begging and other categories of beggar.[3] Those believed to have leprosy, states the legislation, may be removed to a 'leper asylum' (26i), either for the term of their detention or, where deemed necessary in order to administer medical treatment, for a longer period. Furthermore, the BJP, the ruling party in central government during my fieldwork, was increasingly wedded to transnational visions of what a 21st century democratic nation should be: visions that did not square easily with begging as a religious avocation (cf Appadurai 1990). Rather, begging was seen as a social problem to be tackled; a disturbance both to the local population and to India's image on a global stage, impacting negatively on international tourism (Chaudhary 2000: 293–294). Although there were reports of beggars being incarcerated in institutions for the homeless – including members of Bethany's begging population, some of whom it took over six months to get released – there was relatively little action in most cities, outside the capital, to prevent begging by force. Likewise, poverty alleviation measures that might otherwise have served as a deterrent were inadequate to provide realistic alternatives for the destitute. In Andhra, for example, people affected by leprosy qualified for a monthly pension of, at the time of my fieldwork, just Rs 75 each: enough, to use a villager's own example, to pay an average monthly electricity bill for running a couple of light bulbs.

In the absence of a welfare state, punitive measures against begging have been minimal, and control – where it has been exerted at all – has taken a more Foucauldian form. The State has sought not to manipulate beggars themselves, but the symbols by which they are represented, recasting them as a public nuisance rather than religiously justified. A broad coalition of social scientists, aid agencies and donors have been complicit in this construction of begging as a morally negative category, most often framed within a wider discourse on poverty or, after Lewis (1966), as a feature of a 'culture of poverty' (eg, Chaudhuri 1987).

At the macro level, the World Health Organization (WHO) had recognised that disabled people in many developing countries reject the rehabilitation programmes available to them in favour of migrating to the cities to beg, and recommended Community-Based Rehabilitation (CBR) programmes as a possible solution (Kassah 1998). Again, begging is constructed as a highly negative practice; a problem requiring a solution.

Putting it explicitly, one of Bethany's overseas donors declared at a funding meeting that: 'Begging is not a good way for any human being to make a living. What dignity can any man have from begging?' His comment was in response to information he had received from another local project, the director of which had told him that he had spotted Bethany people begging on the streets. Although there were a number of possible answers to the donor's direct question – that dignity from begging might come from being able to support one's family, for example, or that 'dignity' in the European sense might not have been a locally relevant category – his question was rhetorical. He was making the point that begging was bad and that future funding might be contingent on its control. This perceived threat of funding withdrawal clearly limited the ways in which begging could be represented within the community by project leaders and others. Ironically, the meeting itself could be seen as a form of begging, with the project coordinator employing similar forms of 'coercive subordination' (Appadurai 1990: 101) – exaggerated gestures of respect combined with emotional appeals based on the hardships suffered by members of the community – as those used by the beggar on the street. In both cases, as Stirrat and Henkel put it (referring to the grants given by international agencies to local NGOs), 'the receiver is left in a position of indebtedness and powerlessness' (1997: 73).

This certainly fed into the way the community presented itself, with official rhetoric disassociating the community from the practice. When the chief functionary of Bethany's social development programmes met the director of another leprosy project, for example, they discussed having seen leprosy-deformed beggars on the way to their meeting place. 'They couldn't have been mine,' said the latter, 'I wouldn't let *my* patients do that.' The appearance of beggars in public was taken as a sign of lax or incompetent management. Fuelled by fears of losing sponsorship, programme managers resorted to the

19th century argument that beggars should be restrained, forcibly if necessary, within the context of projects established to help them. This also says something about southern Indian NGOs; the personal ambitions and patronage bound up within them; and their relationship to international aid agencies with rather different perspectives on development issues.

Institutional views feed into public perceptions about begging, creating remarkably similar responses, at least in urban contexts, cross-culturally. In New York, for example, Williams (1995: 28) notes that subway passengers claim to prefer giving to beggars who 'do' something (play a musical instrument, for example) rather than those who just ask for cash; travellers on Indian Railways, at least in my presence, expressed almost identical responses. I recorded the following on my train journey back from Mumbai:

> [T]he fattest – and most senior of the three men [*sitting opposite me*] – turned [*the conversation*] to begging, without any prompting from me at all. 'When that man came with no hands, I gave, because what can he do? When the child came and swept the floor, I gave, because he was doing something, he didn't just expect something for nothing,' he said. 'But when they come along and they have nothing wrong with them, when they could work, I don't give, it just encourages them in their idleness. They should get a job, or at least do something for their money.'

An Australian woman I met, a representative of an Alternative Trading Organisation (ATO), expressed similar sentiments – more gently – when I mentioned to her that I was studying begging as part of my research project, and wanted to avoid presenting it as a necessarily negative practice. 'But you surely don't think it's a *good* thing, do you?' she demanded. She added that she never gave to beggars, 'except those small boys who come around on the trains and sweep the floors, because I like that service, and very occasionally I'll give to people if they're handicapped. But I don't give to young, healthy looking people because I think that just encourages it'. Although there remains a religious aspect to giving, there are places and contexts in which begging and receiving is appropriate, and, more often, situations where it is not. People on Indian trains still tend to give, at least some of the time, but their objections are framed nearly always within a more globalised, secular perspective on the practice. The institutional perspectives I have described have a clear impact on the way people beg. Successful beggars understand that they are required either to illustrate why they are deserving, or to provide a service in return for alms. The idioms through which begging can be discussed or represented by those engaged in the practice, as I have shown, are also highly restricted.

CONCLUSION

The examples above demonstrate the range of symbolic, political, and socio-religious resources available to leprosy-affected people within the constraints of a begging identity. Although begging is primarily an economic practice, it is given its social meaning through interaction. At the simplest level, this occurs in the face-to-face contact between the disabled beggar and a member of the giving public. On a larger scale, it occurs between begging communities and donors, both local (philanthropists) and more distant (charities), and between beggars as a symbolic category and the various institutions of State-sponsored and international development.

At street-level, leprosy-affected beggars use their bodies to accentuate their deformities and, as a consequence, to convey the message that they need and *deserve* help. In this context, leprosy becomes more than a social category. It is also a lived, bodily experience that can be manipulated in different ways in different situations. Exposed and exaggerated for the purpose of begging, in other contexts it must become disguised as healthy, requiring people affected by leprosy to navigate their way through multiple, often opposing worlds.

While learning the apparent rules of begging allows a kind of economic freedom – to which other freedoms apart from begging might also be linked – it should be stressed that the 'leper beggar's' power to manipulate the categories he or she lives by, while surprisingly flexible, does have its limitations. Institutional definitions of begging, as a negative moral category, opposed to modernity, dominate the ways in which begging identities are articulated by *all* stakeholders, and restrict the idioms through which other perspectives on the practice can be expressed. These institutional perspectives are further reinforced through their symbolic use by the begging community, gaining them access to other kinds of resources, including government rations or aid from overseas. Having understood the institutional view that donors oppose begging, for example, Bethany leaders' request funding for programmes that, they claim, will help to prevent it. This says more about the needs of donors than it does about the desires of their recipients, and further accentuates the disparities between the visions of both parties. While I am not trying to suggest that practitioners of begging necessarily favour it over alternatives, within the present terms of the debate it is difficult for them openly to express anything other than a reflection of the received wisdom.

Notes

[1] This chapter is an amended version of a chapter published in my book, *Peculiar People, Amazing Lives. Leprosy, Social Exclusion and Community-Making in South India* (2007), Delhi: Orient Longman. I am grateful to the publisher for allowing me to reproduce the material here.

[2] For detailed ethnographic description of this community and its formation see Staples 2003 and 2007.

[3] Full-text of the legislation is published on the government's website: <http://socialwelfare.delhigovt.nic.in/beggpreventact1.htm> (accessed 29 January, 2007).

References

Appadurai, A (1990) 'Topographies of the self: praise and emotion in Hindu India' in Lutz, C and Abu-Lughod, L (eds), *Language and the Politics of Emotion*, Cambridge: Cambridge University Press, 92–112.

Bayly, C A (1983) *Rulers, Townsmen And Bazaars: North Indian Society in the Age of Expansion, 1770–1870*, Cambridge: Cambridge University Press.

Blacking, J (1977) 'Towards an anthropology of the body', in Blacking, J (ed), *The Anthropology of the Body*, London: Academic Press.

Bourdieu, P (1990) *The Logic of Practice* (translated by Richard Nice), Cambridge: Polity.

Brody, N S (1974) *The Disease of the Soul: Leprosy in Medieval Literature*, Ithaca.

Buckingham, J (2002) *Leprosy in Colonial South India*, London: Palgrave.

Caplan, L (1999) 'Gifting and receiving', in Das, V, Gupta, D and Uberoi, P (eds), *Tradition, Pluralism and Identity: In Honour of T. N. Madan*, New Delhi: Sage, 283–305.

Chaudhary, M (2000) 'India's image as a tourist destination – a perspective of foreign tourists', *Tourism Management*, 21(3) 293–297.

Chaudhuri, S (1987) *Beggars of Kalighat, Calcutta*, Calcutta: Imprinta.

de Bruin, H M (1996) *Leprosy in South India: Stigma and Strategies of Coping*, Pondy Paper in Social Sciences: Institute Francais de Pondicherry.

Featherstone, M (1991) 'The body in consumer culture', in Hepworth, M and Turner, B (eds), *The Body: Social Process and Cultural Theory*, London: Sage Publications, 170–196.

Firth, R (1973) *Symbols: Public and Private*, London: George Allen and Unwin.

Goffman, E (1963) *Stigma: Notes on the Management of a Spoiled Identity*, Harmondsworth: Penguin.

Gore, M (1963) 'Social work in India', in Varma, B (ed), *Contemporary India*, New York: Asia Publishing House, 230–246.

Islam, R (1996) 'A note on zanbil: the practice of begging among Sufis in South Asia (mainly 14th century)', *Journal of the Pakistan Historical Society*, 44(1) 5–12.

Kassah, A (1998) 'Community-based rehabilitation and stigma management by physically disabled people in Ghana', *Disability and Rehabilitation*, 20(2) 66–73.

Lévi-Strauss, C (1969) *The Elementary Structures of Kinship* (translated by Bell J, von Sturmer, J and Needham, R), London: Eyre and Spottiswoode.

Lewis, O (1966) 'The culture of poverty', *Scientific American*, 212(4) 19–25.

Makhan, J (1979) *The Beggars of A Pilgrims' City: Anthropological, Sociological, Historical and Religious Aspects of Beggars and Lepers in Puri,* Varansai: Kishor Vidya Niketan.

Malinowski, B (1922) *Argonauts of the Western Pacific: An Account of Native Enterprise and Adventure in the Archipelagoes of Melanesian New Guinea,* London: Routledge and Kegan Paul.

Mauss, M (1979) *Sociology and Psychology: Essays* (translated by Brewster, B), London: Routledge and Kegan Paul.

Mauss, M (1954) *The Gift: Forms and Functions of Exchange in Archaic Societies.* London: Cohen and West.

McIntosh, I and Erskine, A (2000) '"Money for nothing"? Understanding giving to beggars', *Sociological Research Online,* 5(1) <www.socresonline.org.uk/5/1/mcintosh.html> (accessed 10 February, 2007).

Munzer, S R (1999) 'Beggars of God: The Christian ideal of mendicancy', *Journal of Religious Ethics,* 27(2) 305–330.

Navan, L (1998) 'Beggars, metaphors and stigma: a missing link in the social history of leprosy, *Social History of Medicine,* 11(1) 89–105.

Parry, J (1986) 'The gift, the Indian gift and the "Indian gift"', *Man,* 21, 453–473.

Selections from the Records of the Government of India Home Department, No. CCCXXXI, Papers Relating to the Treatment of Leprosy in India from 1887–95, (1896). Calcutta.

Senthilathiban, K and Duraiswamy, S (1999) 'Proposal for training programmes to be conducted at Bethany Leprosy Colony, Bapatla', unpublished consultants' report, Chennai.

Sikhare, V (1920) 'Appendix two', in *Report of the Committee Appointed by the Government of Bombay to Consider and Formulate Proposals for the Purpose of Preventing Professional Beggary in the Bombay Presidency,* Bombay: Government of India Press.

Skinsnes, O K and Elvove, R M, (1970) 'Leprosy in society v. 'leprosy' in occidental literature', *International Journal of Leprosy,* 38(3) 294–307.

Staples, J (1990) 'Bethany Leprosy Colony: the impact of leprosy on social life in a South Indian rural community', unpublished BA dissertation, School of Oriental and African Studies, University of London.

Staples, J (2003) '"Peculiar People, Amazing Lives." A study of social exclusion and community-making among leprosy-affected people in South India', unpublished PhD thesis, School of Oriental and African Studies, University of London.

Staples, J (2005) 'Becoming a man: personhood and masculinity in a South Indian leprosy colony', *Contributions to Indian Sociology,* 39(2) 279–305.

Staples, J (2007) *Peculiar People, Amazing Lives. Leprosy, Social Exclusion and Community-Making in South India.* Delhi: Orient Longman.

Stephen, R (1986) 'Leprosy and social class in the Middle Ages', *International Journal of Leprosy,* 54(2) 300–305.

Stirrat, R and Henkel, H (1997) 'The development gift: the problem of reciprocity in the NGO world', *Annals, AAPSS* 554, 66–80.

Strange, T (1859) *Hindu Law; Principally with Reference to Such Portions of it as Concern the Administration of Justice, in the King's Courts in India,* Third edition, 1, Madras.

The Indian Express (2001) 'Mumbai newsline', 1(356) 3–5.

Tandon, S (1999) 'Social and individual aspects of chronic illness: A case study of leprosy', unpublished PhD thesis, University of Delhi.

Williams, B (1995) 'The public I/eye: conducting fieldwork to do homework on homelessness and begging in two US cities', *Current Anthropology,* 36(1) 25–51.

Wise, T A (1845) Commentary of the Hindu System of Medicine, Calcutta.

Vulnerable in the City: *Adivasi* Seasonal Labour Migrants in western India[1]

David Mosse, with Sanjeev Gupta and Vidya Shah

Chuniya has sent his 14-year-old son Magan to Rajkot with the labour contractor Ramsen. Nobody from the *adivasi* (Bhil) village of 'Khedpada' (in Jhabua District of Madhya Pradesh) had worked in Rajkot before last year when Ramsen moved his business there from Surat and recruited over 40 people (men and women and children) from this and five or six nearby villages. It is rumoured that when he visited the village he brought 50,000 *rupees* cash just to pay advances (remembering last year when several of the labour-gang dropped out, fearful of the unknown place). How could Chuniya resist? He had to take money from Ramsen; the old debt from the *Baniya* (moneylender) in Thandla was gnawing away at the household – 15,000 *rupees* brideprice for his son's wedding two years back, with 7,500 interest, and so 22,500 to repay. Last year his son Rahul and his new wife went to Surat, three months arduous moulding concrete blocks – 'slab work', but the Rs 4,000 they earned didn't even cover the interest and Chuniya had to borrow from the Sarpanch's brother to keep up payment to the *Baniya*. The gang will leave after the festival of *diwali* and not be back before *holi*. (Shah 1997)

Seasonal labour migration for casual work in urban construction and related industries is an irreversible, if painful and socially disruptive, element of the livelihoods of Bhil *adivasis* in western India. These are the rural tribal communities of the borderlands of south Rajasthan, western Madhya Pradesh and eastern Gujarat, whose agriculture has

become precarious over the past generation as a result of land fragmentation and deforestation, but who have long sought supplemen-
tary sources of income to meet family subsistence needs as well as to
'feed the *Baniya*' (Hardiman 1996). Surveys show that only 12 to 20%
of households rely solely on cultivation for their livelihoods (cf Mosse
et al 2002), and even successful cultivators fail to meet basic annual
food needs or save sufficient maize or rice seed for next year's staple
crop.

This chapter examines *adivasi* (tribal) labour migration within the
context of the agencies of the State, unions and non-governmental
organisations (NGOs), contractors, and brokers with whom migrants
engage – those mandated to protect them but who may also be their
most intimate exploiters – and asks how and why these entities fail to
protect some of the most vulnerable among the poor of western India.
Building on earlier research (Mosse et al 2002), this question is raised
specifically in the context of my work with the UK's Department for
International Development (DFID) to set up a programme to support
adivasi migrant labourers in the region.

These days social researchers more or less accept that people move,
that cultures are not fixed by location, that migration partakes in
modernity, but is not itself modern. This paper does not primarily
focus on such debates. Its concern is with hardship and exploitation,
and how to contend with them. This is not to say that migration is
only a matter of hardship. Our earlier study of *adivasi* migration
(Mosse et al 2002) revealed a complex phenomenon in which successful migrants secured incomes and status in the community through
investment in land and symbolic capital, in which women found new
freedoms and in which age hierarchies were challenged. Migration
provided positive opportunities to experience life in the city, in the
sense that, as Farley puts it, 'migration is mostly about survival, but
also a bit about adventure' (cited in Gidwani and Sivaramakrishnan
2003). But arguably recent studies of migration have been captive to
powerful disciplinary narratives. On the one hand, too many anthropologists wed the analysis of migration to narratives of modernity or
progress (Gardner and Osella 2003). On the other hand, too many
developers and environmentalists tie migration to narratives of
decline, loss, de-peasantisation and the creation of 'ecological
refugees' (Gadgil and Guha 1995), or a new itinerant proletarian
underclass (Breman 1996). But migration may index neither transforming social mobility, nor the erosion of rural ways of living. It may,
paradoxically, have become the *only* means by which settled agricultural livelihoods (as ideal and practice) are possible or sustainable.

However, survival that is dependent upon migration and its individ-ualised earning or the loss of reciprocity is also transgressive and brings moral risk.

ADIVASI SEASONAL LABOUR MIGRATION – AN OVERVIEW

From the 1960s, as opportunities for work in forest labour, local canals, railways or drought relief became scarce, Bhil farmers in west-ern India travelled further and further afield to secure employment. At first this migration was to the adjacent regions of commercial agri-culture for harvesting, but with the expansion of the urban/industrial corridor extending from Ahmedabad to Mumbai, Bhil migrants were more likely to be found labouring on distant urban construction sites than in either timber yards or irrigated paddy fields. As the result of a gradual upward trend in seasonal labour migration from the 1970s, according to our 1996–1997 survey of 42 Bhil villages, at a conserva-tive estimate around 65% of households (up to 95% in some villages) and 48% of the adult population are involved in seasonal migration, overwhelmingly for casual urban construction work, which has become the primary source of cash for Bhil families (contributing 86% of cash income) (see Mosse et al 2002 for details). With an average of half of the adult population of Bhil villages migrating for half of the year, leaving only the old, the ill or the disabled, migration has become a massive event in rural life.

Whether for work on construction sites or stone quarries, for brick making or digging cable trenches, the seasonal flow of Bhil casual labourers from upland villages has contributed to the physical expan-sion of industrial growth poles in Gujarat such as Surat, Baroda and Ahmedabad (cf. Breman 1996). *Adivasi* migrants form a sizeable part of the casual labour force in these cities. This labour is entirely in the 'informal sector'– by far the largest component of urban labour. In Surat in 1991, for example, Breman estimates that 700,000 of the city's one million workforce were employed in the informal sector; and about 225,000 of them were engaged in casual labour, street work or domestic service (1996: 54–56). The building industry – the principle sector of employment for Bhil migrants – involved, Breman estimates, at least 60,000 labourers in Surat (*ibid*). Transport is another part of the informal sector attracting migrants, including head-loaders, loaders of trucks, handcart operators, and (a very few) drivers. Migrants also work in industrial plants. They do not work as regular waged and skilled employees, but form a large ancillary body of unskilled labour which is not engaged directly in the production process or employed by factory owners, but hired through labour contractors for construction and building maintenance work, or in loading and unloading raw materials or manufactured produce. In all, today 10–15,000 *adivasis* migrate to each of the major cities (Surat, Ahmedabad, Baroda, Kota) each year.

A highly segmented casual labour market in these cities means that, despite a shortage in skilled labour, *adivasi* migrants are excluded from skilled work as masons, carpenters or textile workers; and ensures that they are absorbed almost entirely as the lowest-paid, most unskilled labour (see Mosse et al 1997). Only 3% of those surveyed had skills as, for example, masons or carpenters,[2] usually relegated to the few young men who get a lucky break when contractors are willing to risk giving them the chance to learn on the job. In particular, it is recruitment through a multi-tier system of labour-gang leaders, jobbing recruiter/supervisors and labour contractors that reproduces this segmentation (and frees the owners of capital from the obligations of an employer, Breman 1996: 157–161), and ensures that Bhil migrants follow well-defined and repeated routes from particular villages to particular urban work sites.

As with other aspects of Bhil livelihoods, the experience and outcome of labour migration is differentiated. In the simplest terms, there are two scenarios: (1) from relatively better-off households with some minimum food security, individual young men take turns migrating opportunistically for interrupted periods to maximise cash earning. This is done in order to manage the inter-year fluctuations in farming, to meet the need for investment (for example, in wells, house-building and marriages), or to repay loans; (2) from poorer households, whole families migrate for long periods for survival, and are tied into relationships of dependence with brokers, contractors and moneylenders. A significant proportion of migrants are women (42% in our study), who tend to be poorer, older and married with children.

There are broadly three systems of recruitment involving variable degrees of dependence and exploitation (see Mosse et al 2002 for details). In the first, opportunistic migrants travel to relatively nearby towns and cities, where they are recruited as daily wage labourers through informal urban labour markets, or *nakas*. Second, people with direct contacts with well-known builders/contractors travel in groups. These are usually kin groups that include younger women, and are often comprised of affinal relations – that is, male migrants are recruited by their *mamas* (maternal uncles) or *behnois* (sisters' husbands) – a practice which serves to protect the core patrilineage from the divisiveness of unequal and individualised migration earning (and gives women more liberty than among their marital kin).

Third, migrants are mobilised in their own villages by gang leaders/brokers or *mukkadams* – former labourers turned supervisors and village moneylenders, a few of whom have settled in town – who negotiate with contractors/employers and arrange cash advances and long-term work. These migrants are those for whom migration is a defensive survival strategy; people who in the monsoon season trade their labour in distant urban sites for cash advances from recruiters to meet the urgent need for food, and who are the most completely tied into relations of dependence and exploitation. They migrate furthest, for longest and with least reward. This is a price paid for the relatively greater security of work, for protection (including shelter at work sites) and patronage offered by ties to *mukkadams*. While the extent of the first kind of positive or opportunistic migration varies with the availability of household labour in any year/village (influenced by domestic cycles), the extent of the last, survival migration, is a factor of poverty.

By whatever route they get there, at worksites migrants experience long hours, hard work, harsh conditions, injuries (with inadequate medical help or compensation), and social isolation and humiliation. Water is scarce at workplaces and encampments, and migrants must negotiate access to it from construction sites or private houses rather than the municipality (DISHA 2002: 45). The costs of living in the city are high, even if food grain can be brought from the village (which is not always possible). Food and fuel are the main expenses. Many spend more than a tenth of a day's earning on fuel, facing competition from angry locals, and in the monsoon season they resort to burning plastic and tyres for cooking (see BMS 1999/2000). Migrants recruited through *mukkadams* depend upon subsistence allowances and shop-credit, which together with earlier cash advances bring deductions at the time of payment. As a result, migrants return home with greatly-reduced earnings, and in extreme cases with nothing or even further in debt (Breman 1996: 156).

Security is another major problem. Most *adivasi* migrants sleep in the open or bivouac under makeshift structures. A study in Ahmedabad (DISHA 2002: 16) found that 54% of the migrants slept in the open, and 41% in huts built from tarpaulins or jute bags. Factors influencing the choice of dwelling place included availability of open ground free from harassment water and fuel availability, and the desire to remain with members of the same village in order to share news and send remittances. Staying in urban spaces, migrants face harassment, abuse, theft, forcible eviction by the police, or the demolition of their dwellings by urban authorities. The abuse of *adivasi* migrants is closely related to their lack of identity or residence in urban places. Here they stand out as marginal, transitional people. They are subject to prejudice, stigmatised and criminalized, falsely accused of theft or looting, and detained and beaten by police. When men are held in remand, women are left without support.

The harsh conditions are indeed amplified for women by their gender roles and the simultaneous demands of work and childcare; by the need to undertake heavy work and long hours when pregnant; and by sexual exploitation by masons, contractors, the police and others, which is routine but silenced by fear and economic or marital insecurity (ie, unreported for fear of loss of work or domestic violence). Migrant women describe fear at night and fitful sleep in exposed places. For the most part children at worksites have no care or shelter – 'they spend their days crying'.[3] Older children either work or are needed to care for younger siblings. Nutrition is poor, and agencies working with seasonal migrant labourers document a catalogue of work-related health problems deriving from the toxicity of materials or the lack of water or sanitation, including reproductive tract infections, spontaneous abortions and pregnancy complications, which are some of the problems women discussed during our earlier fieldwork (Mosse et al 1997, 2002).

Even when paid in full, migrant wages fall well below the legal minimum (especially piece-rate jobs), and payment is often late or withheld, particularly towards 'the end of the season when the balance of power has firmly shifted from employee (coaxed with advances) to the employer, and when migrants are under pressure to return home for the cultivation season' (Mosse et al 2002: 75). The non-payment and under-payment of wages is a regular occurrence, and migrants have no power of redress. Knowing this, if labourers or their *mukkadams* suspect a contractor, they are quite likely to cut their losses by decamping in the night with whatever wages they have.

More important still, work is scarce and irregular. In one study, 91% of labourers at the local labour markets in Ahmedabad were *unemployed* for 10–20 days in a month (DISHA 2002: 27). It is because of this uncertainty that poor Bhil migrants place great store on the reputation of reliable, if exploitative, brokers – *mukkadams* and contractors *(seths)* – who use cash advances to cement control over a fluid labour force by using debt as 'an instrument of coercion' (Breman 1996: 167). Breman argues that this form of 'neo-bondage' differs from the older agrarian type of clientship only by the absence of compensating security (*ibid*). Indeed, he suggests that the relationships of dependence that Bhils historically had with their *sahukars* (moneylenders) have developed and diversified in ways that weaken or eliminate elements of patronage and protection (*ibid*, cf. Hardiman 1987).

The economic and social outcomes of labour migration are as differentiated as the systems of recruitment and employment. For a few, migration provides cash income to supplement agricultural work, and allows savings and investments (in wells, pumps or good marriages) and sometimes, upward mobility as gang leaders and 'recruiters'. It enables investment in social networks, and increases social prestige and creditworthiness. For a majority, however, labour migration is linked to long-term indebtedness, fails to generate net cash returns, and perpetuates below-subsistence livelihoods. The poor, as the opening example of Chuniya shows, find it impossible to work themselves out of debt. In the meantime fresh debts are incurred to meet subsistence and medical needs. Long absences and dependence on distant patrons reduces status, erodes social capital, and makes the poor marginal to the networks through which credit, marriages, or benefits from development projects are obtained.

Migration, then, is both determined by and amplifies existing social inequalities. Some perceive repeated seasonal migration as having a significant negative impact on community institutions at the village level, and on intra-household relations (see Mosse et al 1997, 2002). It is associated with changes that are potentially disruptive of cooperative agricultural life: increased monetisation and the need for cash in Bhil villages; the increase in wage labour at the expense of systems of reciprocal exchange; a decline in joint-cultivation or well management; and significant strains on intra-household relations (gender, marital and inter-generational).[4] Migration itself is dangerous and a source of conflict because it 'stretches the boundaries between the fulfilment of personal/individual ambitions and wider social responsibilities' (Gardner and Osella 2003: ix). And yet seasonal labour migration to urban construction sites has become the means – perhaps the only means – to reproduce valued agricultural livelihoods. Still, *adivasis* conceal their urban-based livelihoods in complicity with rural development agencies who regard migration as an indicator of the failure of rural development programmes. *Adivasis* are not in the habit of discussing their migrant labouring with outsiders whose projects are built around a normative bias towards agricultural livelihoods, *village* resources and investments; access to which requires articulation of goals of autonomous sustainable *rural* livelihoods. Of course Bhils desire to redirect energy from migration to their land; but they face the reality that subsistence farming depends upon migrant earnings (to manage uncertainty, for inputs, investment or debt management), just as 'cultivating' urban work relies on village-based networks. It was no longer a paradox that people in one Dahod Bhil village could perceive themselves as becoming better off, while experiencing a five-fold increase in the number of migrating households. So for most Bhils, migration is not an external factor requiring the limiting of non-agrarian identities, but is integral to the reproduction of subsistence agriculture and village culture. This said, there is a growing minority of households whose land-holdings are so small as to have forced some members (especially younger sons) to move into full-time waged work.

It was growing recognition of the irreversible importance of seasonal labour migration to Bhil livelihoods, even after a decade of intensive development project interventions, that led to my involvement in recent Department for International Development–Western India Rainfed Farming Project (DFID–WIRFP) (GVT) efforts to develop a programme to support *adivasi* migrants (Mosse 2002, 2003). Thinking normatively and practically about *adivasi* labour migration – about what should or could be done – involved new and different enquiries and encounters. It meant understanding the legal and institutional frameworks that could be used to protect *adivasi* migrants and negotiating partnerships with unions, NGOs and government departments that would push a rural development project into new and unfamiliar directions.

The context changed in the five years since our initial study in 1996–1997, in ways that worsened the situation faced by migrant labourers. Further closure of industries in the western region (textile mills, screen printing units and chemical factories) had pushed ex-formal sector workers into construction work, adding skilled workers and swelling the numbers seeking daily wage employment at *nakas* (urban markets). The building industry was facing recession, deepened by a builders' strike (2000), drought and water shortages (1999–2000), an earthquake (2001) that limited high-rise constructions, and serious communal riots (2002). This severely reduced work availability for labourers. By 2002, earthquake reconstruction work in Kuchch provided a new destination, but with reportedly harsh conditions. Still, there was a widespread view (among labourers and those who work with them) that migrants were getting fewer days work for a given period of migration, and women were especially vulnerable to unemployment.

Our research had to be re-directed towards translating the experience of labour migrants into a set of interventions framed by, and addressing, their needs. *Adivasi* migrant labourers clearly had a variety of short-term practical needs relating to shelter, healthcare, information (about jobs) and above all work; many needs were gender-specific. Family members remaining in villages – often the old, children or the disabled – also faced difficulty meeting food, fodder and fuel needs with limited resources, or in accessing assistance or credit. But ultimately, and in the longer-term, the position and welfare of *adivasi* migrant labour would, it was put, only improve by confronting exploitation and the realisation of basic rights – rights to minimum wages, to freedom from bondage and sexual exploitation, to compensation for injury or death, to shelter, and to associate and seek avenues of protection and redress. The approach of the migrant support programme we imagined had, in the new language of development donors, to be firmly 'rights-based' and oriented to the longer-term goal of unionising an especially exploited section of unorganised labour. But in reality what could this possibly mean? If we were to propose interventions supportive of migrant labourers, and if these were not to be naïve normative positions, we had to examine the realities of existing provision and protection of migrant labourers, and the barriers to social protection that would have to be overcome.

EXISTING PROVISION AND PROTECTION: LAW, LABOUR INSPECTORS, LAWYERS AND UNIONS

The Indian State is the guardian of citizen rights and, in principle, offers protection to migrant construction workers through central and state legislation. In 2002, when our planning began, there was an abundance of legal protection *inter alia* under the Minimum Wages Act (1948); the Inter-State Migrant Workmen (*sic*) Act (1979); the Contract Labour System (Regulation & Abolition Act) (1970); the Bonded Labour System (Abolition) Act (1975); and for women, the Equal Remuneration Act (1976), the Construction Workers Act (1996) and the Factories Act (which, for example, set a handling limit for women of 20 kg), as well as through moves towards Indian ratification of the International Labour Office's (ILO) new convention on child labour. Moreover, the Trade Union Act (1926) and cooperative laws enshrined the right of labourers to organise. This legislation contained provisions relating not only to wages, but also health and safety, insurance against accident and injury, and the right to shelter and childcare.

The first point is that these normative frameworks and legal provisions were not, in fact, well-suited to the needs of migrant construction workers. There was a pervasive bias towards formal sector employment, which was recognised in fact through the belated Ministry of Labour policy decision to pay greater attention to the 91% of the 350 million Indian workers who comprised the unorganised sector;[5] and in new proposals such as a Welfare Fund for construction workers providing for accident victims, housing loans or children's education.[6] The Second National Commission on Labour also paid some attention to the 'unorganised sector' and sought a wide range of opinion on appropriate provisions (including from NGOs/unions working with *adivasi* migrant labourers) and in 2002 there was a draft bill for social security and minimum welfare.

The second, and most starkly obvious fact, however, was that the real issue was not formal legal provision, but institutional access and representation. The government Labour Departments (Central and State) are responsible for protecting workers' rights and resolving labour disputes. But at all sites of labour migration, labour inspectors were few even in relation to the government projects that they were supposed to monitor. Junior officers often allied with employers rather than workers and, as Breman points out, engagement in various forms of rent-seeking means that it is often in their interest to conceal rather than act on information on exploitation (1996: 52). *Adivasi* workers have minimal 'social access' to Labour Department officers at every level, and even diligent labour officers, union representatives and lawyers admitted to me that the procedural difficulties of pursuing cases through the labour courts were prohibitive for migrants, and that the Labour Department had little power or influence. Malpractice is anyway hard to detect: illegally low wages are hidden behind piece-rate practices, and compensation or accident claims are diffused by the absence of written agreements, by incomplete registers, and by a long chain of sub-contracting that separates the principal employers (the only actors against whom cases can be pursued) from both the worker and their responsibilities. Labour contractors who negotiate piece-rate work with a *mukkadam* (gang leader) can profess ignorance of the number of workers involved or their terms of employment. For all these reasons very few cases are in fact taken up, and these are mostly at the instigation of social activists or NGO/unions (see below). In practice, disputes rarely go to the Labour Court, and employers are rarely penalised.

Ironically, the State – the guarantor of labour rights – is probably also the largest employer of the most highly exploited *adivasi* migrant labour. Many of the buildings, public works or telecommunications schemes on which migrants worked are State projects contracted to construction companies. These larger established builders and contractors appeared to opt for the dependably compliant, vulnerable and hard-working labour force recruited through *mukkadams* from distant Bhil villages rather than the more independent labour available through urban daily labour markets (*nakas*). In 2001, the Bandhkham Mazdoor Sangathan (Construction Workers' Union, see below) investigated the case of private contractors laying a network of underground cables for the public sector telecommunications company Bharat Sanchar Nigam Ltd (BSNL) in Gujarat, employing around 25,000 labourers, many from *adivasi* districts. Recruited through *mukkadams* and sub-contractors (who take commissions), these labourers were paid piece-rates equivalent to as little as 30 or 40 *rupees* per day.[7] Meanwhile migrant workers received advances (Rs 200 per week) insufficient to meet basic nutritional requirements.[8] In the absence of worker records the practices of contractors on the State's own prestige projects entirely escape the surveillance of labour officers and the regulations of law.

In towns like Baroda, Kota, or Ratlam where we interviewed municipal authorities, officers admit that financial constraints exert pressure to keep project costs down. Given the relatively fixed costs of materials and transport, building contractors make their profits on the labour component through exploiting cheap migrant labour, and regard labour welfare as an avoidable cost or as 'the duty of the Labour Department'. Migrant welfare seems equally peripheral to the concerns of other departments – health, education, women and child development. Medical officers we spoke with in Baroda described *adivasi* migrants as an itinerant inaccessible population, unmindful of their own welfare, potentially bringing infections into the city (Denge fever, malaria, gastroenteritis and sexually transmitted diseases), and they favoured a 'containment approach' for infection including surveillance of migrants, blood testing and treatment at points of entry such as bus stations.

Adivasi migrants face harassment and forced eviction by municipal authorities and the police, for whom they are not regarded as citizens to be served, but a nuisance, whose settlements are illegal encroachments and eyesores. Migrants are 'a traffic hazard', the mayor of Baroda told Sajeev Gupta during the 1996 study. The municipality, he insisted, had no responsibility for those who did not live in the city

(Mosse et al 1997: 17). Labour officers and even labour lawyers also conveyed a general contempt for *adivasi* migrants (derogatorily *mama lok*), whose problems are of their own making, and whose lack of care for their own welfare, ignorance and 'bad habits' are embedded in their culture: 'they are all fond of intoxication ...'; 'they will not care to use [health] services ... just go here and there ...'; 'they are only habituated to construction work, digging, loading ...'; '[they are] easily satisfied with small compensations from employers ...' Even in the pervasive policy environment of reform, accountability or citizen rights, in 2002 it was clear that there was little chance that support for *adivasi* migrant interests could be pursued through formal processes and state departments. There was no space for Bhil migrants to appear as clients, service users or customers, let alone as rights-holding citizens, or members of political society.

There was hardly more hope for support from labour unions. The mainstream party-linked unions were as removed from *adivasi* migrants as rural NGOs or the state departments. The unions have been preoccupied in recent years with fighting widespread closures and retrenchment of workers in the chemical, steel and textile industries (with limited success). From their formal sector point of view, the union representatives I met felt that that the position of illiterate *adivasi* migrant labourers was simply hopeless and beyond reach; or they regarded migrants as competitors with local labour who drive wages down.[9]

Essentially, *adivasi* migrants lack representation; they fail to become regarded as a constituency for labour departments, unions, municipal authorities or political parties (they do not have votes, contribute revenue, or pay subscriptions); they are not consumers or customers; and their interests fail to become a weapon in the struggles within the professional political field (Bourdieu 1991: 188, cited in Gledhill 1994: 139). Making the conditions of migrant labour a moral and political issue is the basis upon which migrants might gain leverage by enrolling elite interests, through pro-poor coalitions, and from competition between elite groups (Moore and Putzel 2000). Today this is a remote prospect. For example, as Breman writes:

> The bureaucratic chief of Gujarat's labour inspectorate told me that state politicians ... constantly bothered him with requests for licences and exemptions from regulations, and supersession from taxation, but not one of them had ever questioned him on the non-implementation of minimal wages or of other labour laws that exist on paper for migrant workers. (2003: 284)

The more administrative and political boundaries migrant workers cross – between *taluk*, district and State – the weaker their political capacity becomes. They not only fail to become a constituency, they also fail to present a recognisable identity so as to press for services and support. They lose identity and minimal belongingness and become criminalised.

Amidst a sea of incapacity remarkable for its indifference to the condition of migrant labourers, there are isolated islands of initiative. First, in recent years a few individuals from left-wing unions have begun working informally with *adivasi* migrants, offering guidance at city *nakas* (morning labour markets) in order to provide a 'space for negotiation' to increase wages or win compensation. Another means to create this space has been through the surveillance of employers, the writing of 'fact finding reports', and publicising bad practices through the media. A few activists have pursued cases for wage payment or compensation through the Labour Commissioner and Labour Court.

The only labour union directly representing *adivasi* migrant labourers in the western region is the politically independent Amedabad-based Bandhkam Mazdoor Sangathan (BMS)('Construction Workers Union'), which is promoted by the NGO Developing Initiatives for Social and Human Action (DISHA). As Mr. Vipul Pandya informed me, enrolling *adivasi* migrants is difficult, and the BMS's membership (of 2,300) presently amounts to only 10% of these workers in Ahmedabad where work began. For the past decade the union has addressed the practical needs of migrants (including information, shelter, health, water, childcare and skill training); generated awareness of rights; and has pursued cases for the payment of withheld wages, compensation for injury, or the prevention of 'forced labour' or forcible eviction from urban settlements. The union's approach to supporting migrants combines welfare provision, rights awareness (through night schools, leafleting, training) and wider campaigns for state-level labour legislation, the implementation of minimum wages and welfare provisions for migrant workers (through *adivasi* migrant labourers' rallies and conventions). BMS runs child daycare centres and has persuaded the Ahmedabad Municipal Corporation to allocate one million *rupees* for a 'night shelter' (*renbasera*) to accommodate 300 migrant families. There are parallel lobbies for a training centre, mobile crèches, and education provision for migrants. Training programmes are run in collaboration with the Central Workers' Education Board and other agencies. The union has a women's wing and a female social worker. BMS receives over 50 group complaints a year relating to the nonpayment or underpayment of wages, and from 1993 to 2000 pressed for payment of Rs 6.05 million unpaid to 2,073 labourers.[10] The union recently successfully exerted pressure to have 'cabling work' included as a scheduled employment under the provisions of the Minimum Wages Act, and to have 'implementation in compliance with this Act' included as a clause in works contracts – including BSNL's – thus increasing the tender rate and wages for migrant workers, to Rs 82.60 per day.

VULNERABLE MIGRANTS AND INTIMATE EXPLOITERS: *MUKKADAMS* AND BUILDER PATRONS

Despite these efforts, most *adivasi* migrant workers lack awareness or representation. But the principle obstacle to pursuing migrants' basic rights is neither the lack of legislation nor the lack of diligence of labour officers, or even the limited reach of inventive unions and activists. Rather it is the self-interest of vulnerable migrant labourers themselves. The overriding problem faced by *adivasi* migrants is the lack of work itself. Since migrants are highly dependent upon their contractor-employers, they are most reluctant to take up cases against them, and almost bound to side with them in an externally instigated case. To complain or to organise is to forfeit employment, and few can afford to do so. Bhil migrants doggedly pursue security, not in alliance with progressive parts of the State, unions or NGOs, but through their patrons and exploiters. Like others facing chronic insecurity, Bhil migrants are tied into a 'Faustian bargain' in which they prioritise the maintenance of relationships with patrons who offer social protection in the short term, even though this limits their capacity for longer-term economic mobility (Wood 2003). Among their most intimate exploiters are their *mukkadams*, gang leaders, foremen or labour brokers.

Mukkadams

The *mukkadam* is probably a poor and indebted migrant's most crucial resource. A *mukkadam* is the route to work, the source of information on the availability of jobs and the trustworthiness of contractors. He is a guarantor and guardian whose role is continuously reinforced by the stories of cheating and non-payment that accompany every gang-labourer back to the village at the end of the season. *Mukkadams* are the intermediaries between contractors and labourers; in many cases contact with contractors is only through them. They recruit labour, arrange travel, assess/estimate the work, establish the prevailing rates (not in the *nakas* but at the worksites), negotiate wage rates and conditions, mediate advances from contractors (during the cultivation season), and make payments.

Mukkadams are mostly from the better-educated or connected Bhil villagers – skilled workers and supervisors who handle wages, attendance registers and deductions, and who have gradually built contacts with urban construction contractors for site-specific recruitment. They may, like Panji, son of a landed family, owe their success to kinsmen who are *mukkadams* and offer introductions to their *seths* (contractors). Or they may be among the few who have worked their own faltering way up the system.

> When he first arrived in Baroda from his village with his wife Shantaben 22 years ago Balabhai sold his shirt so he could break a coconut (an offering) for their future. They got work cart-pulling in a factory, then at a construction site. Winning favour with the *seth* Balabhai was later made a site watchman, then rose to a supervisor managing 22 workers and taking a commission. Through the mediation of a local *dada* he was able to get a place registered for himself in a *basti* (slum). But success had been bought through fidelity to this one *seth*, so when his contractor migrated to Dubai, Balabhai was back on the street as an unskilled labourer; that is, until he made contact with an associate of his old *seth* for whom he now began to work. Over the next 17 years he rose from supervisor to labour contractor (*mukkadam*) handling 35 workers and four masons, and providing a valued focal point in the city for migrants from his village. Although based in Baroda, securing his position as an effective recruiter requires that he invests in village-based networks, for instance through contributing to the *chandla* (an indigenous financial institution) or transporting workers back for village festivals. (Gupta 1997: 20–23)

Most critically, *mukkadams* provide assurances: to labour about reliable employers, and to employers about reliable labour-gangs. Successful *mukkadams* operate well-established networks in villages and cities; they are trusted with sizeable advances from contractors/employers for whom they secure a dependable supply of labour, tying workers (whose creditors they often already are) with advances as they make their rounds of Bhil villages amidst the acute need of the monsoon season or family crises. New *mukkadams* have to risk their own capital to pay the advances or loans that attract labour and create the relationships of dependence upon which recruitment is based, recovering the money from commissions from urban contractors. But there are dangers. In Khedpada, a village influential thought he could profit from labour recruiting, but later found that the contractor on whose behalf he had advanced Rs 15,000 failed to pay up. As this man struggled to recover his money from the labour-gang he not only lost his money, but also his reputation as a *mukkadam* with reliable connections to urban contractors and worksites (Shah 1997). Wary *mukkadams* know that contractors will promise much, but later make excuses in order to delay or withhold payment, saying the builder has not paid and so forth. But a *mukkadam* who recruits workers for a contractor that fails to pay wages is likely to be deserted by his clients, or even to be beaten up by his labourers. Even the best (most trustworthy) relationship with a contractor is subject to failure. When Bhalabai's second *seth* left for the US, suddenly the *mukkadam's* capacity to operate as a broker collapsed.

So *mukkadams* have variable power and effectiveness in negotiating the complexities of urban informal labour markets, and therefore have greater or lesser reputations as sources of work (and generous advances) amongst would-be migrants; as well as equally variable ability to negotiate complex village-based networks of dependency so as to deliver a reliable workforce to their contractor bosses. The number of labourers a *mukkadam* commands and the commissions with which he is rewarded grow with his reputation, usually built up over years. A powerful *mukkadam* like Prabhubhai, boasting a reliable gang of 60 workers, represents himself as a community benefactor, denying that he profits from commissions or advances. But even he is a small player in relation to *mukkadams* in Banswara who have become labour contractors in their own right, reportedly providing as many as 1,000 labourers to big building contractors in Surat (Gupta 1997: 3).

Builders, contractors and patrons

Builders and contractors themselves are also figures with whom Bhil migrants make a 'Faustian bargain'. Without question they exploit Bhil labour through low and irregular pay, advances and deductions; but they are an unavoidable part of the migrants' welfare system. For those directly recruited in groups from their villages, builders are the primary and most immediate source of support. They provide not only paid work, but also a place to stay, water, advances and agricultural loans in the monsoon season. Some builders we interviewed cultivate long-standing connections with villages from which they secure their labour force. They project themselves as benevolent patrons. But at the same time, none I met made any provision for children on their construction sites; moreover they tended to regard the employment of child labour on their sites as a benevolent 'help to poor families'. Most builders probably have insurance policies to cover injury/accident of employees, but do not register their workers, and resort to private hospitals to avoid official attention and compensation claims. If it came to a dispute they would resolve matters out of the court. The builder-labourer relationship is, then, a close patron-client one based on trust and from which rights, bargaining and negotiation are entirely absent.[11] While client labourers have the security of regular (low-paid) work, advances, and a place to stay, the builder has a dependable labour force obliged to supply/replace workers throughout the year, even during the agricultural season. The implication here is that builders/contractors are most unlikely to tolerate the unionisation or organisation of their labour of any kind.

Nakas

Bhil urban labour migrants who are not recruited as labour-gangs in their villages through *mukkadams*, or through kin-links and connections to builders and contractors (and who do not depend upon the security and advances that these patrons offer) try their luck at the bustling early morning casual labour markets or *nakas* dotted around cities such as Ahmedabad, Baroda or Surat, where subcontractors, masons, and others gather together labour-gangs. Depending on their location, between 50 and 700 people – overwhelmingly unskilled and *adivasi* – wait at a *naka* in the early morning looking for work. Some larger builders recruiting directly or through *mukkadams* were suspicious of the wage labour at *nakas,* disparaged as 'more aware' or 'lazy'; and most who do recruit through *nakas* prefer the more vulnerable distant *adivasi* migrants to local labourers. As contractors and migrants alike explain, by ten o'clock when most of the daily hiring is over, the unemployed at the labour markets are most likely to be local labourers (Mosse et al 1997: 17). To some extent individual *nakas* have a particular character, where migrants from one or two regions tend to predominate or certain specialist skills are found.

The flexibility, better and immediate pay (negotiated) of work through *nakas* have to be set against the greater risk of unemployment, conflict with resident casual labour, and the absence of patronage or a place to stay. The poor are forced to find security through membership in labour-gangs recruited through *mukkadams*/ contractors. Now, credit dependency and kinship do not exhaust the connections linking migrants together into gangs. Friendships of various kinds (including those with a shared history of migration) are also important. In any event, membership within a group is a ticket to finding regular, more secure (if under-paid) work and avoiding long unproductive periods. Those in the worst position of all are the very poor without access to groups, whose low credit rating or marginality to dominant kinship grouping means that they fail to forge a relationship with a *mukkadam* or to gain entry into migration groups, and who drift into the *nakas* in the hope of work.

AN *ADIVASI* MIGRANT LABOUR SUPPORT PROGRAMME

Those of us who worked in 2002–2003 to define a programme of support for *adivasi* migrants began with a number of assumptions based on research: first, that seasonal labour migration was central to *rural* livelihoods; secondly, that the position of *adivasi* migrants would only improve by confronting extreme exploitation and the realisation of basic rights; thirdly, that existing institutions responsible for labour welfare – the law, the Labour Departments, employers, NGOs and unions – were systematically failing to meet this need, and that only a handful of union activists had focused on their conditions of work. And fourthly, that these latter actions *had* successfully challenged exploitation by contractors/employers, securing recompense through labour courts or informal settlement, which confirmed the importance of organised union support to achieving welfare. Fifthly, experience showed that there were formidable obstacles to the organised protection of tribal migrants' rights to fair wages and humane working conditions, especially among the least visible and most vulnerable migrant workers recruited directly from villages through contractors and gang leaders. These workers depended upon *mukkadams* and contractors/builders, and had less bargaining power than daily wage labourers recruited through urban labour markets.

From this knowledge base came elements of a programme supporting *adivasi* migrants in 2002–2003 within the DFID-funded WIRFP project. As far as I was concerned, an appropriate strategy would involve interventions that addressed the immediate practical needs of migrant workers in the short term by piloting welfare services, while increasing awareness of rights and encouraging a very gradual process of unionisation. In the long-run, of course, the organisation of *adivasi* migrant labourers for the defence of their basic rights and the provision of welfare services guaranteed by law is the responsibility of labour unions, State government and employers, not a donor-funded project outside of mainstream government. However, DFID-WIRFP could have an important role in piloting initiatives with these agencies, building links, developing partnerships, supporting union organisation and promoting labour rights and welfare issues within the (international) construction industry under the rubric of 'socially responsible business.'

This programme had (in my view) to be collaborative, bringing together very different development approaches – governmental and NGO, service delivery, and the collective defence of rights. The approach would need to be threefold. First, the programme would work in regional city sites of migrant labour, starting where the chances of success were greatest, by extending the work of unions and NGOs amongst the relatively independent daily wage labourers at urban labour markets. Secondly, it would focus on home villages where the less accessible *mukkadam*-recruited, long-distance *adivasi* migrants could be supported. Thirdly, the programme would aim to enhance the visibility of migrant workers to those agencies charged with their welfare, and to build a constituency of support (through NGO and union lobbying, campaigning, networks, research and the media) so as to enable *adivasi* migrants themselves to become a constituency with enhanced political representation.

It is too early to comment on the nature of this work, but as the programme began in 2003 some of the issues and opportunities it presented came more clearly into focus. Let me briefly comment on a few of these.

Work with migrants began in villages where GVT had established a strong relationship with Bhil communities as an effective development agency and patron building.[12] First, the village was a place where labour migrants could inform project and union workers about their experiences and problems. Staff could identify 'route maps', to distinguish the different recruitment and remuneration systems, work conditions, or relations with local workers that are faced by construction workers, brick makers or agricultural workers, and which would demand different approaches. Such 'maps' could also differentiate the experiences of men and women, or workers and recruiters. Secondly, there were opportunities to extend or modify some of the project's existing work to meet the needs of migrants. Interventions in agriculture or micro-finance already promised to increase the returns on migration by weakening its link to high-interest debt; and modifying rules around deposits into village accounts or introducing systems for remittances or saving at migration sites could increase this potential. There was a need to extend community support for the old, the very young and the disabled who remain in the village with demanding responsibilities for cattle or childcare, and to facilitate access to existing State welfare programmes (for nurseries, grain banks, fodder/cattle care, residential schools, and low-cost food grain).

Thirdly, the village would be a site for developing rudimentary legal literacy, rights awareness and negotiation skills involving rights-focused NGOs and union workers (from BMS) who have the opportunity to develop contacts and establish centres in the rural hinterland. But given migrants' dependence upon existing systems of recruitment/patronage, project staff also incorporated village-based *mukkadams* into such training. Working with *mukkadams* presents both opportunities and risks. They do, in practice, represent workers' interests (otherwise they have no clients) and, in principle, enhancing *mukkadam* awareness of labour law, and their ability to negotiate wages and conditions, is key. For instance, it is they who can record the names of contractors or employers in cases of redress, and they who are familiar with the Labour Office and how to make insurance claims. But *mukkadams* also know that the key to their ability to negotiate better wages and work conditions is the protection of their *own* relationship and reputation with contractors. Some *mukkadams* are contractors' men, not easily enrolled onto a migrant labour support agenda or willing to act as advocates of migrant welfare. Still, a talented *mukkadam* who uses negotiation skills to bargain for better wages and conditions without risking loss of work becomes popular and successful, and can see the programme as a resource to this end.

From the migrant's point of view, information on work opportunities and the reliability of contractors/builders is more urgent than literacy in labour law. Fourthly, then, the WIRFP project begun to set up 'migrant information centres' (Palayan Suchna Kendra, or PKS) where migrants can register, located at points of convergence on migration routes (eg, key railway junctions), or more locally in Panchayat (local government) offices. PKS centres have several purposes, of which information on work and employers at different sites is only one. Through a 24-hour telephone link, a message recording and delivery system, and stamped postcards (issued to migrants), they enable communication between migrants and home villages, thereby addressing a significant source of uncertainty and anxiety. The centres can register outgoing migrants, record destinations, employer details or advances paid, issue employment books to record work, and link to official record systems at the block (sub-district) level, which in principle (more than in practice) track migrants and contractors from the area.

In a system in which exploitation depends upon anonymity and concealment, such information and surveillance is potentially a weapon for the weak.[13] However, it remains to be seen how useful these centres will be to migrants: whether they are located in the right places; whether the messaging system will work and be popular, and whether it will substitute for existing messaging via the *Baniya* moneylenders on market days (Gupta 1997: 2); whether PSKs will be able to acquire reliable information on work availability or contractor reputations, to provide usable legal information, or systems for sending money home and continuing payments into savings accounts while away; and, most importantly, whether *mukkadams* will regard these systems as an asset or a threat to their brokering livelihoods.

One thing was clear, and that is that measures to give migrants identities which appear official and can travel with them are important. So, from 2002, the WIRFP project began to develop photo-identity cards authorised by the panchayat *sarpanch* (in early 2003 some 15,000 had been distributed in 25 villages). The cards identify a worker's village of residence and savings group membership. They serve to symbolise a person's social capital (belonging, identity, support networks) when in distant urban centres, and to counter the widespread stigma and 'criminalization' of *adivasi* migrants. The cards identify migrant individuals as a *construction worker*, acknowledging overtly what is subjectively recognised, namely that it is they who have built the major buildings that mark the modern urban landscape of cities like Ahmedabad.

At a village meeting in 2003 *adivasi* men and women waved their cards enthusiastically. Precisely because they can relate to the experience of harassment and exploitation, and a wide variety of abuses (physical, sexual, financial) and false accusations that come with the lack of identity in urban places, these identity cards are hugely popular with migrants; although as yet untested. Of course, ultimately their effectiveness will depend upon their link to official systems of worker registration by employers and contractors, rather than to identities as project clients, self-help groups (SHGs) or Panchayat members.[14] Migrants I spoke with anticipated using the cards strategically (concealing them when looking for work, revealing them when facing difficulty). Encouragingly, the district administration is keen to add its authority to identity cards and to extend their use on a mass scale. Much needs to be monitored regarding these cards, in addition to the various individual and group accident/injury insurance schemes that are currently being extended to migrant workers by the project.

As well as information and identity, WIRFP and other agencies prioritise skill training to increase *adivasi* migrants' earnings through increased expertise, which appears to be in high demand. Increasing the number of skilled *adivasi* workers is important and has other knock-on effects since masons, plumbers, carpenters, machine operators and even *chowkidars* (watchmen) occupy pivotal roles as intermediaries and sub-contactors in the recruitment-information chain that links workers to builders, town to village. However, there are reasons why the simple logic of supply and demand does not apply. For one thing, long-range seasonal workers have to combine migration flexibly with cultivation on their own land. The poorer the household (in material and labour terms), the greater the need for flexibility in moving in and out of urban labour markets. This need for flexibility makes the acquisition of higher-earning skills that require unbroken periods of work, such as masonry, particularly difficult for the poor. Entry into the skilled labour market as a mason is only achieved through a long-term process of apprenticeship and subordination to a master mason 'guru', and requires continuity and the ability to endure low pay, unreasonable demands or humiliation. It is a kind of socialisation – the acquisition of a social identity rather than a technical skill – which involves costs that few can or are willing to bear. This, together with caste-group specialisation and recruitment into the segmented labour market, ties *adivasis* to the lowest-paid unskilled labour. This is especially true of private construction works where builders tend to minimise risk by recruiting through close kin-caste networks.

Perhaps the most important contribution of initiatives like WIRFP-GVT's would be to increase awareness of *adivasi* labour migration and to start promoting these workers as a constituency with various agencies. While this has (so far) been impossible in the urban destinations (where migrants remain marginal to the concerns of municipal authorities, health and labour officers), the rural administration in the *adivasi* districts of western India (especially western Madhya Pradesh) are waking up to the fact that labour migration is a majority concern and in fact critical to their own administrative success. During the recent years of severe drought (1999–2001), administrators explained, they were under pressure to minimise migration by generating employment. In fact, this became a critical indicator of the effectiveness of State interventions (including watershed development programmes). For monitoring purposes, information on work demand and availability (from various government schemes), and migration had to be gathered and passed up the system to the Panchayat or Relief Commissioner. It is not clear how these data were supposed to be used in generating employment at the village or district level, but the exercise had the significant effect of making at least some administrators realise that there was no way that State schemes *could* generate adequate employment, and that migration was in fact essential to government administration. Indeed, one block-level Panchayat CEO regarded migration as a sort of social safety valve. The government could not provide employment for all; and 'if everyone stayed in the village, law and order would be threatened; crime would rise'. Having long regarded helping migrants as only further encouraging migration – an indicator of administrative failure – administrators were now looking at ways to support migrants.

So, at least in some districts, officials are beginning to revise their idea of migration, and appear eager to collaborate with WIRFP in developing a migrant support programme in order to address, among other things, problems of health and education among children. The project built on this by organising village-based public events ('migrant *sammelan'),* involving gatherings of 500 or more returned migrants at which they speak about the problems of migration (or explain through improvised dramas) in front of district, Panchayat and police officials (Gupta report 2003). When development agencies begin to talk openly about supporting migrant livelihoods, and it becomes clear that this is not a threat to continued investment and employment-generation locally, then there is a new licence to speak publicly on these matters. Today, the topic of migration grabs attention in village meetings in Bhil villages. Discussions are animated, and tales of exploitation, of cheating contractors, or false accusations by police, flow quickly. When speaking about migration, as one staff member puts it, 'women show their faces and speak' (ie, unveil in the presence of outsiders).

RURAL COMMUNITIES IN THE CITY

Finding the dispersed and itinerant communities of *adivasi* migrants in the city, and addressing their needs, is altogether more difficult; even the fragments of village groupings of kin or savings groups are hard to locate. Initiatives here rely upon networks within the construction workers' union, the BMS. But the experience of BMS union workers is that it is very difficult to organise *adivasi* migrant labourers for the defence of their basic rights. The union has little access to those labourers who are recruited in gangs directly from their villages, and are tied into deep relations of patronage and dependence. In the more accessible but highly competitive city *nakas,* the risk of losing employment as a result of attempts to negotiate wages is great. For now, enhancing a sense of identity, dignity and self-respect among migrants as workers ('I am a construction labourer, there is someone behind me, someone to help me, somewhere to take my problems') is more feasible than increasing wages through negotiation. Union workers therefore operate through informal guidance rather than formal organisation and, in the first place, address immediate welfare needs relating to shelter, water, health, childcare and education. The DFID-WIRFP programme aims to support the extension of these activities.

Shelter is often a priority. I noted above that the BMS union was successful in getting municipal allocation of land for a night shelter, and in April 2003 I sat with a group of underemployed *adivasi* migrants and BMS members, beside makeshift shelters on land under an Ahmedabad flyover, on which (with BMS help) they had obtained the right to stay, and hence had relief from harassment. Worksites and migrant encampments are widely dispersed in the cities and so also should be the provision of services – health camps, crèches and so on. However, official support for the provision of shelter (and services) for migrants often stems from the desire to give migrants a 'permanent place' as a means to regulate and control what is viewed as an unruly and troublesome itinerant population littering the pavements, thronging the railway station, causing sanitation problems, or bringing disease. (Still others resist the idea of a 'permanent place' for *adivasi* migrants fearing encroachment and that 'temporary shelters' would become permanent settlements in the city.) BMS workers rightly emphasise the need for mobile, dispersed and improvised services – that is, mobile crèches and mobile low-cost shops – rather than standardised packages, which also provide a means of keeping up day-to-day contact and sharing information, especially on who is coming and going from villages. Frequently *adivasi* migrants themselves come up with flexible low-cost practical solutions to problems.

CONCLUSION

Seasonal labour migration is irreversibly part of the lives and livelihoods of many of the poorest sections of rural India. Labour migration is not just a means to cope with below subsistence agriculture and debt, but may, as in Bhil western India, have become the only means by which valued agrarian lifestyles can be reproduced. For a few, migration is a route of upward social and economic mobility; but for the vast majority migration not only perpetuates debt and dependence, but exposes the poorest to extreme hardship and cruel exploitation. Despite the growing significance of labour migration, especially for informal urban and construction work, rural development agencies – State and NGO – have yet to regard this seasonal flow of workers as anything but a problem to be stopped. Meanwhile, those institutions mandated to protect vulnerable informal workers – labour departments, unions, the law – have largely failed to do so. Instead, *adivasi* migrant labourers depend for their work and welfare upon agents, brokers and contractors who are also their most intimate exploiters.

A new initiative with Gramin Vikas Trust backed by DFID as part of its WIRFP project and framed within the now favoured 'rights based approach' to development began in 2002–2003 to address the issue of support for *adivasi* migrant workers in western India. What was proposed was a difficult and ambitious collaborative programme involving State agencies, various departmental authorities, NGOs, unions and business. Like most development initiatives this began as a set of ideas, narratives, and storylines to convince and enrol supporters. It remains to be seen how these policy ambitions will connect to the different (often contradictory) interests and incentives of the several agencies involved, and whether these will render what is an eminently worthwhile initiative practicable. There are certain to be challenges. While anthropologists may now accept the mobility of populations, the institutions of government and rural development remain structured around fixed populations and are still poorly equipped to deal with boundary crossing – a fact which makes labour migrants a particularly invisible and exploitable section of society. At the same time, macro-economic policy encourages a form of capitalist development that creates a growing mass of footloose unskilled labour existing 'outside the law and beyond the benign reach of State agencies [and] subject to repression and exploitation in a capitalist framework remarkable for its nakedness and rawness' (Breman 2003: 284).

Notes

[1] This chapter arises from my work as a consultant for the UK Department for International Development (DFID) and its Western India Rainfed Farming Project (WIRFP) implemented by Gramin Vikas Trust (GVT), and draws on the contributions of former co-researchers Sanjeev Gupta and Vidya Shah. I am grateful for

212 DAVID MOSSE, WITH SANJEEV GUPTA AND VIDYA SHAH

support from the GVT project team, especially Yash Kanungo, Udailal Gurjar, Akhilesh Parey, Divarkar, Meera Shahi, K.S. Sandhu, and P.S. Sodhi, and to consultant colleagues Steve Jones and Andrew Shepherd, among many others. For insights into migrant labour I am indebted to Mona Mehta, Nimita Bhatt, Minali Ben and Ramilaben at SEWA, Vipul Pandya (BMS), Rohit, Kanubhai Brahmabhatt and K. Sagar, and for the support of Jitendra Agarwal (IAS, GoMP). The views expressed here are my own and do not reflect those of DFID, GVT or the WIRFP project. A longer version of this paper appeared in the *Economic and Political Weekly*, 40(28) 9 July, 2005 3025–3038.

2 Only 7% in DISHA's Ahmedabad study were skilled workers (2002: 46). (See DISHA 2002: 10, cf.TRU 1998: 5).

3 Udailal Gurjar 'Migrant Labour Support Programme in Ratlam for Sustainable Livelihood' (in Hindi). Handwritten report on migrants' perspectives on their needs, WIRFP-GVT, Ratlam.

4 The complex and contradictory effects of unequal and individualised earning from migration on household entitlements, on marriage relations, on the division of households, on age and gender hierarchies, and on women's roles and entitlements are discussed in Mosse et al (2002: 81–83).

5 www.indianngos.com/issue/other/labour/politicies.htm (accessed April 2002).

6 Funded by a 1–2% cess on total project cost – part of the move to implement the Construction Workers Welfare Act.

7 The Bandhkam Mazdoor Sangathan (BMS) received complaints against BSNL's contractors regarding the non-payment of Rs 12, 17,445 wages to a total of 876 labourers (letter to Dr Mishra from BMS, 21.3.2002).

8 Letter from BMS General Secretary re: Abolition of 'forced labour' of workers in laying underground cable line for Bharat Sanchar Nigam Ltd (BSNL), Gujarat.

9 In Ratlam I spoke with representatives of the Bhartiya Mazdoor Sangh (BMS), the Chemical Labour Union, and the Indian National Trade Union Congress (District chairman).

10 Migrant Construction Labourers' Welfare Activities, 2000. Report.

11 However, if an unknown builder comes to a village looking for workers, Bhils themselves demand advances against the uncertainly of work and payment.

12 For an account of this rural development programme see Mosse 2005.

13 For example, any worker who can show completion of 90 days of work is entitled to benefits enshrined in central labour acts. But even if employment books and the like are not immediately effective in bringing justice (contractors are unlikely to agree to sign a work schedule), the practice of recording work and identifying employers has important educational and 'empowering' effects (and is perhaps also a means to develop functional literacy/numeracy skills).

14 At present, the cards emphasise the project as 'guarantor/guardian', and SHG credit discipline. The 'conditions' attached to the card include maintenance of group savings; timely loan repayment and so on.

References

BMS (Bandhkam Mazdoor Sangathan) *Annual Reports, 1999, 2000.*
Breman, J (1996) *Footloose Labour*, Cambridge: Cambridge University Press.
Breman, J (2003) *The Labouring Poor in India: Patterns of Exploitation, Subordination, and Exclusion*, Delhi: Oxford University Press.

Bourdieu, P (1991) *Language and Symbolic Power,* Cambridge: Polity Press.
DISHA (Developing Initiatives for Social and Human Action) team (2002) *The Migrant Tribal Construction Labourers in Ahmedabad: A Study* [Originally in Gujarati, 1994, translated 2002], Himmatnagar: DISHA.
Gadgil, M and Guha, R (1995) *Ecology and Equity: The Use and Abuse of Nature in Contemporary India,* London and New York: Routledge.
Gardner, K and Osella, F (2003) 'Migration, modernity and social transformation in South Asia: an overview', *Contributions to Indian Sociology,* (NS) 37(1&2) v–xxviii.
Gidwani, V and Sivaramakrishnan, K (2003) 'Circular migration and the spaces of cultural assertion', *Annals of the Association of American Geographers,* 93(1) 186–213.
Gledhill, J (1994) [2000] *Power and its Disguises: Anthropological Perspectives on Politics,* London: Pluto.
Gupta, S (1997) 'Strategy for survival: migration study of the Bhil adivasis: pattern and intensity; labour market appraisal', KRIBP/West & CDS, Swansea.
Hardiman, D (1987) 'The Bhils and Sahukars of Eastern Gujarat', in Guha, R (ed) *Subaltern Studies V: Writings on South Asian History and Society,'* New Delhi: Oxford University Press, 1–54.
Hardiman, D (1996) *Feeding the Baniya: Peasants and Usurers in Western India,* Delhi: Oxford University Press.
Moore, M and Putzel, J (2000) 'Thinking strategically about politics and poverty', *IDS Working Paper 101,* Brighton: Institute of Development Studies.
Mosse, D (2002) 'Adivasi migrant labour support: a collaborative programme', Consultant's report, Western India Rainfed Farming Project, DFID, India, May, 1–46.
Mosse, D (2003) 'Supporting rural communities in the city: Adivasi migrant labour support programme', Consultant's report, Western India Rainfed Farming Project, DFID, India, May, 1–36.
Mosse, D (2005) *Cultivating Development: An Ethnography of Aid Policy and Practice,* London: Pluto Press.
Mosse, D, Gupta, S, Mehta, M, Shah, V and Rees, J (1997) 'Seasonal labour migration in tribal (Bhil) western India', report to DFID-India, New Delhi (KRIBP Working Paper, Centre for Development Studies University of Wales, Swansea).
Mosse, D, Gupta, S, Mehta, M, Shah, V, Rees, J and the KRIBP Project Team (2002) 'Brokered livelihoods: debt, labour migration and development in tribal western India', *Journal of Development Studies,* 38(5) 59–88.
SEWA (2000) *Labouring Brick by Brick: A Study of Construction Workers,* Ahmedabad: SEWA Academy.
Shah, V (1997) 'Khedpada – a case study in migration', report for KRIBP seasonal labour migration study.
TRU (Trust for Reaching the Unreached)(1998) *Study of Construction Labourers in Vadodara City,* Baroda: Trust for Reaching the Unreached.
Wood, G (2003) 'Staying secure, staying poor: "the Faustian bargain"', *World Development,* 31(3) 455–71.

10 'Moving Up and Down Looking for Money': Making a Living in a Ugandan Refugee Camp[1]

Tania Kaiser

INTRODUCTION

Denied the right to freedom of movement, constrained by an uncertain security situation, frustrated by negligible income-generating opportunities and reductions in food aid, how do refugees survive in camps in Uganda? This chapter, based on ethnographic fieldwork in Sudanese refugee settlements, considers some of the strategies employed by refugees to overcome the legal, political and other obstacles to social and economic survival.

Contrary to popular opinion in many northern States, the vast majority of the world's southern refugee population remain in their regions of origin, moving across the nearest available border when this becomes a necessity. They are subsequently obliged to try to survive in what are often impoverished and sometimes inhospitable environments. In the early stages of a refugee emergency, generous and timely responses are frequently made by the citizens and communities of the countries to which refugees flee from conflict and other horrors. Nevertheless, the extent to which refugees are able to reestablish themselves varies widely, and depends to a large extent on the political and institutional responses made by governments and assistance-providing institutions. Increasingly, once they have crossed an international border, refugee populations remain in exile for protracted periods with no improvement in the conditions from which they fled.

Refugees in the developing world thus tend to live on the margins both literally and metaphorically. Frequently restricted to border regions, they are discouraged, via a range of political and institutional mechanisms, from fully integrating into the host society. Rather, in order to contain and control them, and to maximize the likelihood of their eventual repatriation, host States often insist that they live separately in officially recognised refugee camps and settlements.

This chapter focuses on the experience of some Sudanese communities who have taken refuge in neighbouring Uganda, where they are obliged to live in formal refugee settlements, and on their efforts to overcome consequent constraints on their livelihood activities. Much is routinely made, in refutation of the notion that refugees are by definition prone to dependency, of the 'agency' and 'coping strategies' of refugees. This chapter sets out to show that their best efforts may succeed despite, rather than because of, the legal and institutional structures purportedly designed to protect and support them. It also shows that social and economic processes are inextricably intertwined, and that understanding the values and priorities of refugee communities with respect to subsistence issues must incorporate an awareness of their sociocultural ramifications.

The field research on which this chapter is based was carried out over nine years in refugee settlements in northern Uganda. Ethnographic research was conducted in Kiryandongo Refugee Settlement in Masindi District in 1996–1997, with follow-up visits in 2002 and 2004. Work in other locations has taken the form of shorter research trips to settlements in Adjumani, Moyo, Kitgum (now Pader) and Arua Districts.

REFUGEE LIVELIHOODS

In the first phase of a refugee emergency, the main concern is to address the immediate needs of what are often traumatised and debilitated populations. After initial reception by the host communities, the governments of host States necessarily take an interest in arriving refugees, often appealing for assistance to the international community. As time passes and the situation changes, analysts point to the need for humanitarian and other actors to work towards saving not only the lives, but also the livelihoods of refugee groups (Lautze 1997).

To this end, attempts have been made to apply the learning gleaned from experience in supporting livelihoods among rural populations to the predicament of refugees and other conflict-affected populations. One of the most influential models has been that of the

British government's Department for International Development (DFID 1999). Sustainable Livelihood Frameworks (SLF), which broadly address the context in which people are operating; the diverse resources, assets or forms of capital to which they have access; the institutional or policy environments which mediate these; and the livelihood strategies and outcomes that result from such negotiations (DFID 1999, Schafer 2002, Scoones 1998).

One of the objectives of this chapter is to explore the ways in which a hostile or unconducive institutional or political environment can limit refugees' ability to exploit resources or assets to which they have access. In other words, the extent to which refugees' ability to pursue successful livelihood strategies during their time in exile is contingent not only on the resources and capacity they are able to mobilise, but also on the conditions generated by the policy and practice of host States. Refugees' own responses are also shaped by the experience that has brought them to the present point and their hopes and aspirations for the future.

Communities that have been exposed to conflict and displacement inevitably face particular challenges with respect to their livelihood options. While these conditions are ongoing, the sustainability of livelihoods has to take second place to the survival of individuals and communities in conditions that are far from optimal. A balance between the immediate needs of a population and their hopes for the future has to be found. As Jacobsen puts it, 'In communities facing conflict and displacement, livelihoods comprise the ways in which people access and mobilise resources that enable them to increase their economic security and thereby reduce the vulnerability created and exacerbated by conflict, and pursue goals necessary for their survival and possible return' (Jacobsen 2002: 4). Understanding precisely how people are able to survive, and finding ways to support them in their attempt, are not straightforward tasks.

Sustainable Livelihood Frameworks seek to elucidate the process by emphasising the interrelatedness of economic and other factors – such as the social and the political – that contribute to the establishment of viable livelihoods. DFID's SLF model identifies a diverse range of 'livelihood assets' on which individuals and communities may draw. These include what they describe as 'capital' in various forms – human, natural, financial, social and physical (DFID 1999).[2] Critics adopting a political economy approach have noted that the 'political capital' of communities is critical to their capacity to achieve adequate livelihoods, and that their room to manouevre or ability to mobilise assets may be significantly limited if they are powerless in a given situation (Collinson 2003). Van Hear has further shown that class, 'used as a shorthand for endowments of different forms of capital – economic, social, cultural, symbolic and human' (Van Hear 2004: 1) is extremely influential in 'shaping the forms, patterns and impacts' of forced migration, and this also has implications for livelihoods.

LOSS AND LIVELIHOODS

Becoming a refugee can be characterised as a process of loss: loss of home and country, of people, of protection, of familiar surroundings and activities which have previously been mundane, of networks of social relations and institutions, of a certain kind of identity and, perhaps most immediately, of wealth and property including land, livestock, cash and other assets.

For people who are forced to flee suddenly in the face of human rights abuses or outright conflict, pausing to collect their belongings is rarely an option.[3] For one of the populations with whom this chapter is concerned, a group of predominantly Acholi refugees from southern Sudan's eastern Equatoria who fled to Uganda in 1989, this was certainly the case. One elderly teacher, John Oryem, describing his third flight to Uganda, said, 'We ran when the children were not even dressed. There was no time to look for a shirt for the small ones, we could hear the guns and it was enough.' (Kaiser 1999: 75). Others who had packed some possessions were ultimately obliged to abandon their belongings for the sake of speed. It was not only property that was risked in this way. As one young woman explained, 'There was no time even to look for your own children. If there were children near you, good, you picked them up and ran with them. You hoped that someone had picked up your children.' (Kaiser 1999: 79)

Refugees quite literally experience displacement as a process of impoverishment. If they have not already lost their material possessions or seen them destroyed prior to flight, they may be obliged to abandon all but the most easily portable items when they leave their homes. They may be forced to give up some or all of what they have been able to carry as they negotiate with border guards for entry into the country of exile. Such losses, which will vary significantly depending on socioeconomic status in the country of origin, have immediate and direct consequences for refugees' prospects for reestablishing themselves in the short, medium and long-term.

However, the objects that have been lost – the land, livestock, businesses, houses, vehicles, equipment, clothes and personal property – are not all that has been lost. Gone too, are the ways in which these items were formerly used, managed, negotiated, transacted and understood. These intangible losses speak to the specific social networks, relationships, authority structures and institutions through which people previously engaged with each other and their environment on a day-to-day basis.

As other writers have shown, material and non-material losses of different kinds are inseparable from each other in the sense that they are experienced relationally. John Davis (1992) describes how losses of various kinds can be understood as a process of 'cultural bereavement'. Peter Loizos (1981) shows how lamenting the loss of land and material wealth can be understood as symbolic of the loss of a web of intangible relations, practices and norms which it is much more difficult to articulate.

Recognition of the loss of this almost indefinable sociocultural texture of social life can, however, lead to a mistaken assumption by those providing assistance that refugee 'communities' have been rendered socially bankrupt by displacement, and thus are incapable of facing up to the challenges of exile, both social and material. In the worst cases, this leads to them being dealt with in a way that both assumes an incapacity to manage their own affairs and, arguably, generates dependence on relief assistance (Harrell-Bond 1986).

Typically, it is far from the case that refugees are so negatively affected by their displacement losses that they are unable to respond or mobilise their remaining assets or resources by seeking effective protection and livelihood strategies, even in the presence of enabling humanitarian interventions. Rather, refugees have little choice but to draw on their energy and innovation to overcome the difficulties they face as a result of their displacement. Budget constraints, political impediments and other obstacles mean that refugees would surely perish if they relied exclusively on the largesse of aid providers. Unfortunately, as things stand, they must also respond to the difficulties created by the limiting ways in which they are received by host governments and the international and national organisations that are mandated to protect and assist them.

When people become refugees, there are clear ways in which the losses they have incurred can undermine their livelihood prospects. Having suffered the loss of jobs and of trading and patronage networks, they also lack familiarity with the land or territory on which they are now expected to make a living. These are serious challenges for farmers, traders, businessmen and professionals. This being the case, one might expect that institutional responses would address the need to counteract such disadvantages, perhaps by expediting the integration of the newcomers into the pre-existing livelihood networks of the host population; this occurs infrequently. Instead, the politics of refugee reception and management come into play, and refugees often find themselves further limited and economically disadvantaged by being forced to take up residence in isolated rural refugee settlement schemes.

In isolated and poorly connected refugee camps, refugees are further stripped of their capacity to subsist without external support. Denied the right to move freely and, consequently, to find employment or access adequate agricultural land, they find it impossible to meet all their needs on their own. Under these circumstances, even if refugees enjoyed access to a full range of natural, economic, human and social capital resources (Scoones 1998), they might find themselves prevented from mobilising them to positive effect. Their particular vulnerability is therefore just as much a consequence of the political response to their arrival and its operational consequences, as it is an innate function of their original dispossession (Harrell-Bond 1999, Kaiser et al 2005). What they are able to achieve is a product of the interaction between their own efforts and the limitations of the local political economy (Schafer 2002: 30, citing Le Billon 2000). When the security situation is also uncertain, as is often the case in refugee populated areas, their scope is further limited.

Refugee groups are, of course, not homogeneous. Just as there will have been socio-economic differentiation within communities before flight, so will there be in exile. Individuals' fortunes may rise or fall depending on their particular circumstances and the opportunities available to them in the new environment. It is often the case, however, that the very poorest have the fewest opportunities to improve their situation in the context of flight and exile. Additionally, as Chambers has noted, it is also the case that the poorest hosts are the least well-placed to overcome any livelihood challenges resulting from the arrival of refugees (Chambers 1986)[4].

Refugees are disadvantaged compared to nationals – even of the poorest developing countries – in that they often do not enjoy the fundamental rights that would give them the autonomy to make a reasonable living. Kibreab (2003) argues that it is specifically because refugee populations do not 'belong' in a legal and political sense, and do not enjoy the benefits of nationality and citizenship as nationals do, that they are unable to 'recoup the losses they incur in connection with displacement and to construct sustainable livelihoods in countries of asylum' (Kibreab 2003: 57).

The remainder of the chapter explores some of the issues introduced above, in relation to the experience of Sudanese refugees in Uganda. The next section briefly sketches the Ugandan refugee situation before considering obstacles faced by refugees in trying to pursue effective livelihood strategies. Subsequently, we consider the livelihood activities and strategies employed by refugees in response to such obstacles. Finally, in recognition of the intimate relationship between the social and the economic/material conditions of life, the final section explores some of the ways that social and economic strategies interplay, and to what effect.

UGANDA'S REFUGEE SITUATION

Uganda and Sudan have a long history of hosting each other's refugees. The drawing of the international border between the two countries by colonial authorities divided peoples who had been used to mixing freely. While this continued to some extent, the existence of a border also made it possible for nationals of each country to seek sanctuary on the other side when their own States were affected by political conflict. Many Sudanese spent much of the 1960s in exile in Uganda, returning home only after the signing of the 1972 Addis Ababa Agreement, which was meant to ensure long-lasting peace in Sudan. By the end of the 1970s, perceived supporters of the defeated Ugandan government of Idi Amin were chased into exile in Sudan, where they remained until war recommenced there in the late 1980s. They were joined in their journey back to Uganda by large numbers of Sudanese fleeing renewed violence, many of whom remain in Uganda today.[5]

The 198,000 Sudanese refugees in Uganda today live mainly in the border region, where they are confined to a series of refugee settlements by the government of Uganda (UNHCR 2004). These settlements are serviced by the United Nations High Commissioner for Refugees (UNHCR) and its implementing non-governmental organisations (NGOs) and governmental partners. The long duration of their stay has led to, among other things, the introduction of a 'Self Reliance Strategy' (SRS) for refugees. This initiative, which aspires to the delivery of developmental benefits for refugees and their hosts, is discussed in more detail elsewhere (Dryden-Petersen and Hovil 2003, Kaiser et al 2005 and Kaiser 2005). Broadly speaking, the SRS envisages refugee populations achieving self-sufficiency on the basis of agricultural production and other income generating activities. The objective is thus a situation where they are no longer in need of direct assistance in meeting their immediate and wider needs. Agricultural land has been allocated to refugees for this purpose, albeit often in locations far from markets and disadvantaged by environmental conditions. It should be acknowledged that by offering cultivable land to refugees, the government of Uganda has exceeded the generosity shown by other refugee-hosting States in the region and the continent. Like the Ugandan population, however, the refugees living in the north of the country have been heavily constrained by ongoing insecurity related to the activities of a number of rebel groups, most infamously the Lord's Resistance Army (LRA).

Many of the people of the Kiryandongo Refugee Settlement have managed to achieve some degree of self-sufficiency and the majority, unlike residents of many other settlements, no longer receive food rations from the World Food Programme (WFP). This is partly explained by the fact that Kiryandongo is one of the only settlements for Sudanese refugees in Uganda that has never experienced any insecurity, and it also benefits from relatively fertile land.[6] The livelihoods of its inhabitants were put under serious pressure in 2002, however, after the arrival at Kiryandongo of thousands of their countrymen, displaced from another settlement closer to the rebel-affected border area. The inhabitants of most of the border settlements continue to receive a proportion of the full food ration, and insist that the conditions do not exist for them to achieve self-sufficiency.

Their explanations are broadly convincing. Refugee leaders argue that food rations are inadequate and unreliable and that they are phased-out before people have become established. They complain that the refugees are unable, on the basis of agricultural activity on relatively small plots of land of variable quality, to generate enough produce to meet their basic food needs as well as to fund necessities such as health care, educational expenses and non-food items such as salt and soap. Consequently, they declare themselves unable to cope with unexpected or irregular needs triggered by emergencies or external shocks.

Conditions and experience vary widely from one settlement to another, as well as within settlements. It is the case, however, that in several settlements land quality is known to be extremely poor. Where plots were allocated some years ago, family increases have led to pressure on land that was already exhausted from repeated use. When families are able to generate a surplus, their isolation from markets and the prohibitive cost of transporting produce means that they are obliged to trade with local merchants on disadvantageous terms

(Kaiser et al 2005). Furthermore, many families host unregistered relatives who receive no food aid, either because they have failed to negotiate the bureaucratic system properly, or because they have illegally transferred from another settlement, in many cases because of increased insecurity in those locations.

Given these conditions, men, women and children in Ugandan refugee settlements are engaged in a continual and very active search for income-generating opportunities. In the words of many of them, they spend time 'moving up and down looking for money' in various ways, and draw on a range of resources to do so. In the next section, I sketch briefly three of the structural obstacles to 'finding money', and go on to show some of the ways that people nevertheless contrive to make some sort of a living in Ugandan refugee settlements.

OBSTACLES TO 'FINDING MONEY'

Sudanese refugees' livelihood strategies are limited by the fact that they do not enjoy legal rights in Uganda, as a result of insecurity in the north of the country, and by their exclusion from socioeconomic integration with the host population.

When refugees cross a border, fleeing either their own government or a non-State actor from whom their government is unable to protect them, they find themselves without the protection of a nation-state. The 1951 United Nations Convention Relating to the Status of Refugees and the Statute of UNHCR mandate international protection for refugees, which they attempt to do by putting pressure on host States to respect the rights of refugees. In many cases, including Uganda, this effort is only partly successful and refugees frequently do not enjoy rights in some important respects (Verdirame, Harrell-Bond et al 2005).[7]

In Uganda, the requirement that refugees must live in government-sanctioned settlements in locations of its choosing, means that refugees do not enjoy freedom of movement. This has serious negative consequences for their livelihood outcomes. Not only are refugees unable to choose where they wish to live, they are technically not allowed to take up opportunities to access fertile land if it is available to them outside of the settlements, nor to move freely to access other employment opportunities. The requirement that they live in a settlement and leave it only when equipped with a government-issued travel document means that one of the most important livelihood strategies available to the poor – mobility – is denied to them.

Northern Uganda, where settlements for Sudanese refugees are located, has been in the grip of a series of bitter conflicts for 18 years, with grave consequences for the economy. Developmental activity has been almost entirely forestalled there, and huge numbers of Ugandans have become internally displaced as a result of the conflict between the government of Uganda and the Lord's Resistance Army (LRA). Travel to northern districts is perilous, as the LRA conduct guerrilla warfare and terrorise the population. Government forces, too, have been accused of human rights abuses against civilians (HRW 2003). All civilians living in the conflict zone, whether Ugandan or Sudanese, have been affected, some suffering violent attacks, rapes, abductions, maiming, killings and property theft. Almost the entire border region has been caught up in the violence; and for the Sudanese, reaching the border or attempting to carry out trade across it has become virtually impossible. Trade and other economic activity within central-northern Uganda – an area which is home to people with numerous linguistic and ethnic affiliations with some of the refugees and which would, therefore, be an obvious focal point for their livelihood activities – is also severely curtailed.

Some refugees who were originally registered in settlements in the heart of the conflict zone have fled and taken up residence illegally in other settlements. In order to access food rations to which they are entitled, they are obliged to make a dangerous monthly journey back to their original settlements to collect them. For the Sudanese Acholi in particular, this can be a risky enterprise, since, sharing an ethnicity with many of the LRA rebels, they are subjected to suspicion and some hostility when they move around.

Finally, there are livelihood obstacles related to the refugees' status as outsiders or newcomers to Uganda, which are unmitigated due to their exclusion from local links and integration with the local population. As foreigners and refugees, even educated people are largely excluded from the employment opportunities they had access to at home. Government or civil service posts are no longer open to them, with the occasional exception of poorly-paid teaching jobs. 'Out of place' as they are, refugees have highly restricted access to local business or patronage systems which might bring them some income-generating opportunities.

For peasant farmers too, the context has changed to their disadvantage. In Uganda they do not enjoy ownership of the land they farm, and are restricted from accessing additional land if what they have is insufficient in any respect. They also lack the deep and intimate knowledge of the land that they enjoyed in their home country. Unfamiliar agricultural practices, a function of the way the land has been allocated and is used locally, may further reduce their capacity and opportunities.

REFUGEE RESPONSES

Despite, or even because of, the kinds of limitations discussed above, refugees living in settlements in Uganda have no option but to do what they can to make a living for themselves and their families. While some, such as relative newcomers to the Imvepi Refugee Settlement in Arua District, continue to receive a full food ration from the World Food Programme (WFP), many do not. In all cases, the inadequacy of the ration, even when it is received on time, make additional economic activity a necessity. Given the environmental constraints within which people live, the kinds of opportunities open to them are generally small-scale and modest (for similar findings see Horst 2005). While some strategies rely on finding a niche in the limited market that exists within and around refugee settlements, others are more controversial and require refugees to bend, break or ignore rules, laws or social conventions in order to generate some small amount of profit. This can involve reinventing themselves and their social and economic roles by expanding their sphere of influence and activity. What follows are a number of illustrative examples of these livelihood strategies.

Where refugee farmers are able to generate a surplus, they sell off agricultural produce to local traders and middle-men. Sudanese refugees, like the rural Ugandans with whom they live, grow maize, sorghum, cassava, beans, sesame and vegetables, depending on soil conditions and other environmental factors. In Masindi, maize is the most common cash crop. A minority of refugee farmers in Arua have managed to break into the tobacco trade and sell their produce to firms such as British-American Tobacco. In most cases refugees, like small-scale Ugandan farmers, are unable to produce crops in sufficient quantity or to transport their produce to market centres where they would get a better price for it. In Kiryandongo, traders enter the settlement with lorries at harvest time and buy at predictably low prices. Even those refugee farmers who realise that they could sell more dearly if they were able to wait for the rush to pass, are usually unable to do so as their cash needs are pressing.

After farming their own plot of land when it is available, by far the most common economic activity carried out by both refugee men and women is 'piece work' or '*leja-leja*'. This is a form of day-labour – usually but not exclusively agricultural work – for which refugees are paid in cash or kind. Poor Ugandans also do this kind of work, which may involve setting out from home alone as a 'hoe for hire', or being part of an organised workgang on a larger farm or project. While ubiquitous, this kind of work represents a risk for refugees since payment is not made until the work is completed, and sometimes not even then. Employers are well aware that refugees have little recourse to the police if they are unpaid or underpaid, and some exploit this vulnerability. Refugees may be reluctant to involve the police if they have travelled outside a settlement without the required permit, and many feel that the police would in any case not attend without a bribe, which they are unable to raise. Nevertheless, for many physically fit and able refugees, 'leja-leja' represents a reasonably reliable way of accessing small amounts of food or cash, albeit in exchange for hard labour.

Some refugees have been able to establish themselves as petty traders either within settlements or in local non-refugee markets. Women tend to restrict themselves to selling commodities such as oil, tomatoes, onions, greens, snacks and kerosene which they have bought, made or grown in refugee markets, since market dues are generally lower here than on the outside. They may travel outside the settlement to source goods such as dried fish, which they then re-sell in tiny quantities back inside it. A small number of traders, usually male, accumulate enough capital to run market stalls selling clothes or other manufactured goods in local and refugee markets. Each settlement also has a number of small shops or kiosks, selling a variety of goods including soap, matches, biscuits, candles, drinks and other small items. Start-up capital for such enterprises is constantly sought by refugee men, since to construct and stock a wooden structure requires more cash than most people ever have available.

A related activity, since it also mainly takes place in the central or market area of settlements, is the running of teashops and cooked-food eating houses. These are almost always run by women and, for many of the cultural groups present in Ugandan refugee settlements, represent a break with normal social behaviour for them. In the home area of the Sudanese Acholi, for example, it is reported that this would not be considered a respectable activity for Acholi women. In exile, however, it is accepted as a necessity and is one sign of a transformation of social relations. It is impossible to know at this stage whether changes like this one will sustain after any eventual repatriation.

Close to the teashops in the settlements' trading centres, one can almost always also find a drinking area. Here, men – and some women – can be found drinking locally brewed beers and spirits. For the Acholi, the most commonly enjoyed drinks are a beer called *kwete*, and the *aragi* spirit. It is almost exclusively women who make and sell alcohol, although men do sell bottles of commercially-produced beer in their shops. For women, brewing is a double-edged sword. While many women make their living brewing beer or distilling spirits, for sale both from the homestead and from local bars in the trading centre, the trade can also generate difficulties for them. First, because as wives they suffer when men spend much-needed household resources on alcohol rather than more urgent necessities. Secondly, because observation and research indicates that – as in other contexts – there may be a correlation between alcohol consumption, external stressors and domestic violence (Giles and Hyndman 2004).

There is evidence that refugee communities in Uganda as elsewhere have seen changes in gender relations due to the essential transformation of livelihood strategies. Members of a women's group in Arua's Rhino Camp Settlement, for example, noted that tension arises within households when women are unable to keep up with their domestic responsibilities because they are occupied with crucial income generating activities outside the home. They reported that men felt extraneous to requirements since, in this settlement, more income-generating activities were available for women than for men, yet men felt unable to take on domestic roles for fear of loss of status.

In the confusion of flight and exile many couples are separated, and women may be left supporting children in a settlement, not knowing whether their husbands are alive or dead, or if they have abandoned them or not. Single-headed households, whether male or female, are at a clear disadvantage in a situation where survival depends on being able to mobilise labour in different forms. For women, a judgment has to be made as to whether it is preferable to struggle on alone, or to accept a comparatively unattractive marriage proposal to become a second or third wife of a man who can afford to marry again. If such a woman is lucky, her new husband might agree to feed at least some of her children as well as herself. In addition, marriage brings the added protection of an extended family and increased physical security in an uncertain environment.

In addition to these modest initiatives, each of which makes a small contribution to the household's needs, some individuals and families rely on external inputs. Much has been written about the role and function of remittances in refugee situations (eg, Dick 2002; Van Hear 2002). These represent contributions from friends and families outside the settlement and may be sent from other asylum locations in the region, from the wider diaspora in the developed world, or even from the country of origin under some circumstances.

Remittances may be used for a range of purposes including everyday living expenses including health care, as start-up capital for business ventures, to deal with unexpected expenses and to meet the costs of social, cultural or religious activities. The latter will be discussed further in the final section.

A tiny minority of refugees are lucky enough to gain formal employment in settlements – usually in a very junior capacity – with an NGO or as an assistant in the government office. It is usually, although not always, the case that a few refugees with substantial professional skills, experience and productive networks will find ways of avoiding the settlements altogether. Professional people who are able to find employment find it easier than peasant farmers to acquire permits that allow them to remain outside of settlements. Perhaps more importantly, such people are less likely ever to have registered as refugee, and may be living independently as expatriates in Kampala or other cities. Their experience and contribution as remittance-providers is important, but is not covered further here as this chapter focuses on refugees who remain in settlements.

Only those people with few or no alternatives tend to stay in refugee settlements, unless they have compelling personal reasons for wanting to remain there with families who they could not support outside. This does not mean that there are absolutely no educated and employable individuals within settlements. On the contrary, there are always numerous qualified applicants for any of the junior-level extension and similar posts that are made available by NGOs or the government. Those who are appointed win such jobs for obvious reasons; they speak English fluently, and are knowledgable about the operating mechanisms and cultural language of assistance-providing institutions, and public life in general. Often, in the Ugandan context, they are young men.

In Kiryandongo in 1997, women were employed as 'food basket monitors' (after a well-meant but relatively ineffective directive from WFP), and as health assistants and secretaries. Logistics, agricultural and other posts went to men. As has been noted in other contexts (Turner 2004), the apparent favouring of the younger generation of men can have implications for inter-generational relations and, therefore, for 'community' cohesion. As public practices change, we should not be surprised to see the transformation of social relations following. The broad point is that employment with an NGO or similar group is an avenue open to very few people, and those who are fortunate enough to earn salaries or small 'incentives' immediately find themselves better off than the majority in a differentiated refugee setting.

So far, I have considered some of the legitimate or 'respectable' ways in which refugee families endeavour to supplement what limited assistance they receive in the form of food rations during protracted exile. There are, in addition, a number of crucial strategies that oblige refugees to break the letter or the spirit of the law under which they live.

First, least controversially, and as has been reported widely, large numbers of refugees sell off part of their food rations (eg, Kibreab 2004, Waldron 1992). This practice is disliked by assistance providers, who sometimes take it as evidence that 'too much' food is being distributed or as evidence of bad faith by refugees (Waldron 1992). In reality, refugees often sell what is high in value, such as cooking oil, in order to buy other foodstuffs or non-food items (such as soap) without which they cannot do.

Secondly, and this is also an extremely common phenomenon, some refugees 'cheat' the food ration system in a number of ways (see also Kibreab 2004). They do this by double-registering themselves and their families, by inventing extra children who they claim to be feeding, and by failing to report the death of family members in order to continue receiving their ration, to name but a few examples. As also reported by Horst for the case of Somali refugees in Kenya (2005), some families buy additional ration cards to make up shortfalls in food. As Allen and Turton have noted (1996) it is often the case that when refugees act positively to help themselves, they are seen to be 'cheating', while if they wait dutifully for assistance, they go without. Some entrepreneurs go one step further and turn the project into a business by buying or stealing large numbers of ration cards.

In many Ugandan refugee settlements both men and women are involved in cutting and burning trees to make charcoal, which they sell. While this is strictly illegal without a permit, which is difficult to obtain, in some locations it has been the case that a small 'gift' to the appropriate official makes the risk of prosecution slight. It should be stressed that this is not the case everywhere, but in the face of serious deforestation, the presence of large numbers of people in need of fuel and with no other means to get it nevertheless remains a concern.

Finally, significant but unknown numbers of refugees defy the government's requirement that they live in settlements, and instead move to live, undocumented, outside them in places where they can trade or work. In some cases they are registered in settlements and continue to receive food rations there, even while they live and work elsewhere. A deeper understanding of the experience and strategies of the so-called 'self-settled', who may represent the majority of refugees in sub-Saharan Africa, will also have implications for our understanding of livelihood strategies in camps and settlements (for recent work on self-settlement see, for example, Bakewell 2000, Kaiser et al 2005, Polzer 2005).

'Moving up and down looking for money' is a constant occupation in the settlements, particularly for family heads with unexpected expenses to meet, or for students seeking a way to pay school fees. Poverty is boringly, frustratingly omnipresent in this context, and all the worse for appearing insurmountable. Aware that the agencies expect them to be grateful that they are not starving, for many people this is not enough, and they are frustrated by living in an environment which offers so few economic opportunities or prospects.

As is often the case with difficult or sensitive issues, poverty has become a subject about which people joke in the settlements. Outsiders who come to visit are scrutinized and if they are 'fat', enjoyment is had in speculating about the amount of meat they must eat in the wealthy city from which they come. To be 'fat', it should be noted, is to be attractively prosperous-looking. Eating well is associated with wealth and is even used as a metaphor for enrichment through corruption. Newspaper reports of politicians who have 'eaten' or 'consumed' money corruptly are viewed as much with admiration as with outrage. Residents of refugee settlements take some pride in the fact that they are able to endure the hardship of the settlement, and assume that soft city types would not last long there.

ECONOMIC AND SOCIAL GOALS AND ASSETS

As elsewhere, in refugee contexts the social and economic dimensions of life are tightly interwoven. Refugees need to meet their immediate subsistence needs, but they also have sociocultural and political needs and aspirations that may require a financial investment. If they lack sufficient economic resources, some of these may have to be reduced, or go by the board. While considerable attention has been paid to the idea that livelihood strategies may draw on social as well as other resources, it is also the case that the preservation and maintenance of social relations, networks and practices are themselves not cost-free activities.

As noted earlier in the chapter, when refugees are forced to leave their homes and go into exile, they suffer a series of losses, including non-material losses. As they strive to reestablish themselves in exile, they make choices about the sociocultural relations and practices without which they cannot do, and invest in reasserting these in exile.

As Davis (1992) puts it, 'It is probably the case that the first reaction to suffering is to preserve the social relations which are disrupted and threatened; partly so that... there should be some people you can rely on; and partly because it is important to maintain those characteristic forms of life which define what it is to be human' (1992: 157). Davis's formulation succinctly reminds us that social relations, institutions and practices may be revived or re-asserted by refugees in exile both because they generate order which may prove useful in practical terms, but also because they are meaningful and significant in and of themselves.

While a functionalist reading of refugee behaviour which interpreted sociocultural activity as an form of economic investment would be overly simplistic, it is important to recognise that people, albeit for different reasons, may not distinguish concretely between 'social', 'political' and 'economic' activity. As Brun writes, 'Constructing livelihoods is about how individuals and groups strive to make a living, attempting to meet their various consumption and economic needs, cope with uncertainties, respond to new opportunities, *and choose among different value positions.*' (2003: 32, emphasis added)

One of the ways in which refugees re-make meaning is by participating in sociocultural or ritual activity, even when this requires an investment of money, despite their reduced circumstances. In some cases, poverty makes full participation impossible, but some symbolic contribution is accepted as a sign of commitment. One of the most common examples of this, in Kiryandongo Refugee Settlement, relates to the negotiation and payment of bridewealth, a regular feature of marriage arrangements prior to exile for most of Kiryandongo's residents. In exile, the majority find themselves without the wherewithal to make the necessary bridewealth payments. This is acknowledged by most families, who nevertheless allow marriages to go ahead on the basis of a reduced or notional payment and the promise of further payments in the uncertain future. Wedding parties or celebrations, however, are out of the reach of most refugees and with few exceptions, marriages take place without fuss or ceremony in the settlement.

By contrast, for the Acholi residents, it has proved impossible to find much less-expensive ways of meeting funeral obligations and to continue large-scale funeral rituals while in exile. While expensive and time-consuming to organise, since they require hospitality and entertainment on a grand scale, elaborate funeral rituals are still held, at least for clan leaders and elders. Other cultural or ritual activities may continue in modified forms, as resources become available within a family or other network, even if it means delaying a ritual which should take place at a specified time. In one example from Kiryandongo, a married woman whose husband had been absent from the settlement for several years, had been unable to hold a ceremony for the twins which she bore him after his departure. The ritual occasion, *rut*, should have taken place shortly after their birth, but it was only after the death of one, when the other was already a toddler, that her father accumulated enough money to buy a ram to slaughter at the ritual. In her husband's absence, his clan relations had the obligation to conduct the ceremony on his behalf. When they failed to do so, her father stepped in to ensure that when it was possible, the ceremony was carried out. In this way, the spiritual and social requirements of her situation were met despite her impoverished circumstances and the absence of her husband.

Finding the money to participate in these kinds of activities is, of course, difficult for most people living in refugee settlements in Uganda. Nevertheless, great efforts are made to participate in at least some explicitly cultural or ritual activity. This kind of activity strengthens social relationships and facilitates the (re)emergence of a collective consciousness within refugee communities, also contributing to the generation of an environment within which people are more likely to work productively together in the economic domain.

Such economic activity may take new sociocultural forms. In Kiryandongo, for example, refugee women have creatively reinvented 'traditional' Acholi work groups – formerly a male, clan-based system of labour organisation – and transformed them into female, network-based cooperative work groups. Such groups come together to work collectively according to a precise set of rules and conventions, so that what none of them can do alone, can be managed together. One such group, *mon poro* or 'women who dig', has so named itself to emphasise that in this case, women are taking on what were previously male agricultural roles.

Some of the coping or livelihood strategies employed by refugee men and women in Kiryandongo are thus grounded in the very social networks and institutions – albeit transformed to suit the new context – which assistance providers had assumed the communities had lost as a consequence of displacement.

CONCLUSION

The Sustainable Livelihood Framework encourages us to consider the different types of livelihood assets available to individuals and communities, and to recognise that these can be deployed selectively and strategically to maximise advantage, as well as the importance of viewing them relationally.

This chapter discussed some of the ways that Sudanese refugees in Ugandan refugee settlements contrive to make a living despite the constraints inherent in the political and institutional context in which they operate. In order to meet their immediate goals of feeding their families, accessing healthcare and education, and feeling like useful members of society, refugees deployed all the assets or forms of capital at their disposal. These, it was argued following Kibreab (2003), were limited by their political positioning as 'refugees' who do not enjoy the same rights as non-refugees in Uganda. In some cases, certain 'coping strategies' required refugees to break rules or social conventions in order to effect positive livelihood outcomes.

The chapter has also highlighted the close relationship that exists between financial and social resources and activities, and some of the ways that Sudanese refugees have innovated to derive financial benefit as well as meeting wider social and community needs. Many of the livelihood strategies discussed here would be much less effective in the absence of the kind of information-sharing, relationship-building and collaborative activity described and implied in the examples provided; in particular, the investments of various kinds that are required to ensure the maintenance of social networks and relations on which refugees may rely in the context of economic activity. Finally, it has suggested that there are limits to what a rural population can be expected to achieve in the absence of a conducive or enabling environment. Removing restrictions on freedom of movement and enabling access to markets and employment opportunities for Sudanese refugees in Uganda would transform their livelihood options by allowing them to capitalise more effectively on what assets they do have. Whether this is likely to be achieved in the near future will depend partly on the success of the increasingly vocal advocacy campaign against the long-term encampment of refugees in the developing world (Kaiser et al 2005, USCRI 2005). It will also depend on persuading the government of Uganda that it has more to gain than to fear from the dispersal of refugee populations, whom it would dearly like to see returning home in the near future.

Notes

[1] I would like sincerely to thank the refugees of the Kiryandongo and other refugee settlements in Uganda for their willingness to participate in the field research on which

this chapter is based. I am also grateful to the numerous institutions and bodies that helped to fund the field research on which this chapter is based. Principal funding came from the Education Department of Basel, Switzerland, with additional grants from the Godfrey Lienhardt Memorial Fund, the Orisha Studentship of the Inter-Faculty Committee for African Studies, University of Oxford and the Royal Anthropological Institute. I would also like to thank the Uganda National Council for Science and Technology for providing research clearance, and personnel at the Office of the Prime Minister in Uganda for facilitating access and providing information, and staff of UNHCR. Thanks also to the Refugee Law Project research team with whom I worked on related issues in Uganda in September 2004, the work of which informs this chapter. Warm thanks also to Cindy Horst and Tara Polzer for helpful comments on a draft of this chapter.

[2] It should be noted that there is no consensus in the literature on how best to characterise these categories. 'Social capital' in particular, remains a phenomenon whose definition and use is highly contested. See, for example, Fine 1999, and Harriss and de Renzio 1997. For the purposes of this chapter what is important is that the Sustainable Livelihood Framework recognises that in their search for effective livelihood strategies, individuals and communities are likely to need to mobilise a range of diverse and inter-related resources to achieve successful outcomes.

[3] Of course, people flee under a wide range of circumstances and in many cases the nature of flight itself varies for different members of the community. The old, young or sick may be sent on in advance if danger threatens, male youths may leave alone to try to seek employment in urban areas, and so on.

[4] There has been a lively debate about whether a refugee presence represents a burden or a potential economic opportunity. See, for example, Jacobsen 2002b and Harrell-Bond 1986. Space constraints prevent coverage of this important question here, but it would be a critical component of any attempt to resolve some of the problems discussed here in relation to the use of developmental approaches to refugee management.

[5] The signing of a new peace agreement in January 2005 between the Government of Sudan and the former rebel Sudanese Peoples' Liberation Army holds out the promise of a return home for the Sudanese still in Uganda.

[6] Kiryandongo is located south of the Victoria Nile, only two-and-a-half hours' drive northwest of Kampala and within reasonable reach of markets and traders in a peaceful part of the country. Unusually, many of its residents were relocated from a transit camp in Kitgum District in the early 1990s, after repeated rebel attacks on the refugees there.

[7] As set out in the UN Convention on the Status of Refugees, 1951, and the Protocol Relating to the Status of Refugees, 1967. International human rights instruments relating to non-refugee populations also, of course, apply. Relevant instruments include but are not limited to the Universal Declaration of Human Rights, 1948, the International Covenant on Civil and Political Rights, 1966 and the International Covenant on Economic, Social and Cultural Rights, 1966.

References

Allen, T and Turton, D (1996) 'Introduction' in Allen, T (ed), *In Search of Cool Ground: War, Flight and Homecoming in Northeast Africa*, London: James Currey.

Bakewell, O (2000) 'Repatriation and self-settled refugees in Zambia: bringing solutions to the wrong problems', *Journal of Refugee Studies*, 13(4) 356–373.

Brun, C (2003) 'Not only about survival: livelihood strategies in protracted displacement', in Shanmugaratnam, N, Ragnhild, L and Stølen, K A (eds), *In the Maze of Displacement: Conflict, Migration and Change*, Kristiansand: Norwegian Academic Press, 26–45.

Chambers, R (1986) 'Hidden losers? The impact of rural refugees and refugee programs on poorer hosts', *International Migration Review*, 20(2) 245–263.

Collinson, S (ed) (2003) *Power, Livelihoods and Conflict: Case Studies in Political Economy Analysis for Humanitarian Action* (HPG Report 13), Overseas Development Institute: London.

Davis, J (1992) 'The anthropology of suffering', *Journal of Refugee Studies*, 5(2) 149–161.

Dick, S (2002) 'Liberians in Ghana: living without humanitarian assistance', *UNHCR New Issues in Refugee Research Working Paper*, 57.

DFID (1999) *Sustainable Livelihoods Guidance Sheets*, London: DFID.

Dryden-Peterson, S and Hovil, L (2003) 'Local integration as a durable solution: refugees, host populations and education in Uganda', *UNHCR New Issues in Refugee Research Working Paper*, 93.

Fine, B (1999) 'The developmental state is dead, long live social capital', *Development and Change*, 30(1) 1–19.

Giles, W and Hyndman, J (2004) *Sites of Violence: Gender and Conflict Zones*. Berkeley and Los Angeles: University of California Press.

Harrell-Bond, B E (1986) *Imposing Aid: Emergency Assistance to Refugees*, Oxford: Oxford University Press.

Harrell-Bond, B E (1999) 'The experience of refugees as recipients of aid', in Ager, A (ed), *Refugees: Perspectives on the Experience of Forced Migration*, London: Pinter.

Harriss, J and de Renzio, P (1997) '"Missing link" or analytically missing? The concept of social capital: An introductory bibliographic essay', *Journal of International Development*, 9(7) 919–937.

Horst, C (2005) *Transnational Nomads; How Somalis Cope With Refugee Life in the Dadaab Camps of Kenya*, Oxford: Berghahn.

Human Rights Watch (2003) *Abducted and Abused: Renewed War in Northern Uganda*, HRW Index No. A1512.

Jacobsen, K (2002) *Livelihoods in Conflict: The Pursuit of Livelihoods by Refugees and the Impact on the Human Security of Host Communities*, Expert Working Paper prepared for the Center for Development Research study: Migration – Development Links: Evidence and Policy Options. Feinstein International Famine Center, Tufts University.

Jacobsen, K (2002b) 'Can refugees benefit the state? Refugee resources and African statebuilding', *Journal of Modern African Studies*, 40(4) 577–596.

Kaiser, T (2005) 'Participating in development? Refugee protection, politics and developmental approaches to refugee management in Uganda', *Third World Quarterly*, 26(2) 351–367.

Kaiser, T (1999) 'Living in limbo: insecurity and the settlement of Sudanese refugees in northern Uganda', unpublished DPhil thesis, University of Oxford.

Kaiser, T, Hovil, L and Lomo, Z (2005) *We Are All Stranded Here Together: The Local Settlement System, Freedom of Movement and Livelihood Opportunities in Arua and Moyo Districts*, Refugee Law Project Working Paper No. 14. Kampala.

Kibreab, G (2003) 'Displacement, host governments' policies, and constraints on the construction of sustainable livelihoods', *International Social Science Journal*, 55(175) 57–67.

Kibreab, G (2004) 'Pulling the wool over the eyes of the strangers: refugee deceit and trickery in institutionalized settings', *Journal of Refugee Studies*, 17(1) 1–26.

Lautze, S (1997) *Saving Lives and Livelihoods: The Fundamentals of a Livelihood Strategy*, Feinstein International Famine Centre: Tufts University.

Le Billon, P (2000) *The Political Economy of War: What Relief Agencies Need to Know,* HPN Network Paper, London: ODI.

Loizos, P (1981) *The Heart Grown Bitter: A Chronicle of Cypriot War Refugees,* Cambridge: Cambridge University Press.

Polzer, T (2005) 'Negotiating rights; the politics of local integration', paper presented at the 9th conference of the International Association of the Study of Forced Migration, Sao Paolo, Brazil 9–12 January, 2005.

Schafer, J (2002) *Supporting Livelihoods in Situations of Chronic Conflict and Political Instability: Overview of Conceptual Issues,* London: ODI, Working Paper 183.

Scoones, I (1998) *Sustainable Rural Livelihoods: A Framework for Analysis,* Brighton: IDS Working Paper 72.

Turner, S (2004) 'New opportunities: angry young men in a Tanzanian refugee camp', in Essed, P, Frerks, G and Schrijvers, J (eds) *Loss and Recovery; Refugees and the Transformation of Societies,* Oxford: Berghahn.

UNHCR (2004) *Global Report 2003,* Geneva: UNHCR.

USCRI (2005) *World Refugee Survey 2005,* Washington DC: USCRI.

Van Hear, N (2002) 'Sustaining societies under strain: remittances as a form of transnational exchange in Sri Lanka and Ghana' in Al–Ali, N and Koser, K (eds) *New Approaches to Migration: Transnational Communities and the Transformation of Home,* London and New York: Routledge, 202–223.

Van Hear, N (2004) *'I Went as Far as My Money Would Take Me': Conflict, Forced Migration and Class,* Centre on Migration, Policy and Society Working Paper No. 6: University of Oxford.

Verdirame, G and Harrell-Bond, B with Lomo, Z and Garry, H (2005) *Rights in Exile: Janus Faced Humanitarianism,* Oxford: Berghahn.

Waldron, S (1992) 'Food for thought: refugee survival strategies and administrative control in organized settlements', unpublished paper presented at international meeting of 'Population Movements, Food Crises and Community Response' at the Centre for the Study of the Administration of Relief, New Delhi, India.

'In-betweenness' on the Margins: Collective Organisation, Ethnicity and Political Agency among Bolivian Street Traders

Sian Lazar[1]

This chapter explores the relationship between commerce, ethnicity and political agency in a city that is both on the margins and increasingly at the centre of Bolivian political life. El Alto has around 700,000 inhabitants and lies on the Andean high plain at 4,100 metres above sea level.[2] It began in the early 20th century as 'overflow' from the city of La Paz (which is located in a crater), but grew to the point where it became a city in its own right in 1985. As a satellite of the capital city of Bolivia, El Alto can reasonably be called marginal. Certainly, its residents frequently complain about being forgotten by the central State authorities; and it is the poorest city in the poorest country in South America.[3] It is also a highly 'informal' city, with most of its inhabitants working in untaxed commerce, transport or production activities. Newspaper estimates cite up to 200,000 informal street traders in the city. The leaders of the El Alto Federation of Street Traders estimate the number of their affiliates at around 160,000. Since people are often affiliated with more than one traders' association under the federation's umbrella, the actual number of trading families is lower. Yet even an estimate of 100,000 street traders would mean that at least one in seven of El Alto's entire population is involved in some way in street trading. Compare this with a 1998 estimate of 200,000 traders in Mexico City out of a population of around 20 million (Cross 1998).

On indicators of impoverishment and 'informality' then, El Alto is a city 'at the margins'. However, in other senses, El Alto and its street traders are squarely 'in the middle'. El Alto's inhabitants are mostly rural-urban migrants, which does not mean a linear progression from the countryside to the city, but rather that they participate in a series of flows between city and countryside. Migrants come and settle in the city but tend to move backwards and forwards between there and their home villages in the rural provinces of the department of La Paz or further afield. In fact, the La Paz provinces have become increasingly urbanised in recent years, but they are usually regarded as rural by city-dwellers, of all classes. [4]

El Alto is also 'in the middle' of several sets of flows of objects, as goods produced in the provinces are brought to the city to sell, alongside contraband transported from the borders with Chile and Brazil. Linda Seligmann (1989) has highlighted the importance of the intermediary position of market traders, as they connect the rural economy with the national market. She argues that being 'in-between' in this sense gives them considerable political power, which is linked to their ethnicity. Traders in El Alto have a fluid and 'in-between' ethnicity: the archetypal market-woman is known as a '*chola*', which is an ethno-cultural category somewhere in between Indian and *mestizo*, that is, people of mixed Indian and Spanish background. Geographically also, it lies in between La Paz and the rest of the country, as all the four or five roads out of the capital city go through El Alto. The main roads converge at the *Ceja* (literally, 'eyebrow'), which is the transport and commercial hub of El Alto. Thus, if *alteños* – those who live in El Alto – choose to blockade the few roads down to the city of La Paz, they can wield significant political power. This was demonstrated in October 2003, when a general strike called by the city's residents' association combined with a series of other protests to force the president to resign. In this chapter, I discuss the role of the *chola* middle-woman in trade, focusing on the chain of 'production' and distribution of fish. I explore the fish sellers' relationship with the State and with a rival organisation, and consider the importance of the different kinds of 'in-betweenness' as experienced by the fish sellers for *alteño* and national political life.

ORGANISING THE INFORMAL ECONOMY IN EL ALTO

El Alto can be called an informal city. This is a reasonably good description of its economy, while acknowledging the various academic debates over the definition of the informal sector, the impossibility of cleanly separating out formal and informal sectors, or of clearly distinguishing criminal from informal; and even the usefulness of the term "informal" itself (eg, see Cross 1998; Hart 1973; Peattie 1987; Portes and Castells et al 1989). Despite (or because of) its imprecision, the term retains some descriptive power in a broad sense, and the informal economy in El Alto is characterised by small-scale production or vending, unregulated and untaxed by government, with people mostly self-employed rather than receiving a wage. According to the National Statistics Institute, 49.7% of the economically active population (EAP) of El Alto were 'self-employed' in November 1997. Seventy-three per cent of the EAP worked in establishments that employed 1–4 people. Most of the work in the informal sector is small-scale commerce on the streets or in markets held either daily or once or twice a week. About 30% of the EAP work in commerce, and in 1995, there were 150 associations of market traders, each with 200–1,000 members (Choque Mamani 1997). In 2003, there were nearly 200 associations of street traders who were politically active in the El Alto Federation of Street Traders – The Federation of Organised Workers, Artisans, Small Traders and Food Sellers of the City of El Alto,[5] to give its full title (hereafter 'the Federation of Street Traders' or 'the federation'). Others had broken away from the federation, whose leaders estimated that in total there were probably around 300 associations in El Alto.

The informal economy of El Alto is informal in the sense that it is more or less unregulated by government for taxation purposes.[6] However, it is neither clandestine nor entirely separate from the State. The relationship between those in the informal sector and the State is mediated by membership in collective organisations. Most adult *alteños* belong to trade unions within the informal sector. In the case of the predominantly male jobs (as drivers or artisans), the collective organisations are called unions (*sindicatos*), and in the case of the predominantly female street traders, they are called associations (*asociaciónes*).

An association consists of all the women (and men) who sell in the same area in markets that are held weekly, twice-weekly, or daily, depending on the neighbourhood. Associations mediate between individuals and the State and represent the traders in negotiations with other civic bodies in the neighbourhood where they work, principally the local neighbourhood council (*Junta Vecinal*) and other associations of traders. The associations are affiliated with the citywide federation, which mediates any conflicts between two associations and assists associations when they must deal with the State authorities.

The federation is led by an executive committee, which is headed by an executive secretary who, in 2003, was Don Braulio Rocha Tapia.

These trade associations and the federation fit into a highly organised collective structure that is parallel to the State, and which interacts with the State at multiple levels. Residents (*vecinos*) are organised through the neighbourhood councils, which also have a citywide federation similar to the traders' associations, called the FEJUVE (*Federación de Juntas Vecinales*, or Federation of Neighbourhood Councils). The third main organisation at the city level is the COR (*Central Obrera Regional*, or Regional Worker's Centre), a coordinator of workers' trade unions including factory workers, teachers, journalists, artisans, and the federation of market traders.[7] There is a further layer of civic organisations at the national level. At all levels, the organisations represent their affiliates in negotiations with each other and with different parts of the State.

As well as mediating between their members and the State, the civic organisations also often substitute for the State, doing regulatory work in its stead. Under everyday circumstances, the street traders' associations control how many traders can sell in their part of the street or fixed market and formalise the ownership of particular stalls, including overseeing changes in ownership, and defining and regulating the size of the stall and which products are sold. The leadership keeps watch to see if someone is not attending their stall regularly, keeping it orderly, or taking part in cleaning their part of the street. In the last few years, they have also taken on the responsibility of organising the policing of their market by raising quotas to hire private security.

As in other parts of the world, the street trader associations seek to protect their ability to self-regulate as far as posible (Basile and Harriss-White 2000). This is also compatible with the neoliberal 'solution' to the informal sector that has inspired Bolivian governments since the 1990s, namely deregulation as advocated in Hernando de Soto's influential book *The Other Path* (1989). De Soto argued that the costs of being legal in developing countries were too high for poor traders, largely because of the bureaucracy involved in setting up a stall, getting a permit, and so on. His solution was to reduce State regulation in all sectors of the economy, which would have the effect of merging the informal with the formal. In this scenario, governments have different options for dealing with the black market: either trying to instigate a clampdown in order to force people to formalise or legalise their businesses, or allowing (parts of) the informal sector to self-regulate, thus delegating the costs of regulation to entities such as the trade unions, who become *de facto* State agents. Bolivian national governments did not follow De Soto's advice in its entirety, but they did remove sales tax for those with small amounts of capital, and left the regulation of street trading in the hands of local governments and trade unions. The trade unions defend this arrangement fiercely, because it gives them influence with the State and access to State resources, enabling them to serve their members' interests and bolster their political power generally. However, it can lead to some insecurity for the unions, as what are *ad hoc* arrangements are vulnerable to conflicts with other unions. In a conflictual situation, there is always the danger that affiliates will choose to abandon the organisation they perceive to be on the losing side.

THE FISH SELLERS

The street traders' role in the parallel structure outlined above creates a relationship with the State that is not solely one of antagonism or resistance to State measures, as proposed by Clark (1988) but rather, allows the organisations considerable agency, as Cross has argued in the case of Mexico City (1998). In El Alto, the collective organisations can at times drive the strategic decisions of the State. This section discusses one of the associations affiliated with the Federation of Street Traders, an association of fish sellers (*pescaderas*) whose market is located at Final Los Andes in the northern part of the city. They have a history of problems with the municipal authorities, and in 2003 were embroiled in a particularly difficult conflict with a federation of fishermen from the provinces. Their story highlights the ways in which informal traders must interact with the State even if they do not pay sales tax or buy licences to sell; and how differently organised groups interact with each other. Informality cannot be easily equated with marginality.

Don Alberto Mamani, a member of the executive committee of the Federation, filled me in on the history of the fish sellers' association. The commercialisation of fish is relatively recent in Bolivia: about 20 years ago, fish was mostly eaten only by those who lived in the provinces around the banks of Lake Titicaca, to the north of La Paz. At that time, a few women travelled from the lake to the *Ceja*, to sell fish 'directly from the producer [the fishermen] to the consumer'. They founded an association in the *Ceja*, but were moved a few years later, to a site a bit further out from the centre of El Alto. Throughout this time, El Alto was growing at an average of 9.23% a year, and with it the market for fish. [8] By the late 1980s, a system of 'intermediaries' had developed. The women who went to the lake, bought fish from the fishermen there, and then transported the fish to El Alto became wholesalers. In the city, they sold the fish to a further level of inter-mediaries, that is, women who sold small quantities in other markets in the city, called *detallistas*.

The fish sellers were then forced by municipal authorities to leave their site, and so they relocated still further out from the centre. The site the fish sellers chose this time was good for them, situated as it was at the entrance to the biggest street market in El Alto. However, it also stood opposite the prestigious airforce base, and despite sup-port from the federation, the authorities were reluctant to grant the fish sellers legal permission to sell in that area. So they moved once more, to Final Los Andes, where they have stayed since, putting con-siderable energy into organising themselves as an association. Their association gradually grew, and by 2003 had around 200 members. While the association has its legal personhood, they still do not have the municipal order recognising their right to sell on that site. This makes them vulnerable to harassment from municipal authorities who want them to move, harassment they have suffered periodically over the last few years.

The insecurity of their position became a particular problem when Don Roberto[9] Quispe, the executive of the La Paz Departmental Federation of Fishermen, came on the scene. In early 2002 he led a protest march, demanding among other things a 'fish terminal' in El Alto, where fishermen from the provinces could sell directly to con-sumers. By mid-2003, the La Paz Departmental Prefect's office appeared to be taking this demand seriously. Don Roberto Quispe told me that the Final Los Andes fish sellers had not demanded any-thing like this from the prefecture themselves, and that only when it subsequently appeared that the prefecture was responding to his demand did they want to be involved. He said that there was a large amount of money belonging to the Final Los Andes association which had simply disappeared, and which could have bought a piece of land for development as a commercial centre had they really wanted it; a thinly-veiled accusation of corruption on the part of the Final Los Andes leaders. He also said that the fish sellers had intimidated women who occasionally came from Lake Titicaca to the city to sell fish. The middle-women of Final Los Andes prevented them from selling directly to consumers, and further demanded that even those women who sold fish only occasionally should affiliate with their association, for substantial amounts of money. He argued that the middle-women earned a good profit, which was money that the fish-ermen and women should be earning. Both his affiliates and some *detallistas* wanted to bypass the Final Los Andes middle-women, hence the demand for a fish terminal.

Don Alberto Mamani (from the executive committee of the federa-tion) argued that many of the participants in the protest march of 2002 were fish sellers from Final Los Andes. The fish sellers were angry with Quispe for using photographs from Final Los Andes in his appli-cation to the Spanish Embassy for funds for the proposed fish termi-nal, pretending that it was his association. According to the fish sellers, Quispe had also begun to harass them. He told fishermen not to sell to those who belong to the Final Los Andes association; and 'his' people attacked 'their' people in one incident, physically injuring them and overturning and spoiling their merchandise. In a meeting of the fish sellers in early July of that year, some also accused him of sexual harassment. Quispe had also encouraged the formation of a rival fish sellers' association, led by an ex-leader of the Final Los Andes group, who was keen to unify with Quispe's federation. Both sides in the conflict accused one another of corruption and high-handedness, and both vigorously denied that they were either. This is quite common in conflicts of this kind, as accusations of corruption are one of the most important ways in which trade union and local politics are conducted – an issue I have discussed elsewhere (Lazar 2005).

In mid-2003, it looked as though the prefecture was ready to find land for the fish terminal. The political context for this was the suc-cess of the Aymara peasant mobilisations of 2000 and 2001 (Lazar and McNeish 2006; Patzi Paco 2003), one of the results of which was the prefecture agreeing to grant the national peasant union control over land in El Alto for two 'peasant markets' where producers could sell directly to consumers. Since the prefecture can only transfer land to other State bodies, and not private entities, they made an arrange-ment with the mayor of El Alto to swap plots of land with the munic-ipality so that a fish terminal could be built, with financial assistance from the Spanish Embassy. Because Don Roberto Quispe was friends with the people in the Fisheries department of the prefecture, he was best placed to control the fish terminal. Rumours had it that he was pro-posing to charge an affiliation fee of (US)$500 to each person who wanted to sell fish there, but he energetically denied this to me, say-ing it was 'calumny and lies'. The Final Los Andes association argued that they should be in charge of any terminal, which in their opinion should be a 'commercial centre of fish', because their association had supervised the sale of fish in the city for over 20 years. The difference in terminology is significant, because Quispe was arguing in favour of a direct producer-consumer relationship, while the fish sellers wished to preserve their position as intermediaries. They might have had a stronger case in the eyes of the State authorities if they had had full documentation, including the municipal order. However, their legal personhood helped, and the federation was prepared to vouch for their antiquity.

By August 2003, the fish sellers and Roberto Quispe had signed an agreement promising mutual respect. That meant that women from Don Roberto Quispe's federation would not be prevented from selling their fish at Final Los Andes, although they would be expected to support the activities of the association with small financial contributions. In return, Roberto Quispe promised not to harass the fish sellers from Final Los Andes. However, the dispute over who would control the commercialisation of fish in El Alto remained. When I interviewed Don Alberto Mamani (from the federation), he said that the mayor was more or less amenable to the creation of a commercial centre for fish supervised by the Final Los Andes association but accessible to members of Don Roberto Quispe's federation. The prefecture remained convinced that Quispe should run the terminal. However, both the mayor and the prefecture stressed that neither organisation could charge extortionate amounts to those who wanted to sell in areas they controlled, because that would go against the free trade provisions of the 21060 law. Their use of this law was rather ironic, since it is notorious in Bolivia as the structural adjustment decree of 1985, which led to the firing of thousands of miners and other workers. The 21060 decree is known as the *'ley maldita'*, or 'evil law'.

ETHNICITY: THE RURAL, THE URBAN AND THE IN-BETWEEN

One of the key issues for all the bodies involved in the dispute was how to negotiate the rural-urban relationship. In their arguments on behalf of the Final Los Andes fish sellers, federation leaders persisted in articulating this as a *split* between rural and urban. They argued that the Final Los Andes association had been selling fish in the city of El Alto for 20 years, and jurisdiction over any urban activities therefore belonged to them. One leader, for example, asked rhetorically in one of their meetings: 'they're two things – one is urban, another rural ... are we urban or are we rural?' He used the fact that their association 'belonged' to the Urban Federation of Street Traders to underline this point. When Don Braulio (the executive secretary) met with the fish sellers, he consistently emphasised that he did respect the fishermen and women, but in their place; that is, in the provinces.

It is certainly the case that both sides organised themselves in different spheres: one focused on the urban space where the fish was sold, while the other focused on the catching of the fish, mainly in Lake Titicaca. However, of necessity the two regions shaded into each other. The Final Los Andes women had to go and buy fish from fishermen at the lake, while Roberto Quispe's federation wanted the right to bring fish from the lake into El Alto to sell there. The matter was further complicated by the fact that the women and men of the Final Los Andes association did not all live in El Alto. Some of them had dual residence, some lived in the provinces. The majority of those who lived mainly in the city had originally come from the lake area, and bought fish from their family members and *paisanos* (fellow countrymen) who still lived there. Quispe's affiliates were probably in a similar situation. Quispe himself certainly spent much of his time in the city, going through all the legal processes associated with the dispute. It is understandable that, according to one of those involved, the mayor thought that Don Roberto Quispe's federation and the Final Los Andes association were one and the same. Certainly it was easy for Quispe to convince the Spanish Embassy that they were.

The distinction was quite subtle, focused as it was on individual personalities within the different organisations, as well as on the site of the central locus of the legal personhood of each organisation. Legally and politically, however, the distinction was crucial, not least because the different areas fell largely under different State jurisdictions: the El Alto municipal government was responsible for the city, while the prefecture was responsible for the provinces. The different trade unions attempted to play one part of the State off against the other: the Final Los Andes fish sellers using the federation and Don Alberto's personal connections to influence the mayor, while Quispe used his friendship with Fisheries department functionaries to influence the prefecture (cf Cross 1998). The prefecture was particularly responsive to Don Roberto Quispe's demands because he had presented them during a protest march held in 2002. In the context of pressure from the national government to respond to the peasant union's list of demands around the same time, it was very important that the prefecture respond as far as possible to a similar set of demands from Quispe. This illustrates one of the main ways in which collectively organised groups drive State decisions or policy. In this particular instance, different parts of the parallel structure vied with each other to influence State institutions. The prefecture was not overly concerned if their response to Quispe's protest meant that they went against the interests of another group of people, even if they had participated in the protest march. For the functionaries, it was more important to appear responsive to peasant demands.

The conflict was essentially a dispute between rival associations of fish sellers and organisations of fishermen, both of which spanned the rural and urban spheres. However, when it suited their purpose, members of the two organisations would make a distinction between urban and rural, and they wanted it respected. One man said in a meeting at the federation's office: 'As a migrant, I am a resident of the city of El Alto. I defend my province, of course, but over there. Here [in the city] I defend myself.' Others argued that the fishermen and women of the provinces had their own markets in the countryside where they could sell their produce, and that the urban area was properly under the federation and Final Los Andes association's jurisdiction.

At the heart of the conflict then was a struggle over the position of commercial intermediaries. The Final Los Andes women were most aggrieved at the fact that Quispe was preventing people who lived by the lake, and with whom they had a special trading relationship, from selling fish to them, especially since their trading partners were in many cases also their kin. When fishermen and women did sell fish to the Final Los Andes fish sellers, Quispe's people apparently prevented them from going out on the lake to fish. By agreement with the prefecture, his federation was responsible for organising the environmental regulation of fishing in Lake Titicaca, which meant that he could easily enforce his sanctions against those who sold to the Final Los Andes fish sellers instead of to their rivals. However, he presented his demands in the context of the right to sell from (rural) producer direct to (urban) consumer, and the functionaries at the prefecture considered this to be an important principle.

Florence Babb's work describes a similar case in Peru in the 1970s, when State agencies attempted to bypass the market-women and create fairs where producers could sell directly to consumers. There, the campaigns were unsuccessful, as producers generally preferred to sell in bulk to regular buyers, rather than spending their time selling small quantities. They recognised the value that market-women added to the products they sold, in the considerable work of packaging, transporting and building up a client base (Babb 1988). The Final Los Andes fish sellers pointed out that fishermen generally do not catch enough fish to warrant spending the time and money to travel to El Alto, and instead merge together small quantities of fish from different sources in order to make it worthwhile. As one would expect, Don Braulio and the federation leaders were utterly opposed to bypassing commercial intermediaries. Don Braulio said in a meeting: 'we can't defend the direct sale from the producer to the consumer; what a disgrace when there are no jobs around'. His point reflects another argument made since Hart's seminal article (1973), which is that employment in the informal sector absorbs the surplus labour of the formal sector, a crucial function in the present economic crisis.

As many scholars have pointed out, commerce in Andean countries is ethnically marked (Larson and Harris 1995; Peredo Beltrán 1992; Rivera Cusicanqui 2002; Seligmann 1989; Seligmann 1993; Weismantel 2001). Market-women are known as *cholas*, an ethno-cultural category which has been used since colonial times to describe an Indian who has moved to the city, and who is therefore somewhere between Indian and *mestizo* (ie, of mixed Spanish and indigenous background). *Cholo/a* is both a racial and a social category, signified by indigenous physical features plus particular clothes and economic activities, most especially commerce. *Cholos* are indelibly associated with the urban service sector and the informal economy: commerce, transport and, in earlier times, mining. Depending on who is using the word and whom they are addressing, *cholo/a* can be pejorative. However, people in El Alto do call young single women '*cholitas*', the diminuitive of *chola*, and the phrase '*gran chola Paceña*' ('great *chola* from La Paz') is used admiringly about women who have been very successful in commerce. The most important signifier of being a *chola* or *cholita* is dress: that is, layered and gathered skirts (called a *pollera*), a shawl, specific shoes, and a bowler hat. Mary Wiesmantel (2001) notes the ways in which women make 'indexical statements' about themselves through their clothes and behaviour, even if they do not explicitly refer to themselves as *cholas*. Market-women self-consciously assume what Lynn Sikkink (2001) calls an 'ethnicity for consumption' by the purchasers of their products.

Of course, ethnic identities are not stable. Susan Paulson illustrates this point with her discussion of a woman who is a peasant in her village, but puts on her *pollera*, hat and shawl to go and sell her produce in the urban market. She thereby moves from Indian to *chola* during her travel to the city, and back to Indian once she returns from the day's selling (Paulson 2002). Once in the market, women's ethnic positionings are constantly under negotiation, as sellers will insult market-women by calling them Indian, whereas the market-women will assert their superiority over the (Indian) peasants from whom they buy their products, or when they come to the city to buy items such as rice, sugar and kerosene (Seligmann 1993).

The story of the fish sellers highlights one way in which ethnicity and commerce relate to each other in El Alto and the surrounding provinces. At first glance, it appears to be a conflict between the *chola* market-women and the peasants of the provinces (the fishermen). The market-women are the classic intermediaries between the latter and the *mestiza* (and *chola*) consumers in the urban sphere. However, look more closely and we see that in the first place, the Final Los Andes fish sellers are part of a rather longer chain of commerce in the urban sphere. They do sell to some consumers, but sell more to the *detallistas*, the women who go to markets in El Alto and La Paz and sell small quantities to consumers there, and who are also *cholas*. Secondly, they buy their fish from fishermen in the provinces, but these are frequently their family members. Alternatively, they may actually base themselves in the provinces and come to sell at the market of Final Los Andes a few days a week, perhaps staying with relatives in El Alto; or they may own one house in the city and one in the provinces. Their ethnic identity shifts as they move from the countryside to the city and back again, and the boundaries between the two spheres are blurred. Yet at the same time they make a distinction between the two spheres for political purposes in order to defend their right to work and to sell.

POLITICAL AGENCY: RURAL AND URBAN IN THE OCTOBER 2003 UPHEAVALS

This dynamic of rhetorical separation between rural and urban and the practical porousness of the boundaries between the two is not confined to groups such as the fish sellers, but is a key characteristic of El Alto in general, one that has important political implications. El Alto's position 'in the middle' of flows of objects between the rural provinces, and between the borders and the city of La Paz, can be a source of political power. Linda Seligmann has argued, for the case of highland Peru, that this power drives from three different 'capacities' of the *cholas*:

> The capacity … to (a) speak and understand the language and behaviour of the peasants; (b) withdraw the services they provide to the *mestizos*; and (c) ally themselves with the indigenous peasantry increases their prospects for successful political resistance to the existing economic and social order. (1989: 717)

The urban *mestizos* and whites are dependent on the *cholas*, whose linking of the peasant economy and the national market make them 'crucial nodes of the national economy' (Seligmann 1989: 707). The combination of the *cholas'* broker position, and El Alto's position as the linking point between the city of La Paz and the rest of the country, means that concerted action to blockade the city of La Paz by well-organised groups can result in a situation where food supplies simply cannot enter the city, and people cannot get out. The siege tactic has a long historical pedigree, at least as far back as the indigenous revolt of 1780 led by Tupac Katari.

A siege or blockade affects different classes and ethnicities differently, because of the way that marketing and food provisioning is organised in La Paz and El Alto. People of all classes do the majority of their shopping in markets, even the very wealthy, who tend to complement their market shopping with produce brought from the growing number of supermarkets. The price differentials are simply so great, and the food in the markets so fresh and flavourful, that the supermarkets have not yet achieved complete hegemony; even though more people are deciding to sacrifice taste for (perceived) hygiene and buy products like meat from the supermarkets. However, those from the wealthier classes tend to buy fresher goods more frequently. Their diet is richer in vegetables and fruit, for example, which they buy on a weekly basis, whereas ordinary residents of El Alto often buy staples like potatoes, *chuño* (freeze-dried potatoes), rice and pasta in bulk, or bring potatoes and other vegetables from their fields in the countryside. Between 2000 and 2003, families I knew in El Alto increased the proportion of these kinds of staple foods in their diet and reduced their meat consumption, because their economic situation became more difficult. So when there is a blockade, although poorer *alteños* suffer more from price increases for food and do not have refrigerators to preserve goods, they also have greater stocks of food available to rely upon, and their diet changes relatively less than that of those residents of the wealthy parts of La Paz. During the blockades of April 2000, my landlady said to me:

As far as I'm concerned, it's fine. That way, perhaps the government will think a little bit. We're fine here – we have potato, *chuño*, meat. It's the people who live in Obrajes and Calacoto [ie the rich areas of La Paz] who will suffer, because they buy their food each week, don't they?

Furthermore, ordinary *alteños* mobilise their relationships with the countryside to bring back vegetables for family consumption; groups such as the fish sellers can use the commercial relationships with kin and those from their *pueblos,* which they have developed over the years. Those who are from the areas where the peasants are protesting are frequently let through the blockades because they know the protestors, and can therefore bring back provisions for their families, whereas trucks transporting supermarket goods are prevented from proceeding along the main roads, and the supermarkets have to shut down.

Seligmann assumes that *cholas* will identify with the peasants in any political struggles between whites and Indians. In fact, in Bolivia, '*cholo* politics' has tended to favour urban populist leaders more than indigenous and/or peasant movements (Lazar 2002), although this may be changing. *Alteños'* relationship with the peasants and the countryside is not quite as straightforward as an automatic identification. Many do strongly support the peasants when it comes to political mobilization, yet on the whole, they feel that they are different from the people who live in the countryside, largely because they have become accustomed to city life. Nevertheless, although the peasants from their birth villages might be different – they might drink more, eat better food, be stronger or work harder – they are still kin, both figuratively and literally. This can be compared with the strong kin relations that even the most 'urban' fish sellers had with the fishermen and women of Lake Titicaca.

For many of those who migrated from the countryside, and often for their children, their *pueblo* (village of birth) is regarded as a stronger affiliation than that towards their place of residence in El Alto, even if in practice they spend more of their time as city-dwellers than as peasants. When I asked schoolchildren from Rosas Pampa to talk about 'my *pueblo*' in group interviews, they generally agreed that it was one's place of birth. But in practice, children called their parents' village their *pueblo* even if they were born in El Alto, and no one I spoke to ever called El Alto or Rosas Pampa their *pueblo*. *Pueblo* is a very emotive term, which can also mean 'people' or 'nation', particularly when used by politicians or community leaders. Many *alteños* have strong emotional attachments to their *pueblos*, and to the countryside in general.

The peasants themselves have an ambiguous relationship with those who have migrated from their village, as the conflict between the provincial fishermen and the women's association and urban fish sellers also illustrates. David Llanos Layme (1998) has studied the effects of return migration on the rural community of Chari. While many return migrants reintegrate into the community well, some create resentment when they express attitudes of superiority and individuality, and when they expect to enjoy all the rights accorded to community members without being prepared to fulfil their responsibilities. These tensions occur also when migrants visit their *pueblos*, but equally, migrants can be seen as members of the community even if they spend relatively little time in the *pueblo*, as long as they attend the important fiestas and are present for planting and harvesting (Canessa 1998).

Few political movements have effectively capitalised on the links between *alteños* and their *pueblos*. The most important Aymara movement in Bolivia, Katarismo, has in the past not directed its appeal to ordinary urban Aymaras in El Alto or La Paz. Katarismo has targeted its political efforts at rural areas since its inception in the late 1960s. Despite the fact that many of its leaders were educated urban Aymaras, its rhetoric appealed to indigenous peoples as noble peasants with an alternative social, political and economic logic based upon either the *ayllu* (the 'traditional' indigenous community of the Andes) or the peasant union (eg, see Untoja 2000; Quispe 2001). There is a sense in which the rural-urban migrants are seen as already assimilated into Hispanic society, by virtue simply of having moved to the city; at best a sort of bastardised category of Aymara, lying outside of the essentialised scheme of identification that is perhaps necessary for indigenous politics. Katarismo found it difficult to deal with the ordinary people like the fish sellers who are both rural and urban, and who move between the two spheres with relative facility.

However, an 'ethnic identification' between *alteños* and the countryside was of particular salience in October 2003.[10] Then, a coalition of Aymara peasants from the department of La Paz and the El Alto Federations of residents (FEJUVE), workers (COR) and street traders gradually came together, and led a series of protests and blockades throughout September and October. The protests incorporated multiple sectoral demands but coalesced around opposition to the export of Bolivian natural gas. The heavy-handed government response, which eventually led to over 80 deaths, was felt first in Warisata, a village in the department of La Paz. On 21 September, the army killed six people there in a 'rescue mission' to release tourists trapped by peasant blockades in the nearby town of Sorata. Thereafter, as the protests escalated and confrontations between *alteños* and the army took an increasingly heavy toll on *alteño* lives, the clamour for the president's resignation grew. He eventually resigned and fled the country on 17 October, leaving his vice-president to take over.

El Alto was the epicentre of the protests, which spread down to La Paz to other parts of the country in the few days prior to the president's resignation. The most radical parts of El Alto were those in the northern part of the city, which holds some of its newest (and poorest) neighbourhoods. The residents of these zones tend to be people who have migrated more recently, and who therefore have very strong ties to the provinces. Villa Ingenio was one such flashpoint, in part because its residents mostly come from the province of Omasuyos, the province to which Warisata belongs.[11] Rio Seco was another turbulent neighbourhood; something which was attributed by one of its residents to the fact that there are a lot of '*Achacacheños*' living there. Achacachi is the territory of the main peasant leader of the blockades, Felipe Quispe. Furthermore, *Achacacheños* are known for being warriors, even cannibals according to some stories. Don Braulio Rocha described the reaction to Warisata as follows:

> That was where the problem was born. The government sent military and police forces to Warisata where... they unleashed a great fury in order to save the tourists. There were deaths, injuries, and this problem affected El Alto; and in El Alto we organised support for our peasant brothers.

Alteños also objected strongly to the government's plans for exporting the gas with terms that they considered extremely unfavourable to Bolivia. The gas was the latest in a long line of natural resources to leave the country since colonialism – principally silver, tin and oil. For many it came to symbolise the fact that successive Bolivian governments were more concerned about appeasing the International Monetary Fund (IMF) and the US Embassy, and serving their own personal interests, than in looking after the Bolivian people who were (and still are) suffering a severe economic crisis. The deaths at Warisata and increasingly in El Alto meant that leaders of the different civic organisations had little difficulty in persuading their members to unite against the government. Indeed, the most common phrase I heard when I asked leaders about the upheavals was that 'the people overruled [*rebasó*] the leaders'.

However, this was not an automatic unification of *cholos* and peasants as Seligmann proposes, and there is a gap between the rhetoric and the actual ability of these groups to unify. As the fish sellers' story shows, the high degree of civic and trade union organisation in El Alto can lead to fractious and conflictive relationships as well as to strong and unified action. The potential for confrontation over who controls the market for different products in the city is as great (if not greater) as the potential for unification and thus political power. In October 2003, a number of factors came together with the result that the political power correctly identified by Seligmann was realised at that particular time. For example, the decision that the peasant union took in early September to begin a hunger strike in a radio station's buildings in El Alto took advantage of the linkages between the rural provinces of the department of La Paz and many of the residents of El Alto. Local residents mobilised themselves to hold bonfire-lit vigils outside the buildings in order to protect the peasants from rumoured army interventions, and the peasants' protest was brought firmly into the middle of the city. It was this decision that showed that the peasant blockade had much more impact in October 2003 than in 2000 and 2001, even though in the earlier blockades more peasants had participated, and even though there was widespread sympathy in El Alto for the peasants at that time too. And I suspect that it was not a random decision: in political meetings during mid-2003 which evaluated the riots from February of that year, analysts and politicians debated the importance for the Indianist movement of gaining a foothold in the cities, particularly El Alto.

In recent years there has been an increasing realization by oppositional political movements of the strategic nature of El Alto, as well as a growing ability among intellectuals and community leaders to articulate its identity as an indigenous city, and to convert that into concrete and effective political action. What October 2003 illustrates is the fact that such an indigenous identity is based upon the mixing of the rural and the urban, and the state of being 'in between' the two. When leaders in El Alto talk of 'our peasant brothers', they are making use of a rhetorical distinction between urban and rural which enables them to make claims upon an indigenous authenticity in opposition to the (white) governing elites. Indigeneity is linked to a rural identity in the Bolivian imagination. So, for inhabitants of El Alto, the peasants are *and* aren't 'us' – they are our kin, but not us. El Alto is really 'in the middle', between the provinces and the city, even if it is also usually on the margins of national Bolivian political life. Nevertheless, as October 2003 showed, its strategic location in both a geographical and ethnocultural sense makes the city a force to be reckoned with when it does erupt into national political life. Terms like 'informal' and 'marginal' describe one set of aspects of El Alto, politically and economically. However, it would be wrong to imagine those who revolted in October as entirely marginal and outside of the State. Even if 'the people' did overrule their leaders, they organised themselves through neighbourhood-level associations (of residents, and street and market traders), which are part of a structure that interacts with the State on a day-to-day basis, and which at times even drives State policy in Bolivia. 'In-betweenness' can be a significant source of power if the political conditions are right.

Notes

[1] I am very grateful to John Gledhill and Barbara Harriss-White for comments on an early draft of this paper.

[2] El Alto's population according to the 2001 Census was 649,958. Between 1992 and 2001, its population increased at a rate of 5.1% per year.

[3] The UN Human Poverty Index for 2003 puts Bolivia behind Haiti, Nicaragua, Guatemala, Honduras and El Salvador in terms of Latin American countries. See <http://hdr.undp.org/reports/global/2003/indicator/indic_16_2_2.html> (accessed 20 February, 2007).
The 2001 Census found that 66.9% of the population of El Alto is 'poor', which is calculated on the basis of housing conditions, sewage and water services, use of 'inadequate fuels', education levels and access to health services. Specifically, the Census calculated that only 7.5% of the population of the city had their 'basic necessities satisfied'; 25.6% were 'on the verge' of poverty; 49.3% in moderate poverty; 17.1% in conditions of 'indigence'; and 0.5% in conditions of 'marginality'. Source: 2001 National Census, Instituto Nacional de Estadísticas, Bolivia. Available at: <www.ine.gov.bo/PDF/PUBLICACIONES/Censo_2001/Pobreza/PBolivia.pdf> (accessed 20 February, 2007).

[4] I am grateful to Andrew Canessa for pointing this out.

[5] The Federación de Trabajadores Gremiales, Artesanos, Comerciantes Minoristas y Vivanderos de la Ciudad de El Alto.

[6] Street traders are in theory liable for a series of municipal taxes, which used to be collected by municipal agents who visited the street markets each day. However, the federation reached an agreement with the Mayor in 2000 whereby traders would stop paying these taxes. The municipality would prefer traders to pay once a year, but the federation was not happy with the amount the municipality proposes, and decided to negotiate after the municipal elections of December 2004. Trader organisations can also get a series of legal documents which give them some formality – the most important being legal personhood for their association and a municipal order recognising their right to sell where they have set their stalls up. Not all associations have this documentation.

[7] There is a distinction between those traders who sell at street markets and those who sell every day on a fixed and permanent site in residential zones. The latter are organised into their own federation, which is affiliated with the COR.

[8] El Alto's population increased by an average of 9.23% a year between the Censuses of 1976 and 1992. (Information retrieved from Instituto Nacional de Estadísticas, <www.ine.gov.bo>) (accessed 20 February, 2007). The influx of migrants to the city during this time is usually attributed to the structural adjustment measures of the mid-1980s, which meant that thousands of miners lost their jobs. Some went to the Chapare region to grow coca leaves, others migrated to El Alto.

[9] This is a pseudonym.

[10] Bruno Rojas, personal communication.

[11] Silvia Rivera, personal communication.

References

Babb, F (1988) ' "From the field to the cooking pot": Economic crisis and the threat to marketers in Peru', in Clark, G (ed), *Traders Versus the State: Anthropological Approaches to Unofficial Economies*, Boulder: Westview Press, 17–40.

Basile, E and Harriss-White, B (2000) 'Corporative capitalism: civil society and the politics of accumulation in small town India', Working Paper No. 38, Oxford: Queen Elizabeth House.

Canessa, A (1998) 'Procreation, personhood and ethnic difference in Highland Bolivia', *Ethnos*, 63(2) 227–247.

Choque Mamani, T (1997) *Agenda Municipal Para el Desarrollo*. El Alto: HAMEA.

Clark, G (ed) (1988) *Traders Versus the State: Anthropological Approaches to Unofficial Economies*, Boulder: Westview Press.

Cross, J (1998) *Informal Politics: Street Vendors and the State in Mexico City*. Stanford: Stanford University Press.

de Soto, H (1989) *The Other Path: The Invisible Revolution in the Third World*, London: I.B. Tauris and Co.

Hart, K (1973) 'Informal income opportunities and urban employment in Ghana', *Journal of Modern African Studies*, 11(1), 61–89.

Larson, B and Harris, O (eds) (1995) *Ethnicity, Markets, and Migration in the Andes. At the Crossroads of History and Anthropology*, Durham: Duke University Press.

Lazar, S (2002) 'The "politics of the everyday": populism, gender and the media in La Paz and El Alto, Bolivia', Goldsmiths Anthropology Research Paper No. 6, London: Goldsmiths College.

Lazar, S (2005) 'Citizens despite the state: everyday corruption and local politics in El Alto, Bolivia,' in Haller, D and Shore, C (eds), *Understanding Corruption: Anthropological Perspectives*, London: Pluto.

Lazar, S and McNeish, J-A (eds) (2006) *'The millions return? Democracy in Bolivia at the start of the 21st century'*, Special Issue, *Bulletin of Latin American Research*.

Llanos Layme, D (1998) 'Diaspora comunal y sistema productivo altoandino: una aproximacion al impacto de la migracion y participacion popular en la organizacion social y productiva de la comunidad Chari (Prov. B. Saavedra), La Paz', unpublished Masters thesis, Sociology Department, La Paz, Universidad Mayor de San Andres.

Patzi Paco, F (2003) 'Rebelion indígena contra la colonialidad y la transnacionalizacion de la economia', in Hylton, F, Patzi, F, Serulnikov, S and Thomson, S (eds), *Ya es Otro Tiempo el Presente. Cuatro Momentos de Insurgencia Indigena*, La Paz: Muela del Diablo editores, 199–279.

Paulson, S (2002) 'Placing gender and ethnicity on the bodies of indigenous women and in the work of Bolivian intellectuals', in Montoya, R, Frazier, L. J, and Hurtig, J (eds), *Gender's Place. Feminist Anthropologies of Latin America*, London: Palgrave, Macmillan, 135–154.

Peattie, L (1987) 'An idea in good currency and how it grew: the informal sector', *World Development*, 15(7) 851–860.

Peredo Beltrán, E (1992) *Recoveras de los Andes: La Identidad de la Chola del Mercado: Una Aproximaciòn Psicosocial*, La Paz: TAHIPAMU.

Portes, A, Castells, M et al (eds) (1989) *The Informal Economy: Studies in Advanced and Less Developed Countries*, Baltimore: John Hopkins University Press.

Quispe, F (2001) 'Organizacion y proyecto politico de la rebelion indigena aymara-quechua', in Garcia Linera, A, Gutierrez, R, Prada Alcoreza, R, Quispe, F and Tapia Mealla, L (eds), *Tiempos de Rebelión*, La Paz: Muela del Diablo editores, 163–189.

Rivera Cusicanqui, S (2002) *Bircholas: Trabajo de Mujeres: Explotaciòn Capitalista y Opresión Colonial Entre las Migrantes Aymaras de La Paz y El Alto* (2da edicion), La Paz: Mama Huaco.

Seligmann, L (1989) 'To be in between: the Cholas as market women,' *Comparative Studies in Society and History*, 31(4) 694–721.

Seligmann, L (1993) 'Between worlds of exchange: ethnicity among Peruvian market women', *Cultural Anthropology*, 8(2) 187–213.

Sikkink, L (2001) 'Traditional medicines in the marketplace: identity and ethnicity among female vendors,' in Seligmann, L (ed), *Women Traders in Cross-Cultural Perspective. Mediating Identities, Marketing Wares*, Stanford: Stanford University Press, 209–228.

Untoja, F (2000) El *Retorno del Ayllu* La Paz: Fondo Editorial de los Diputados.

Weismantel, M (2001) *Cholas and Pishtacos. Stories of Race and Sex in the Andes*, Chicago: University of Chicago Press.

Index

About the Contributors

Laura María Agustín currently works for the ESRC-sponsored project 'Regulating the spaces of sex work' and is author of *Leaving Home For Sex* (forthcoming, Zed Books), the product of 12 years' research in Latin America and Europe on migrants who sell domestic, caring and sexual services in Europe and the large social sector which proposes to help them.

Alyson Brody received her doctorate from the School of Oriental and African Studies, University of London, in 2003. She has since been part of an action-research initiative on micro-finance at the Institute of Development Studies, Sussex. Her research interests include rights, citizenship, migration and gender issues in the workplace.

Udi Butler has conducted research with children, adolescents and young adults who live or have lived on the streets of Rio de Janeiro. He is a researcher affiliated to CIESPI in Rio de Janeiro, and Goldsmiths College, University of London, where he teaches Social Anthropology.

Alessandro Conticini is a post-doctoral fellow at the Institute for Development Policy and Management (IDPM) at the University of Manchester, and affiliated researcher to the Chronic Poverty Research Centre. He has been working for UNICEF where he is responsible for programmes addressing vulnerable children.

Stan Frankland is a Lecturer in Social Anthropology at the University of St Andrews, where he is responsible for the development of Visual Anthropology.

Tania Kaiser is a Lecturer in Refugee Studies at the School of Oriental and African Studies, University of London. She first carried out ethnographic research with Sudanese refugees in Uganda in 1996 and has also conducted agency commissioned work with refugees and IDPs in West Africa and Sri Lanka.

Sian Lazar is a Lecturer in Social Anthropology at the University of Cambridge. She completed her PhD in Social Anthropology at Goldsmiths College, University of London, in 2002, before moving to the Centre of Latin American Studies at the University of Cambridge as a Research Officer.

David Mosse is a Reader in Social Anthropology at the School of Oriental and African Studies, University of London. He is author of *The Rule of Water: Statecraft, Ecology and Collective Action in South India* (Oxford University Press, 2003) and *Cultivating Development: An Ethnography of Aid, Policy and Practice* (Pluto Press, 2005).

Atreyee Sen has recently been appointed Research Council United Kingdom (RCUK) Fellow at the Centre for Interdisciplinary Research in the Arts (CIDRA), University of Manchester, following lectureships in anthropology at Sussex and the School of Oriental and African Studies, University of London. Her areas of interest include female militancy, child-soldiering and right-wing vigilantism.

James Staples is a British Academy post-doctoral research fellow in Social Anthropology at the School of Oriental and African Studies, University of London, where he also teaches on the Anthropology of Disability. He is author of *Peculiar People, Amazing Lives: Leprosy, Social Exclusion and Community.*